Supervising and Being Supervised

A Practice in Search of a Theory

Edited by

JAN WIENER, RICHARD MIZEN AND
JENNY DUCKHAM

First published 2003 by
PALGRAVE MACMILLAN
Houndmills, Basingstoke, Hampshire RG21 6XS and
175 Fifth Avenue, New York, N.Y. 10010
Companies and representatives throughout the world

PALGRAVE MACMILLAN is the global academic imprint of the Palgrave
Macmillan division of St. Martin's Press, LLC and of Palgrave Macmillan Ltd.
Macmillan® is a registered trademark in the United States, United
Kingdom and other countries. Palgrave is a registered trademark in the
European Union and other countries.

ISBN 0–333–96269–9

This book is printed on paper suitable for recycling and made from fully
managed and sustained forest sources.

A catalogue record for this book is available from the British Library.

Library of Congress Cataloging-in-Publication Data

Supervising and being supervised: a practice in search of a theory/edited by
Jan Wiener, Richard Mizen, and Jenny Duckham.
    p. cm
  Includes bibliographical references and index.
  ISBN 0–333–96269–9 (pbk.)
    1. Supervision of employees. 2. Supervision of employees—Moral and
ethical aspects. I. Wiener, Jan. II. Mizen, Richard, 1957– III. Duckham, Jenny,
1946–
HF5549.12.S854 2002
658.3′02—dc21   2002028681

10   9   8   7   6   5   4   3   2   1
12   11   10   09   08   07   06   05   04   03

Printed and bound in Great Britain by
J.W. Arrowsmith Ltd, Bristol

Contents

Notes on the Contributors   ix

Introduction: Thinking about Supervision   1
Jan Wiener, Richard Mizen and Jenny Duckham

PART I THE SUPERVISORY RELATIONSHIP

1. The Individuating Supervisor   19
   Robin McGlashan

2. Reflections on the Therapist–Supervisor Relationship   34
   Jane Knight

3. Empathy in the use of Countertransference between
   Supervisor and Supervisee   49
   James Astor

PART II APPLICATIONS AND SETTINGS FOR SUPERVISION

4. Supervising Work with Children   67
   Elizabeth Urban

5. Supervision in Analytic Training   82
   Barbara Wharton

6. Supervising in Institutions   100
   Catherine Crowther

7. Supervision in Groups   118
   Victoria Graham Fuller

PART III PROBLEMS IN PRACTICE

8. Problems and Ethical Issues in Supervision   135
   Edward Martin

  9. Boundaries in Supervision   151
     Hugh Gee

 10. Supervising the Erotic Transference and
     Countertransference   167
     Joy Schaverien

PART IV EVOLVING A THEORY OF SUPERVISION

 11. Into the Labyrinth: A Developing Approach to
     Supervision   187
     Christopher Perry

 12. Learning about Supervision   207
     Ann Shearer

 13. From Practice to Theory: Evolving a Theory of
     Supervision   224
     Richard Mizen, Jan Wiener and Jenny Duckham

     Index   241

To our supervisors and supervisees, with thanks

With thanks also to Victoria Graham Fuller for permission to use 'A Practice in Search of a Theory' as part of the title of the book

Notes on the Contributors

James Astor BSc, M.Psych.Psych, C.Psychol is a Training Analyst of the Society of Analytical Psychology. He is author of *Michael Fordham, Innovations in Analytical Psychology* (1995) and numerous clinical papers. He is in private practice in London.

Catherine Crowther is a Professional Member of the Society of Analytical Psychology, working in private practice and in Child and Adolescent Psychiatry at the Royal Free Hospital, London. She was previously Senior Tutor in Psychotherapy at the Maudsley Hospital. She supervises counsellors and psychotherapists in general practice and trainees at the Westminster Pastoral Foundation. She is interested in disseminating analytic and systemic ideas within organisations, especially the NHS, and is co-convenor and supervisor for the Jungian Programme in St Petersburg, Russia.

Jenny Duckham BSc, MRCP is a Professional Member of the Society of Analytical Psychology and Medical Director of the C.G. Jung Clinic. She trained originally as a doctor working in hospital medicine and later in general practice. She is also a group analyst and trains on behalf of the Institute of Group Analysis in London and Dublin.

Victoria Graham Fuller BA is a Professional Member of the Society of Analytical Psychology, and a qualified member of the Institute of Group Analysis. She has conducted theoretical seminars and supervision groups for both organisations, as well as for various psychotherapy training programmes in London and NHS Trusts. She is in private practice and a Tutor at Birkbeck College, London.

Hugh Gee, MA, DPSA (Oxon), DMH is a Training Analyst of the Society of Analytical Psychology, the British Association of Psychotherapists and the London Centre for Psychotherapy. He has written many articles on analytical psychology. He is in private practice in London.

Jane Knight MA, AIMSW trained originally as a Medical Social Worker. Later, she attended the Advanced Casework Course at the Tavistock Clinic. She worked in general hospitals, specialising in work with patients of the maternity department. This led to family case-work and supervision of student and newly trained social casework-ers. Having completed analytic training with the Society of Analytical Psychology, she became a member of the Society in 1975. She has held various offices within the Society, including Director of Training, and is a Training Analyst with the Society.

Edward Martin MA, MSc, is a Professional Member of the Society of Analytical Psychology. He is a course organiser, supervisor and trainer of supervisors for WPF (Counselling and Psychotherapy). He is co-editor of *Supervising Psychotherapy* (2001).

Robin McGlashan MA, is a recently retired Professional Member of the Society of Analytical Psychology. He is an Anglican priest, taught theology in India and was chaplain in a London psychiatric hospital. He worked in private practice in London for many years, teaching on a number of psychotherapy courses, including the supervision course at the Maudsley Hospital. Since retiring, he has been visiting Professor of Pastoral Theology at Tamilnadu Theological Seminary, Madurai, South India and visiting analyst and teacher to the Developing Groups of Analytical Psychology in St Petersburg, Russia, and in Poland.

Richard Mizen MA DSW CQSW is a Professional Member of the Society of Analytical Psychology. He is in private practice in London and Devon.

Christopher Perry BSc is a Training Analyst and Supervisor for the Society of Analytical Psychology, of which he is a former Director of Training, and of the British Association of Psychotherapists. He is the author of *Listen to the Voice Within: A Jungian Approach to Pastoral Care* and of several articles on analytical psychology. In private practice, he also has a great interest in the application of understandings derived from analytical psychology to supervision and organisational consul-tancy.

Joy Schaverien PhD is a Member of the Society of Analytical Psychology in private practice in Rutland. She is Professor Associate in Art Psychotherapy at the University of Sheffield, a Professional Member of the West Midlands Institute of Psychotherapy and a teacher for the C.G. Jung Institute of Copenhagen. Among her many publications, she is the author of *Desire and the Female Therapist: Engendered Gazes in Psychotherapy and Art Therapy* (1995) and *The Dying Patient in Psychotherapy* (2002).

Ann Shearer MA is a Senior Analyst and past Convenor of the Independent Group of Analytical Psychologists, in private practice in London. She lectures widely on Jungian psychology, with a particular interest in archetypal approaches. Before training with IGAP, she worked as a journalist and international consultant in social welfare. Her books include *Disability: Whose Handicap?* (1981); *Woman: her Changing Image* (1987*); Athene: Image and Energy* (1996) and *When a Princess Dies* (1998), co-edited with Jane Haynes.

Elizabeth Urban BA, MA is a Professional Member of the Society of Analytical Psychology, where she trained in child analysis and later in adult analysis. She works in private practice in London and in the NHS. Together with another child analyst, she has recently become Organising Tutor for Child Analytic Training. Her interest in Michael Fordham's model of development and early infancy has prompted a number of published papers.

Barbara Wharton MA (Oxon) is a Training Analyst of the Society of Analytical Psychology and a recognised Training Therapist and Supervisor for the British Association of Psychotherapy. She was an editor of the *Journal of Analytical Psychology* from 1993 to 2000, and has published a number of papers on analytical psychology.

Jan Wiener BA, MSc is a Training Analyst of the Society of Analytical Psychology, where she is Director of Training, and the British Association of Psychotherapists. She works as a Senior Adult Psychotherapist at Thorpe Coombe Hospital (formerly Claybury) and in private practice in London. She is joint co-ordinator and teacher/supervisor to the Developing Group of Analytical Psychology in St Petersburg, Russia. She is author of several papers on analytical psychology and co-author of *Counselling and Psychotherapy in Primary Health Care: A Psychodynamic Approach* (1998).

Introduction: Thinking about Supervision

Jan Wiener, Richard Mizen and Jenny Duckham

History and evolution of the book

The idea for this book emerged from a series of twelve-week supervision events called *Thinking about Supervision*, developed and organised in the late 1990s by the editors on behalf of the Society of Analytical Psychology (SAP) for qualified analysts, psychotherapists and counsellors. Some of the ideas to evolve from these events, both in the talks given by members of the society, and in the subsequent small group case discussions, prompted us to think further about the nature of the supervisory process. We then invited some of the contributors who gave lectures and others with a special interest in supervision, to develop their ideas into cohesive chapters. We hope the book will be of interest to Jungian analysts around the world as well as to psychotherapists and counsellors supervising therapy in different institutional settings and in private practice.

All except one of the authors are Jungian analysts and supervisors trained at the Society of Analytical Psychology (SAP). The exception is Ann Shearer, a member of the Independent Group of Jungian Analysts (IGAP), who participated in one of the events. The book has our contemporary Jungian orientation but, because many SAP analysts have integrated much psychoanalytic theory and practice into their clinical work – the essence of a London post-Jungian approach – we hope it will appeal to readers from different schools with an interest in reflecting about the supervisory process in all its manifestations.

The nature of supervision

To be in supervision is now an essential constituent of any training, whether to become a counsellor, a psychotherapist or an analyst. Qualifying actually implies being able to work with patients without supervision. However, the ethos of our profession, reinforced by the relative isolation of working as an analyst, promotes the continuation of supervision as part of ongoing professional development. In contrast to many other professions, this generally proceeds until retirement, rather like a craftsman who sometimes seeks out different master craftsmen to learn about new techniques or consults now and again with a respected fellow-craftsman about a difficulty. Given the psychological pressure under which we work, a discipline of continuing supervision protects us (and, therefore, our patients) from deterioration in technique.

The ethos of this book, embraced in its title, *Supervising and Being Supervised*, implies the idea of a *relationship in which both parties can be changed* and, since we are analysts, an interest in the unconscious processes that are constellated within the relationship. This idea is central for both Jungian analysts and psychoanalysts in their analytic work and is equally true in supervision. Berman (2000, pp. 284–5) puts it well:

> The ethical option is to create in supervision a tolerant and attentive atmosphere, which will make it easier for trainees to share personal associations and feelings whenever they appear to be potentially relevant to the task in hand . . . the inner freedom achieved can evolve into a transitional space, within which the dyad generates new meanings not accessible by the intrapsychic work of each partner in isolation.

Mollon (1997, p. 33) too reflects on the supervisory space, describing it as a space for thinking:

> This thinking is not linear, logical 'left-brain' cognition, but a kind of free-associative mulling over, perhaps a characteristic of right-hemispheric functioning. Wishes to understand quickly, to appear competent, or to compete with peers or with the supervisor can all interfere with this thinking space. The supervisor must work to understand and counter the potential impediments to the space for thinking.

As the reader will discover in perusing this book, the supervisory space and the relationship evolving within it are complicated, and different authors draw on a range of different concepts and metaphors to elaborate its aims, processes and theory. To quote Clarkson (1998, p. 143):

At any one moment of time, any supervisor may need to be a Cerberus guarding the territories and boundaries, or a Psyche-sorter of the wheat and barley of primary and secondary realities. Or a Zeus-like referee between warring internal or external factors, or a Chironic mentor teaching and modelling the skills of healing, or even a Hestian flame of spiritual (professional?) direction.

Zinkin (1995, p. 240) thinks that 'supervision can be a delight, but may often be a torment'. He goes on to discuss how supervisors are rarely trained and tend to be chosen without having demonstrated their ability to supervise. While the progress towards the state regulation of our profession means that this is unlikely to continue, we are sympathetic to his point of view. Zinkin's ambivalence about supervision is obvious, 'supervision is actually a shared fantasy . . . it works best if both remain aware that what they are jointly imagining is not true. Both can profit enormously . . . there is teaching and learning to be found in this joint imaginative venture' (Zinkin, 1995, p. 247). For all its complexity then, Zinkin does believe that supervising the work of our junior colleagues is worthwhile. I do not think we, as editors of this book, would have embarked on two years of preparation had we not agreed with him!

Not all experiences in supervision are positive. Crick (1992), talking to supervisees, found that the definition of a 'good supervision session' meant leaving with a sense of having understood something new about the therapy, but a 'bad supervision session' left the supervisee feeling that taking on their supervisor's views was a burden. 'Bad supervisors' were described as narcissistic and competitive or as using 'not knowing' or 'uncertainty' in an idealised way, inhibiting proper attempts to 'know'.

Authors choose different metaphors or analogies to evoke the nature of the supervisory process. Hughes and Pengelly (1997, p. 47) quote Hawkins and Shohet's (1989, p. 37) belief that a supervisor requires *helicopter ability* being able to move in close, but also pull away to a broader perspective. This might be relatively easy for the well-trained helicopter pilot but less easy for an apprentice supervisor trying to hold in mind a matrix of complicated but relevant dynamics. Several authors (Marshall, 1997; Hughes and Pengelly, 1997; Mander 1998) use the concept of a *triangle* or *triad* as the basic shape to supervision. Perry, in this volume, prefers the idea of a *matrix*. Berman (2000) similarly positions supervision at the crossroads of a *relational matrix of at least three persons*. Clarkson (1998) describes *over-*

lapping supervisory systems, Henderson (1998), the *archetype of the Hermit*; Ekstein and Wallerstein (1972), the *clinical rhombus* with four related points of contact and Hahn (1998) evokes *a parental couple in dialogue about a child*. Berman's (2000) metaphors of the *chaperone on a honeymoon* and the supervisor as *Cyrano de Bergerac*, putting words into his supervisee's mouths, remind us of the shadow and more intrusive sides of supervision.

The role and function of supervisors will vary depending on the context in which they are working. Is it private practice or in an institutional setting? Is it a voluntary arrangement with a qualified analyst or a compulsory part of a supervisee's training? Is it individual one-to-one supervision or in a group? Is this supervision of work with adults or with children? The content of this book has been selected to highlight some of these subtle differences.

In the broadest sense there are four primary tasks of supervision:

(a) To facilitate, encourage and inform analytic work with patients, supporting the individuation and analytic attitude of the (trainee) analyst throughout his or her professional life;
(b) To attend to the dynamics of the supervisory relationship including the role of the organisation and any specific issues arising from the context of the work;
(c) To ensure that the supervisee is practising competently and ethically and, in the case of trainees, evaluating the stage of development reached;
(d) To maintain the good reputation of the profession as a whole by giving attention to professional standards and clinical governance.

The main disagreements amongst authors about the nature of supervision seem to centre on whether it should focus on helping supervisees to learn about their own evoked feelings with patients, and how to use them effectively, or to learn about therapeutic techniques and strategies. How therapeutic should supervision be? To understand the arguments contributing to this debate, we must turn to the history of supervision.

History of supervision

The need for critical reflection about clinical case material in the presence of a trusted confidante or colleague has been strongly felt since the early days of analysis. Even before the concept of supervision was formulated, the requirement for this sort of intense personal and professional discussion arose spontaneously from difficulties encountered by our founding fathers in their relationships with their patients. Freud, Jung and their contemporaries had no supervisors, no training analysts and no training courses to attend. Supervision, if we can call it that, happened informally. Colleagues chose to consult with Freud and Jung about clinical matters by letter, in personal meetings, at international congresses and, significantly, in their own personal analyses. Until the 1920s, these were the means by which analytic knowledge was unsystematically transmitted. Fleming and Benedek (1983, p. 7) quote Bibring's word *schlampigkeit,* meaning sloppy or untidy, to describe these early informal structures of learning through experience.

Jung was the first analyst to propose that trainee analysts should undergo a personal analysis (Mattoon, 1995, p. 31), and in 1918 psychoanalysts formally adopted the idea. Jacobs *et al.* (1995, p. 20) quote the perhaps apocryphal tale that the idea of supervision was conceived in Berlin when the psychoanalyst Hans Sachs complained to his colleague Eitingon that he was tired of hearing his patients going on about their own patients in analysis, reflecting in his remark that, in the early days, analysis and supervision were usually combined. This tradition, of combining personal analysis with supervision has been described by Ekstein (1960) as ahistorical and by Balint (1948) as prehistorical! Two terms – *Kontrollanalyse,* to describe supervision, including analysing a trainee's countertransference responses to his patients, and *Analysenkontrolle,* to describe personal analysis – lay at the heart of early disagreements about the nature of analytic training and, within it, the role of supervision.

Among the early psychoanalysts, it was the tense debates between the Hungarians and the Viennese during the 1930s about who should supervise that determined the evolution of contemporary attitudes to supervision. The central issue was about who should work with trainees' countertransference. Kovacs (1936), from the Hungarian group, thought that a trainee's countertransference to a patient was best understood when considered in personal analysis. In other words, a training analysis was the best place for supervision. Trainees could explore their feelings and resistances emerging in the work with their patients with their analysts. Following Freud, trainees could not go further with their patients than they had come themselves. Bibring (1937) from Vienna and the Berlin psychoanalysts, on the other hand, were firmly of the view that a trainee's analyst should not supervise his work. Another analyst should be the supervisor. They made the case for separating personal analysis and supervision, the latter being suitable for teaching and understanding the dynamics between patient and analyst. The Hungarian proposal was discussed at both Four Countries Conferences in 1935 and 1937. Eventually a compromise was reached and the Hungarians conceded that trainees needed teaching (from supervisors) for their training cases and the Viennese agreed that supervisors might sometimes have to work with counter-transference in supervision, rather than leaving it all up to the analyst. Gradually, the tradition to separate analysis and supervision has become the norm in analytic training institutes, although the bound-aries between the two continue to remain a subject for heated debate and controversy.

This separation between analysis and supervision took longer in Jungian circles. After his split with Freud in 1912 and four dark years in a near psychotic state of mind, Jung, perhaps rebelliously, sought to develop analytical psychology as a vocation rather than a profession (Eisold, 2001), and he set up a 'Psychological Club'. Many other Clubs followed and by the Second World War there were Clubs in London, New York, Los Angeles, San Francisco, Paris, Berlin, Rome and Basel, as well as in Zurich. As Fordham questioned (1979, p 280):

> how anyone became an analytic therapist in those days is vague and must be regarded largely as a matter of vocation, though there was an unwritten law that any person who wanted to be called a Jungian analyst was expected to go out to Zurich, make a relation with Jung himself, and undergo analysis with either himself or one or more of his close colleagues.

There were no guidelines for training or supervision, rather an apprenticeship model without structures. It was only in 1946 when the Society of Analytical Psychology was founded, that Jungian analy-sis began to acquire a formal professional identity, with entrance requirements and criteria for training.

For Jungians in the 1920s and 1930s, 'training' meant personal analysis with Jung and what we might view as informal supervision in his many training seminars/clinical case consultations. Jung himself decided when someone was 'ready to practice' (Mattoon, 1995, p. 30). The increasing numbers of professionals wishing to train as analysts after the Second World War probably contributed to the enforced introduction of bureaucracy and more systematic structures. In 1958, the International Association of Analytical Psychology (IAAP) was founded and the 1962 membership byelaws called for eighteen months in supervision. In 1971, this was changed to a requirement of fifty hours and, in 1983, one hundred hours (Mattoon, 1995, p. 34).

Fordham (1995, p. 41) describes the development of a training programme in the SAP, highlighting the ease with which it was possible, following Jung, to stipulate that each trainee should have two training cases – learning on the job, so to speak – but more difficult to decide on criteria for supervision. For Fordham, analysis was best separated from supervision and the two considered as different functions. His view endures today in the SAP, in which personal analysis is kept entirely private between analyst and analysand, in contrast to societies in which analysts are asked to report on their trainees.

A brief overview of the development of supervision over the past seventy-five years shows how, with the evolution of our knowledge, especially of transference and countertransference, attitudes to supervision have also evolved. Methods have changed from what in the early days Balint (1948) rather critically called 'superego training' – telling supervisees what to do and how to do it, a kind of learning by imitation or identification – to a more relational model. Here, the personalities and attitudes of both supervisor and supervisee may be changed. It seems likely that attitudes to supervision have evolved in parallel with attitudes to the practice of analysis, a kind of parallel process in itself. Ekstein and Wallerstein (1972) were the first to produce a model of the supervisory relationship that took account of patient, therapist, supervisor and institution. Searles (1965) introduced the idea of a 'reflection process', a transference–countertransference dynamic between patient and analyst that affects the dynamics of supervision and, if talked about, can be productive.

The growing literature on the subject of supervision is a testament to the interest that now exists (Gabbard and Lester, 1995; Jacobs *et al.*, 1995; Kugler, 1995; Hughes and Pengelly, 1997; Martindale *et al.*, 1997; Rock, 1997; Shipton, 1997; Clarkson, 1998; Driver and Martin, 2002). However, debates about how supervisors work with trainees' countertransference are no less emotionally loaded now than in the past. Moore (1995, p. 52) summarises helpfully the relationship between supervision and training analysis: 'analysis is always the centre of training . . . supervision is different, although a candidate's affective response comes into it, he does not tackle these countertransference reactions (leaving that to analysis)'. She goes on to describe her experience of Fordham as a supervisor:

the setting of supervision with Fordham was almost analytic, boundaries being strict in many ways. Although not analysis, being about patients' material, it had some correlates, each session starting with a not-knowing attitude and with something like an open system view in reportage and discussion, using unconscious as well as conscious information. (Moore, 1995, p. 57)

Grinberg (1970) distinguished between the obvious countertransferences to emerge in supervision, which the supervisor indicates the supervisee should take to her analyst, and cases where projective counteridentifications were taking place and where the supervisor could appropriately intervene (Gabbard and Lester, 1995, p. 169). Astor (2000, p. 372) is against sending supervisees to their analysts with countertransference difficulties: 'I strongly disagree with supervisors who *tell* their supervisees to take such and such a feeling to their analyst. We are analysts, so let us proceed analytically, not as traffic policemen'. As the above quotations illustrate, the perils of the split transference to personal analyst and to supervisor remain as pertinent as ever.

The nature of theory

The subtitle of this book – *A Practice in Search of a Theory* – highlights our hope of making a contribution towards thinking about the theory of supervision. There is little existing formal theory about supervision and, for the most part, supervisors learn on the job, drawing on their own internal supervisor which they acquired through good and problematic experiences of being supervised themselves. In the present climate of regulation and registration, this is unlikely to continue. Supervision courses of different orientations are mushrooming and attendance can be a mandatory component to meet employment prerequisites.

It may be an over-ambitious expectation that the thinking and writing of a number of accomplished authors will assist us in our aims of emerging with some helpful theory or useful concepts for supervision. However, the absence of any substantial theory about supervision, and the possible reasons for this, is in itself interesting and worthy of thought. Our own motivation for writing this book gathered energy from our personal experience that supervising is difficult, more difficult than analysis in a way. As has been outlined above, supervisors must negotiate carefully the narrow and thorny path of working with their supervisees' countertransferences to their patients.

The search for a theory also raises questions as to whether there *is* a theory specific to supervision or whether the familiar concepts and theory we borrow from our analytic practice with patients can adequately give meaning to the process of supervising and inform our practice.

Wissentrieb – the search for knowledge – is probably archetypal, that is, a universal instinct. It is often called the epistemophilic impulse. Britton thinks of *Wissentrieb* as

> on a par with and independent of other instincts; the desire for knowledge exists alongside love and hate . . . Unlike Freud and Klein, I do not think of Wissentrieb as a component instinct, but as an instinct with components. Exploration, recognition and belief are among such components. (Britton, 1998, p. 11)

The cumulative wisdom of our profession is embodied in our theory and it is worth reflecting on its nature. The word 'theory' comes from the Greek word *theoria* meaning contemplation or speculation. It also implies a 'system of ideas or statements explaining something, especially one based on general principles independent of the things to be explained' (New Oxford Shorter English Dictionary). While we may have no difficulty with the first part of this definition, the second seems dissonant with the method and process of depth psychology. It is now generally accepted that analytical psychology (and psychoanalysis) may have outgrown its initial classificiation as a 'pure' natural science in favour of an approach more familiar to the social sciences taking account of both the observed and the observer (Sandler, 1983; Rustin, 1985; Wright, 1991; Duncan, 1993; Frosh, 1997; Parsons, 2000). Forrester (1997, p. 235–6) thinks that, rather than debate whether or not psychoanalysis is a science, we should ask what kind of discipline it is. In his view, it is a stable discipline which produces knowledge, 'an observational, naturalistic science of human beings; coping with complexity and variety'.

Frosh (1997) evaluates the arguments for and against psychoanalytic theory. He considers that the making of analytic theory represents an excellent example of a new paradigm approach in the social sciences, which includes the investment of the researcher in the material she or he is exploring. He values its engagement with subjectivity and emotion and its concern with intentionality and agency, the limits of consciousness and the role of fantasy and therapeutic integrity. In contrast, he criticises its weak evidence and research base and its ethnocentricity. Significantly, he highlights how the central interest of psychoanalysis and analytical psychology – the unconscious – means that theory can never be completely objective:

> A dynamic unconscious explodes all claims to absolute knowledge. If there is always unconscious activity, then one can never stand outside the system in order to observe its operations in a perfectly 'objective' way. (Frosh, 1997, p. 233)

We live in a contemporary culture of pluralism when it comes to thinking about analytic theory. For Samuels (1989, p. 1), pluralism is 'an attitude to conflict that tries to reconcile differences without imposing a false resolution on them or losing sight of the unique value of each position . . . it tries to hold unity and diversity in balance . . . to hold the tension between the one and the many'. He goes on to describe the goal of pluralism as 'reform, as a portmanteau term to include renewal, rebirth, spontaneous and well-planned evolutions and imaginative productivity generally' (Samuels, 1989, p. 230).

Wallerstein (1988, p. 5) also emphasises the increasing psychoanalytic diversity, 'a pluralism of theoretical perspectives, of linguistic and thought conventions, of distinctive regional, cultural and language emphases'. And later 'psycho-analysis today consists of multiple (and divergent) theories of mental functioning, of development, of pathogenesis, of treatment and of cure' (Wallerstein, 1988, p. 11). He believes that we are united by the work we do in our consulting rooms.

Pluralism though, despite its democratic attractions, can be confusing and chaotic. Many of the concepts so familiar to us as analysts, such as transference, projective identification and so on, do not necessarily have a shared meaning. Sandler (1983, p. 36) values the elasticity of analytic concepts since it allows for new developments to take place without disrupting our overall theories; 'the elastic and flexible concepts take up the strain of theoretical change, absorbing it while more organized newer theories or part-theories can develop'. He advocates the search for a 'nucleus of appropriateness' in our theoretical and technical ideas (Sandler, 1983, p. 36). Tuckett (2001, p. 643) is more pessimistic about our use of theory:

> within our profession and within most schools there is a wealth of clinical experience and a wealth of good psychoanalytic practice. It is also true that there has been a *collective intellectual failure to establish secure, consensually agreed*

and demonstrable propositions concerning key questions of theory and technique. [emphasis added]

Parsons (2000, p. 63) defines (analytic) theory as 'a set of propositions, or hypotheses, impersonally available in the same way to anyone who informs himself or herself, which can be applied from the general to the particular in a given instance'. This is *the public face of theory*. Parsons goes on to say that 'the power of theory to inform clinical practice depends on linking this external aspect to the internal, less articulate aspect of it . . . that finds its personal meaning through lived experience'. This seems to suggest a more *personal face of theory*. In reality, – the public and the personal – are difficult to separate.

Jung (1946, para. 181) was ambivalent about theory:

> If you begin the analysis with a fixed belief in some theory which purports to know all about the nature of neurosis, you apparently make your task very much easier; but you are nevertheless in danger of riding roughshod over the real psychology of your patient and of disregarding his individuality.

He emphasised the need for a theory for every patient:

> Since every individual is a new and unique combination of psychic elements, the investigation of truth must begin afresh with each case, for each 'case' is individual and not derivable from any preconceived formula. . . . We miss the meaning of the individual psyche if we interpret it on the basis of any fixed theory, however fond of it we may be. (Jung, 1946, para. 173)

Jung (1938, p. 7) clearly also had strong *feelings* about theory:

> Theories in psychology are the very devil. It is true that we need certain points of view for their orienting and heuristic value; but they should always be regarded as mere auxiliary concepts that can be laid aside at any time.

Perhaps Jung is overstating his case in this last point and theories are not 'mere auxiliary concepts' but, rather, need to be worked with cautiously and appropriately. The defensive use of theory is dangerous. Wright (1991) reminds us of the tyranny of concepts, which leads to doctrine or dogma in analytic institutes and a failure to resolve disagreements except on the basis of loyalty. He thinks that theory can also represent a refuge from reality, 'a kind of solace' or illusion of predictability when the chaos of our own subjectivity threatens to overwhelm us.

Analytic theory evolves directly from our experience with patients in the consulting room and our use of our 'selves'. In the words of Jung, 'every psychotherapist not only has his own method, he himself is that method' (1945, para. 198). Parsons (2000, p. 53) would agree with Jung: 'understanding grows by integrating what is learned from outside with what acquires meaning from within, and the theory that has a real effect in the consulting-room is that to which analysts have themselves given meaning through their own experience'.

Parsons makes his case with great elegance:

> Analysts need an evolving, interactive relationship with their theories so that, as they discover their patients by listening to and responding to them, they discover their analytic knowledge by listening to and responding to it as well. An analyst serves truth not only by trying to see it and point it out to his patient, but by embodying it in his relationship to his patient and to his theory . . . Psychoanalysis uniquely combines the scientific and the personal . . . Its scientific nature is embedded in its personal nature: it is scientific only in so far as it is personal as well. (Parsons, 2000, p. 67)

Simon (1988) writes about Bion's analysis of Beckett whereby the therapeutic contact had a profound and prolonged impact on both men and informed the work of both for years to come: 'something unfinished, unsatisfying, unresolved, but intriguing and attractive gets into the 'system' of the analyst and does not let him alone' (Simon, 1988, p. 331). Freud and Jung both found a 'private space' that included stringent (although unsupervised and unanalysed) self-examination to develop their own theories. Freud's idea of the Oedipus complex came first from his own dreams and Jung used his personal psychological crisis and his journals to develop his theories. The first clinical cases of Freud and Jung served as the scaffolding for the concepts and theoretical themes that preoccupied them and their writings may be seen as a kind of self supervision.

If the making or holding of metapsychological theory goes on in the unconscious (Parsons, 2000, p. 54), we may not easily be able to articulate it to ourselves. It is not available for introspection or thought since it remains essentially unconscious. Perhaps we re-find what we already know, giving theory-making an archetypal quality, whether at a micro or macro level, in one session for one patient or for several patients.

In summary, there is both public, official theory, that is conscious, and also private, personal theory, that 'is cooking' less consciously.

What is significant is the relationship between them. The authors writing in this book can be observed in their struggles to make and re-make theory in each and every session with their patients. Writing a chapter has a different objective – to clarify an argument and then evaluate it (Tuckett, 2001, p. 646) – but we need clinical material to make our theories conscious. Without it, they can remain disembodied ideas. In this book, some authors are drawn more to the external, public aspects of theory that have a common language recognisable to colleagues. Others are more comfortable with drawing meaning from private, internal theory-making.

Like Janus, then, our theory has two faces looking simultaneously inwards and outwards. Whether we are thinking about analysis or supervision, there is a continuous search for meaning in our work with patients and supervisees. Looking inwards, this can be a very private activity in the consulting room, yet we also look outwards to share our knowledge. It becomes public theory when people write and give papers. To learn (about supervision) is to match up public theory with our own private, sometimes unconscious, theorising and finding the courage to challenge public theory when it seems to contradict our personal beliefs. This book is an example. Writers approach it from their own unique and different perspectives and some chapters may appeal in style more to some readers than others. Some authors are more personally revealing of what goes on in the consulting room and share with us their activities in this significant space. Others are more drawn to the public face of theory. Since practice and theory are always linked, readers may make their own meaningful links.

Reading the book

We imagine that the reader will approach this book with existing beliefs, will recognise some of the themes developed in the chapters as familiar and relevant and, we hope, find they want to explore the territory further. Each author was invited to focus on a particular aspect of supervision, paying attention to his or her own theoretical ideas and how they have evolved in the course of the author's experience as a supervisor. The range of styles and approach is a testament to the many different ways to practise as a Jungian analyst today. In our view, this gives a depth and variety of approach to supervision that we hope readers will appreciate. Although some chapters overlap in terms of the authors' clinical experience and theoretical orientations, they each focus on a particular aspect of supervision and the supervisory relationship.Readers may choose to start at the beginning and progress to the end or dip into those chapters that attract their interest. To ensure some consistency in style, we have asked authors to refer to themselves as supervisors using their own gender (he or she) and to refer to their supervisees using the alternative gender designation he or she. We have also asked contributors to preserve the confidentiality of their patients and supervisee in clinical vignettes by adequately disguising personal material and, where possible, obtaining appropriate permissions. We have cross-referenced some common themes across chapters within the main body of the text. A number of central themes run through the text. Part I presents the supervisory relationship in all its subtle manifestations, then Part II considers how the supervisory process is affected by the setting in which it is practised. Part III focuses on specific problems observable in practice and finally, Part IV deals with ideas about the theory of supervision and the extent to which we can discern specific concepts and theories as relevant for supervision, as opposed to those which come from our day-to-day analytic work. The final chapter summarises our thoughts about theory and practice. We draw not only on the significant common and discrepant themes to emerge in the preceding text, but also develop those ideas about the relationship between theory and practice that have stimulated and puzzled us over several years since the seeds of the idea for this book first germinated.

References

Astor, J. (2000) 'Some Reflections on Empathy and Reciprocity in the Use of Countertransference between Supervisor and Supervisee', *Journal of Analytical Psychology*, **45**(3), 367–85.

Balint, M. (1948) 'On the Psycho-analytic Training System', *International Journal of Psychoanalysis*, **29**(3), 163–73.

Berman, E. (2000) 'Psychoanalytic Supervision: The Intersubjective Development', *International Journal of Psychoanalysis*, **81**(2), 273–90.

Bibring, E. (1937) 'Methods and Techniques of Control-analysis', *International Journal of Psycho-Analysis*, **18**, 369–70.

Britton, R. (1998) *Belief and Imagination* (London and New York: Routledge).

Clarkson, P. (ed.), (1998) *Supervision: Psychoanalytic and Jungian Perspectives* (London: Whurr).

Crick, P. (1992) 'Good Supervision: On the Experience of being Supervised', *Psychoanalytic Psychotherapy*, **5**(3), 235–45.

Driver, C. and Martin, E. (2002) *Supervising Psychotherapy* (London: Sage).

Duncan, D. (1993) 'Theory in Vivo', *International Journal of Psychoanalysis*, **74**, 25–32.

Eisold, E. (2001) 'Institutional Conflicts in Jungian Analysis', *Journal of Analytical Psychology*, **46**(2), 335–55.

Ekstein, R. (1960) 'A Historical Survey of the Teaching of Psychoanalytic Technique', *Journal of the American Psychoanalytic Association*, **8**, 500–16.

Ekstein, R. and Wallerstein, R. S. (1972) *The Teaching and Learning of Psychotherapy* (2nd edn.). (Madison, CT.: International Universities Press).

Fleming, J. and Benedek, T. E. (1983) *Psychoanalytic Supervision: A Method of Clinical Teaching* (New York: International Universities Press).

Fordham, M. (1979) 'Analytical Psychology in England', *Journal of Analytical Psychology*, **24**, 279–97.

Fordham, M. (1995) 'Suggestions towards a Theory of Supervision', in P. Kugler (ed.), *Jungian Perspectives on Clinical Supervsion* (Einsiedeln Daimon), Chapter 3.

Forrester, J. (1997) *Dispatches from the Freud Wars: Psychoanalysis and its Passions* (London and Cambridge, MA: Harvard University Press).

Frosh, S. (1997) *For and Against Psychoanalysis* (London and New York: Routledge), Chapter 9.

Gabbard, G. O. and Lester, E. P. (1995) *Boundaries and Boundary Violations in Psychoanalysis* (New York: Basic Books), Chapter 9.

Grimberg, L. (1970) 'The problems of supervision in psychoanalytic education', *International Journal of Psycho-Analysis*, **51**, 371–4.

Hahn, H. (1998) 'Super Vision: Seen, Sought and Reviewed', in P. Clarkson (ed.), *Supervision: Psychoanalytic and Jungian Perspectives* (London: Whurr), Chapter 6).

Hawkins, P. and Shohet, R. (1989) *Supervision in the Helping Professions* (Milton Keynes: Open University Press).

Henderson, J. (1998) Solitude and Solidarity, in P. Clarkson (ed.), *Supervision: Psychoanalytic and Jungian Perspectives* (London: Whurr).

Hughes, L. and Pengelly P (1997). *Staff Supervision in a Turbulent Environment* (London and Philadelphia: Jessica Kingsley).

Jacobs, M., David, P. and Meyer D. J., (1995) *The Supervisory Encounter* (Newhaven, CN, and London: Yale University Press).

Jung, C. G. (1938) 'Psychic Conflicts in a Child', foreword to the Third Edition, *Collected Works Volume 17*.

Jung, C. G. (1945) 'Medicine and Psychotherapy', *Collected Works Volume 16*.

Jung, C. G. (1946) 'Analytical Psychology and Education', *Collected Works Volume 17*.

Kovacs, W. (1936) 'Training and Control-analysis', *International Journal of Psycho-Analysis*, **17**, 346–54.

Kugler, P. (1995) *Jungian Perspectives on Clinical Supervision* (Einsiedeln: Daimon).

Mander, G. (1998) 'Dyads and Triads: Some Thoughts on the Nature of Therapy Supervision.', in P. Clarkson (ed.), *Supervision: Psychoanalytic and Jungian Perspectives* (London: Whurr), Chapter 4.

Marshall, R. J. (1997) 'The Interactional Triad in Supervision', in M.H. Rock (ed.), *Psychodynamic Supervision* (London and Northvale, NJ: Jason Aronson), Chapter 3.

Martindale, B., Morner, M., Roderiguez, M. E. C. and Vidit, J.-P. (1997) *Supervision and its Vicissitudes* (London: Karnac Books).

Mattoon, M.A. (1995) 'Historical Notes' in P. Kugler (ed.), *Jungian Perspectives on Clinical Supervision* (Eisiedeln: Daimon).

Mollon, P. (1997) 'Supervision as a Space for Thinking', in G. Shipton (ed.), *Supervision of Psychotherapy and Counselling* (Buckingham: Open University Press), Chapter 3.

Moore, N. (1995) 'Michael Fordham's Theory and Practice of Supervision', in P. Kugler (ed.), *Jungian Perspectives on Jungian Supervision* (Einsiedeln: Daimon).

Parsons, M. (2000) *The Dove that Returns, The Dove that Vanishes: Paradox and Creativity in Psychoanalysis,* The New Library of Psychoanalysis, **39** (London and Philadelphia: Routledge), Chapter 1.

Rock, M. (1997) *Psychodynamic Supervision* (Northvale, NJ: Jason Aronson).

Rustin, M. (1985) 'The Social Organisation of Secrets: Towards a Sociology of Psychoanalysis', *International Review of Psycho-Analysis,* **12**, 143–61.

Samuels, A. (1989) *The Plural Psyche* (London and New York: Routledge).

Sandler J. (1983), 'Reflections on some Relations between Psychoanalytic Concepts and Psychoanalytic Practice', *International Journal of Psycho-Analysis*, **64**, 35–47.

Searles, M. (first pub. 1955) 'The Informational Value of the Supervisor's Emotional Experiences', in J. D. Sutherland (ed.) (1965) *Collected Papers on Schizophrenia* [New York International Universities Press).

Shipton, G. (ed.) (1997) *Supervision of Psychotherapy and Counselling* (Buckingham: Open University Press).

Simon, B. (1988) 'The Imaginary Twins: The Case of Beckett and Bion', *International Review of Psycho-Analysis*, **15**(3), 331–53.

Tuckett, D. (2001) 'Towards a more Facilitating Peer Environment. Editorial', *International Journal of Psychoanalysis,* **82**, Pt 4 643–51.

Wallerstein, R. S. (1988) 'One Psychoanalysis or Many', *International Journal of Psycho-Analysis*, **69**(1) 5–23.

Wright, K. (1991) *Vision and Separation: Between Mother and Baby* (London: Free Association Books).

Zinkin, L. (1995) 'Supervision: The Impossible Profession', in P. Kugler (ed.), *Jungian Perspectives on Clinical Supervision* (Einsiedeln: Daimon).

PART I

The Supervisory Relationship

1

The Individuating Supervisor

Robin McGlashan

Introduction

Individuation is a process of personal development whereby a person becomes more conscious of who they are. It can be seen as 'a movement towards wholeness by means of an integration of conscious and unconscious parts of the personality' (Samuels, 1985, p. 102). The term is normally employed to denote a process that encompasses the whole person and spans the whole course of his or her development. In this chapter, it is used in a limited sense, in relation to one particular aspect of a person's functioning, that is to say, development in the clinical task of supervision. So, here, the concept of individuation is being used in a way that could be called metaphorical, in order to discover what light the concept can throw on the specialised process of becoming a supervisor. It is, of course, assumed that anyone who gets to the point of supervising others, although he may only be at the beginning of the task of individuating as a supervisor, will already have taken steps along the path of individuation as a whole person.

One aspect of this process is that the individuating person becomes more free to make conscious choices about his behaviour and the direction of his life. To say that individuation involves becoming 'more conscious' or 'more free' implies that at the outset, before the process sets in, the individuating person (in this context, the individuating supervisor) was at least relatively unconscious and unfree. Thus, when embarking upon this process, the new supervisor is likely to be bound by his own anxiety and the unfamiliarity of the role, and to react in instinctual, unthought out ways, in order to mitigate his own discomfort. To illustrate this, we shall first look at some typical examples from Greek mythology of the ways in which people react when exercising responsibility in roles comparable to that of the supervisor.

Mythological anticipations of the supervisory process

1. Nestor, King of Pylos, was the oldest of the Greek leaders in the Trojan War, the survivor of an older generation. As such, he had a rich store of accumulated wisdom from battles long ago, which he was anxious to pass on to the younger leaders around him. However, he was painfully aware of his age and realised that his advice might not be welcome. Actually, it was usually sound, but he managed to ruin its impact by becoming overly garrulous and self-consciously apologetic. As a supervisor, we could say that Nestor was ambivalent about his authority. Undoubtedly his experience conferred an authority upon him, but he did not know how to own it or use it, and so was reduced to being anxious, defensive, falsely modest and self-effacing. He became paralysed by the fear of a hostile reaction, which no doubt reflected his own unconscious hostility to authority.

2. Eurystheus, King of Argos, was born on the same day as Herakles, but two hours earlier, so Zeus granted to Eurystheus pre-eminence and authority over the younger hero. In spite of this, Eurystheus was consumed with fear, envy and rivalry towards Herakles, and set him the twelve labours, in the hope that each time Herakles would fail and be destroyed. When Herakles returned to report to Eurystheus after successfully completing each task, the latter was mean and tight-fisted in the appreciation and reward that he offered. In this, Eurystheus represents the envious supervisor who is intensely insecure about his own competence and feels threatened by the potential of his students. As a result he becomes destructively critical and disparaging of their efforts, demanding from them ever higher levels of achievement.

3. Procrustes was an ogre who lived in a castle commanding the strategic highway between Athens and Troizen. He used to lure travellers to his castle, where he laid them on his bed. If they were too long to fit, he lopped off the excess, and if they were too short, he stretched them out until they fitted exactly. He eventually met his death at the hands of Theseus, who journeyed along that road to claim the crown of Athens. Procrustes can be seen as the proto-

type of the supervisor who cannot tolerate individual differences, and attempts to make everyone conform to the same mould, at whatever cost. This is a more drastic version of Gee's 'Pygmalion complex' (Gee, 1992). Basically the Procrustean supervisor acts towards his supervisees as he acts towards himself. He is trying to force himself and them into a fixed, pre-set ideal mould because he is not at ease with himself. He has not learned to recognise and accept his own individual characteristics, but can only see them as failures and deviations from a rigid norm.

4. With Pallas Athene, goddess of wisdom and the arts, we come to the realm of the gods and goddesses. A particularly unattractive trait of hers was that she liked to be the patron and protectress of favourite heroes, and supported them with her divine resources against their human rivals. One of her favourites was Odysseus, who was caught up in bitter rivalry with Ajax after the death of Achilles during the Trojan War. In Sophocles' tragedy, Ajax, in order to further the interests of Odysseus, we see Athene bring upon Ajax such intolerable disgrace as to lead directly to the latter's suicide. Here the parallel is with the kind of supervisor who is parentally possessive and protective towards his supervisees and wins vicarious triumphs through their successes, for example, through favourable assessments of their work and advocacy of their merits at supervisors' meetings. This kind of supervisor seems to be using his supervisees to compensate for his own painful sense of inadequacy.

5. For our last example, we go to Delphi, the site of the most prestigious oracle of the ancient world, where Apollo Pythius was the presiding deity. Here the oracles were delivered by a priestess inspired by the god. She was seated in the innermost recesses of the temple in a state of trance, over a cleft in the rock from which issued mephitic vapours. Her highly prized deliverances on matters of religion, politics and personal conduct were imbued with a mysterious wisdom, and were often highly ambiguous and difficult to interpret. For example, in 546 BC Croesus, King of Lydia in central Asia Minor, was threatened by the power of Cyrus of Persia, whose empire was expanding up to the river Halys on Lydia's eastern frontier. In fear and perplexity Croesus consulted Apollo at Delphi. He was told, 'If you cross the Halys, you will destroy a great empire'. Thus reassured, he crossed the Halys and destroyed a great empire – not Cyrus', but his own. Supervisors, too, can clothe themselves with a similar divine and mysterious

authority, which cannot be questioned or challenged, and to protect that authority they can carefully avoid giving direct, unambiguous direction when it is called for.

In their early days as supervisors, beginners fall into similar patterns of behaviour and relating, not out of conscious choice but out of blind instinct, in order to ease the anxiety which the responsibility of supervising arouses in them. In most of the examples sketched above, the anxiety arises at root from a painful sense of emptiness, ignorance or incompetence within the supervisors themselves, of which they may be unaware or only dimly conscious. The reactive pattern serves to defend against the pain of that inadequacy by warding off anticipated criticism and exposure and/or by arming the supervisor with an apparently polished and competent persona (see Chapter 12, p. 207).

Learning by identification

In many cases, the particular pattern of supervisory behaviour may have been acquired from outside. For example, the beginner's own supervisor may have acted in that way, and so have provided a model for them to adopt spontaneously. Such imitation of a given model in fact constitutes a necessary factor in the process of learning a role: the beginner learns a role by identifying with an existing bearer of it. The external model combines with, or activates, the learner's own innate archetypal potential, to produce a pattern of behaviour that will meet the new demands. That is how boys learn to be fathers, and girls to be mothers. In object-relations terms, the subject forms an attachment to an external object and takes that object into him or herself. Thus an internal object is established within the psyche, an object with which the subject can identify and which becomes an essential part of the subject's own developing identity. The subject may then, under appropriate circumstances, come to be, or act as, the internal object.

That is of course an oversimplified account of the process of identification, which may in practice run nowhere near so smoothly. For example, if the learner/subject is particularly anxious about not being an adequate supervisor and not meeting the expectations of the supervisees, he may overidentify with the presented pattern. This may lead in turn to an exaggerated and overly rigid development of the defensive persona, which effectively inhibits further growth and development. Alternatively, a 'bad' or rejected model can influence, distort and dominate the process of identification. For example, the supervisee who has a bad experience in supervision may bend over backwards to be supergood, and not repeat the failings of his or her own 'bad' supervisor when it comes to learning to supervise. But still, the 'bad' supervisor will remain as an internal object within the learner and so constitute the potential for the learner occasionally to act out or embody that 'badness' as a supervisor despite his or her best efforts and intentions. Another possibility is that, if the learner's own experience of receiving supervision was vitiated by an excess of envy and rivalry, it may, in the end, turn out that he or she becomes incapable of identifying constructively with any role model at all. As a supervisor he or she will be left floundering at the mercy of instinctual impulses, without any solid point from which to take off on the learning process.

Identification with an available model, then, is a necessary first step in the development of a supervisor, but it is not the final or only one. It is best seen as the prelude to the process of individuation, which remains the goal. This brings us to what Jung himself says about individuation, although as previously noted, he is writing in the context of the development of the whole personality not of the partial development of one particular aspect of a person's potential.

Jung on individuation

'Individuation', Jung writes, 'means becoming a single homogeneous being', one's own unique self. Again, individuation is 'a process by which a man becomes the definite unique being he in fact is' (Jung, 1945, para. 267). To unpack these statements a little, we may say that being an individual or being individuated means being a separate entity, distinct from other people and from the collective psychology, free from external pressures to conform. Etymologically, the word 'individual' carries the root meaning 'not divided'. This points towards another dimension, that of inner wholeness, reconciliation and integration, developing and achieving one's potential beyond the tension of internal conflicts and the constraints which they impose. In short, individuation means being who one really is, the supervisor that you really are and only you can become, with a growing measure of freedom from unexamined controlling pressures both from within and without.

In the quotations cited above, Jung defines individuation in terms of its aim or goal. It is well, however, to remember that individuation is essentially a process in which we are continuously involved without ever reaching the point where we can claim to have achieved its completion. That is as true for the supervisor as it is for the individual human being. Hence the title of this chapter: not 'the *individuated* supervisor' but 'the *individuating* supervisor'.

In its focus on aim, the following quotation is no different from those cited above: 'The aim of individuation is nothing less than to divest the self of the false wrappings of the persona on the one hand, and the suggestive power of primordial images on the other' (Jung, 1945, para. 269). However, a new image of the individuation process is introduced here – that of divesting. Just as the attainment of consciousness and freedom imply a previous state of unconsciousness and a lack of freedom, so a process of divesting implies a previous state of vestedness, that is, of being clothed. That state has been described above in the examples from Greek mythology and in the discussion of identification. The new supervisor starts off metaphorically vested in the wrappings of the persona, taken on (as we have seen) to cope with anxieties about adequacy and competence, and at the mercy of powerful instinctual impulses and reactions which can be pictured in such suggestive images as mythology affords. Vesting is like putting on someone else's identity by identifying with them. That brings us to the questions: 'From such a starting point, how does the individuation process actually operate?', 'For the already vested, how does divesting occur?'. To answer those questions, we shall draw on the work of Fordham, Bion and Kolb in the field of learning theory.

Individuation in wider perspective

Fordham

In describing the interaction between the infant and its maternal environment, Fordham postulates the existence of an original or primary self, which is the integrated repository of all the infant's psychological potentials. When the infant encounters its environment, the primary self unpacks, or in Fordham's term 'deintegrates' (Fordham, 1957). That is, one particular potential (one 'deintegrate') comes into operation to guide the infant's actions and reactions in the encounter. That deintegrate includes affect, behaviour and primitive cognition in the form of phantasy or image. When the environment mother responds in a way that meets the needs of the infant, a fit occurs between the deintegrate and the environment, and the infant enjoys a good experience. When such an interaction reaches its natural conclusion, 'reintegration' occurs. This means that the deintegrate is withdrawn, the original wholeness of the primary self is restored and the infant reverts to a state of rest, until the next encounter takes place and the process of deintegration is repeated.

The deintegration–reintegration process described above represents a good cycle. When such good cycles are repeated and good experiences accumulate, the result is that a good internal object in the Kleinian sense is established within the psyche. However, when a harmonious fit does not occur between the deintegrate and the environment, for example, when the mother does not come to meet the infant's need, or the feed does not proceed satisfactorily, then what can happen is disintegration, a traumatic shattering of the infant's nascent world of consciousness. As a result of such an experience, a bad object is formed within the infant's psyche and the process of the development of consciousness and adaptation is thereby impeded or distorted.

The title of the essay in which Fordham introduced the idea of deintegration is 'The Origin of the Ego in Childhood'. He is talking here about the birth of consciousness. It is in the instinct-led encounter between infant and environment that the primitive ego comes to be formed. Fordham also talks about a process of individuation that begins in infancy through this cycle of repeated deintegrations (see Chapter 4, p. 68). This is a gradual process whereby the subject's awareness is differentiated from the unconsciousness of instinctual and archetypal domination. On the same theme, Jung described in figurative terms how, to illuminate the original darkness of unconsciousness, *scintillae* of light are struck in that same encounter of organism with environment (Jung, 1954 para. 389). Lambert further suggested that if the organism–environment fit is too snug, such sparks would not be ignited (Lambert, 1981). It demands a tolerable degree of friction or nonfit to occur, if the light of rudimentary, spasmodic ego-consciousness is to dawn.

Although it is sometimes so presented, Fordham's formulation is not specifically a theory of *infant* development. The repeated process of deintegration–reintegration is one that occurs throughout life, whenever instinctual patterns of behaviour and their accompanying archetypal images are elicited in the encounter between organism and environment. So in the context of the supervisory relationship, at times the supervisor may react to the supervisee's presentation on the spur of the moment in an unthinking, spontaneous way. At that point we may say that a deintegration occurs in the supervisor's encounter with the environment. Alternatively we might say that the supervisor is acting out of his original 'vested' condition, wrapped in the suggestive power of primordial images, as Nestor and the other mythological figures acted in the examples given above. What we still need to know is how divesting occurs, how the *scintillae* of consciousness are ignited. What happens in the infant's (or individuating supervisor's) inner world to make such ignition possible in that deintegrative encounter with the environment? Fordham himself does not go any further towards describing what goes on at this point. Rather, he refers the enquirer to the work of Wilfred Bion: 'as to the nature of early object relations', Fordham writes, 'I cannot improve on Bion's β elements transformed into α elements' (Fordham, 1995, p. 71). So it is to Bion's work that we must now turn, after a brief preliminary excursion into that of Freud.

Freud, Bion

For Freud, the process of learning through experience was intimately connected with the function of thinking (Freud, 1911). He proposed a schema whereby, when the organism is subjected to overstimulation by sensory perception, a state of tension or frustration arises, and that tension seeks relief through motor discharge. If such relief is delayed, tension increases. Thinking makes it possible to tolerate such delay and the consequent increase of tension, so that immediate action through motor discharge can be postponed. Bion's contribution is to spell out further the place of thought within this sequence (Grinberg, Sor and Bianchedi, 1985).

Again with reference to the interaction of infants and mothers, Bion describes how the hungry infant cries for its needs to be met. For Bion, all needed objects are bad objects, so this experience of need is *ipso facto* an experience of the 'bad breast'. Such an experience produces unpleasant resonances within the infant's awareness, which he calls 'β elements'. The infant cannot tolerate or process these within itself, but expels them into the environment mother by projective identification. Then two outcomes are possible. Either the mother comes to feed and comfort the infant within a time frame that the infant can tolerate. In addition, by virtue of her own 'reverie', she is able to accept and deal with the infant's distress within herself without rejection or retaliation, and so she serves as a good enough 'container' for the distressed infant. Thus she receives the β elements projected into her, processes them, transforms them and returns them to the child as α elements, that is, as thoughts. So, in a word, the intolerable and unthinkable experience is transformed into something that can be thought about and tolerated. Alternatively, the mother does not come, or comes too late, or in some other way fails to accept the projective identification. Then there is no container for the infant's distress, the β elements remain untransformed, projective identification is reinforced, and thought is impossible. The infant is left prey to its β elements, and all it can do is blindly to act out its distress.

All this relates most immediately to mothers and infants. At another level, of course, it also relates to analysts and their patients: the analyst enables the transformation of the patient's β elements into α elements by virtue of the containment that he offers. Beyond that, this pattern of mother–infant interaction also reflects what happens in the supervisor–supervisee dyad, in which the supervisor may offer sufficient containment to a stressed supervisee to enable the process of thought to emerge in relation to the supervisee's experience with the patient. Beyond that again, the learning supervisor himself is enabled to think about his work by the presence of an available container, rather than acting out compulsively in the supervision session in response to the supervisee's presentation. In this instance, containment may be offered to the supervisor from outside by a more experienced trainer/supervisor, or it may be provided intrapsychically, depending on his level of development. In Jungian terms we could summarise this process as the compelling power of a bad archetypal experience that becomes modified by good enough, human, mothering.

What Bion crucially adds to Freud's work is the need for thought as the essential factor in breaking free from the power of the archetype, and the need for adequate containment as the matrix in which thought may germinate. In other words, for individuation as divesting to occur, thought enabled by containment is necessary to interrupt the compulsive sequence (in Freud's terms) of overstimulation, tension and motor discharge. Nestor and his mythological colleagues need to have their anxiety contained sufficiently for them to think about what they are doing. Then he, for one, might stop rambling on in the Greek council of war about what happened decades ago and find a way to present his ideas more effectively. And *mutatis mutandis*, the supervisor, too, might be enabled to do the same.

Kolb

We now move on to look at the work of a group of American psychologists who have studied the processes of adult, experience-based learning in professional and work settings (Kolb, 1993). Their work differs from that of the writers already considered in several ways. They are concerned with the learning process in adults rather than in infants and mothers, and their focus is on conscious rather than on unconscious processes. Their stance is behavioural rather than analytic. However, there is a degree of convergence between the two groups.

To describe the process of learning, Kolb reproduces a four-part cycle, developed by Lewin, in which all four elements are necessary for the optimal facilitation of learning.

(i) The initial phase of the cycle is the concrete experience of the learner in the learning situation. This is not something theoretical or secondhand, but raw personal exposure to the experience. For the learning supervisor, it is the experience in the session with the supervisee that constitutes this essential starting point.

(ii) Following that initial experience, the learner withdraws to recall and reflect on it as fully as possible. He explores the experience, observing what happened and what it felt like from as many angles as possible. The learning supervisor may be encouraged to do this on his or her own, but preferably it may be done through a presentation of the work to his trainer, by verbatim report or whatever other method is chosen.

(iii) The learner seeks to develop and apply concepts in order to understand the given experience more fully and to form judgements about it. At this stage, theory may be applied to, or drawn out from, the material and thought encouraged.

(iv) Lastly, on the basis of the conceptualisation carried out in the third stage, the learner can begin to apply the understanding gained and to work out provisional strategies for the next stage of the learning process. So armed, he will be ready for a return to the arena of concrete experience where he will reenter the cyclical process at the first stage. That is to say, the learning supervisor will think about the application of the results of the total reflective process, in preparation for the next meeting with his supervisee(s).

On this view, learning is a process that requires the judicious integration of action and reflection. Kolb quotes Dewey to that effect: 'the crucial educational problem is that of procuring the postponement of immediate action upon desire until observation and judgement have intervened' (Kolb, 1993, p. 140). Essential to learning, then, is the ability to tolerate the tension that arises when immediate action upon impulse is postponed (cf. Freud, p. 26). That check on impulsive action gives opportunity for observation and judgement, in the sense of reflection, evaluation and choice. In this way the spontaneous, unconsidered initial feelings and impulses can be transformed into purposeful, deliberate action.

To clarify further the processes described above, we shall now look at a clinical example:

On the acute ward of a psychiatric hospital ward, a senior staff nurse, John, was the supervisor of a newly qualified junior colleague, Mary.

1. *Mary was on night duty in the ward, when a patient threatened her with a knife. Mary was very frightened, and her fear subsequently turned to anger. She drafted a strongly worded letter of protest to the unit manager regarding safety procedures on the ward.*

2. *In supervision Mary told John the story of the incident and brought the draft letter to show to him, looking for his approval and support. However, deep down John strongly disapproved of the letter, because he was anxious about the ripples which it would set in motion. In the supervision session he argued against Mary sending it, saying that it would not do any good, and anyway a review of security was already planned. But Mary was adamant, and determined to send the letter. She attacked John's response as 'pussy-footing around'. John tried to explore Mary's feelings about the incident in greater depth but met with a brick wall.*

3. *As a new supervisor, John was lucky enough to have a group to attend where he could receive supervision on his supervisory work with Mary. In the group, John expressed his distress with the way that the supervision with Mary had gone. He felt that he had failed utterly in not having dissuaded Mary from sending the letter, and he pressed the group for an immediate practical solution to his quandary. John wanted to protect Mary from what he saw as the harmful consequences of her plan, which could well rebound on Mary herself.*

4. *The members of John's supervision group initially tried to explore with him the feelings of all the parties involved in the situation: the patient with the knife, the supervisee Mary, John himself and his colleagues. Attention was focused on Mary's fear and anger and also on John's fearful reaction to Mary's angry letter. The group members themselves also felt somewhat*

intimidated by John's forceful demand for concrete, practical direction.
Eventually, through the discussion in the group a theoretical formulation
emerged, based on the work of Ekstein and Wallerstein on the parallel
process (1972).

In this example, the parallel exists in the resemblance between the
angry patient–frightened nurse couple in the clinical situation and the
angry supervisee–frightened supervisor couple in the supervisory
context. What happened on the ward is reproduced in Mary's supervision. A further parallel can be drawn in the next stage of the story,
when John as forceful supervisee intimidates the group and, thus,
reproduces the pattern. A pattern of feeling and action between one
pair of actors in the drama (patient and nurse Mary) is transmitted
outside its original context and reproduced between further pairs
(Mary and supervisor John, then John and his supervision group) in
an extending series of parallels by a kind of psychic infection. This can
be represented as follows:

patient : Mary || Mary : John || John : supervision group

Thus the supervisor, standing outside the original context, and,
subsequently, the supervision group are given the possibility of experiencing what is going on within the original pairing. The supervisor
can then use this insight to help the supervisee to relocate the immediately overpowering emotions back into the interactive situation
where they originated and properly belong.

5.   *By understanding the situation in this way, John was enabled to see that*
      the feelings he was experiencing and expressing both in the supervision
      with Mary and in the subsequent group supervision could be used to
      throw light on Mary's internal process. Before they were transmitted to
      John and then to his supervision group, the fear and the anger belonged
      primarily to Mary. If they could be given back to her, John could recover
      his own strength and poise. He could then allow Mary to take responsi-
      bility for her own action over the letter, after due reflection and discussion,
      without trying desperately to impose on her his own hesitations. So, hope-
      fully, he could now return to Mary's supervision with a new awareness
      and an enhanced freedom from the constraint of the archetypal reactions
      unconsciously communicated by the supervisee.

Viewed from the perspective of Bion's formulation, Mary was
initially overwhelmed by β elements, which she projected into John
(para. 1). As supervisor, John too was overwhelmed and unable to

contain Mary's intense emotion, which therefore remained unmodified. Thinking remained impossible, and Mary persevered in her intention to act out her feelings (para. 2). John's experience in supervision was different. He too came to the session full of β elements, the force of which the members of the supervision group also experienced (para. 3). However, their capacity for reverie and reflection was not entirely disabled, so John experienced sufficient containment in the group for thought to emerge and the β elements to be transformed into α elements (paras 4 and 5). Moreover, it was precisely the impact on the group of John's desperate demand, recognised by the members through a process of deliberate introspection, that enabled them to be aware of the dynamics of the situation.

When we look at these two supervisory processes in the light of Kolb's four-part formulation, we can see how, in Mary's supervision with John no full report or reflection on Mary's experience is undertaken (stage ii). In consequence, no adequate conceptualisation or thinking about the experience can take place either (stage iii). Instead, Mary jumps straight from the first to the fourth stage of the process and plans her next action. There is no postponement of immediate action upon desire. Thus the whole process becomes defective and ineffectual. However, when John takes all this to his own supervision, the deficiency in the reporting/reflection stage is not allowed to recur, by virtue of the careful exploration of the reported events within the group (para. 3 above). On that basis, concepts and judgements can be formulated (para. 4), and John is equipped for his next encounter with Mary (para. 5), so fulfilling the third and fourth stages of Kolb's prescription. In this way, the supervision group helps to make it possible for John to learn from his experience and to develop as a supervisor.

This chapter opened with a quotation from Samuels, on the relationship between conscious and unconscious processes. Further clarification of that relationship is needed in the context of learning within the supervisory process. The analysts (Fordham, Freud and Bion) are dealing for the most part with the relationship between mothers and infants in which the infant's reactions are largely unconscious. They are not wholly unconscious however because in Fordham, for example, the nascent ego emerges out of the process of deintegration, and that emergence is what he is seeking to describe. Moreover, when the processes described by the analysts take place in adult life, although they will not be wholly conscious, consciousness may be expected to participate to a higher degree than was the case in infancy. Similarly, as the adult learns to supervise, there will be many creative factors in his professional functioning which will remain unconscious. However, some of those factors will need to be brought into consciousness if they are to become resources for growth and learning, if damage to the supervisory process is to be avoided and if the supervisor is not perpetually to fly by the seat of his pants. That is the perspective from which Kolb is writing. However, the weakness in Kolb's presentation is the tacit suggestion that everything is under the sway of consciousness. In fact, as we saw in the clinical illustration (para. 2), the failure to secure an adequate place for observation and reflection on what has occurred may very well be due to unconscious factors. It is Bion who helps us to understand such phenomena more fully.

Conclusion

At the beginning of this chapter, we recalled five characters from Greek mythology who exercised responsibilities in similar ways to modern supervisors. By acting on unconsidered and unreflective impulse, they demonstrate the kind of starting point from which the process of individuation for the supervisor may begin. As the supervisor seeks to find his way in the new role, identification with a paradigm offered from without, which matches up with a potential within, may also play a part. According to Jung, individuation requires that a person differentiate himself or herself from such identifications in order to discover and become who he or she truly is. To explore this notion, we used Jung's metaphor of vesting and divesting. If, in the role of supervisor, a person may initially clothe himself with whatever vestments are available in order to ease his anxiety and enable himself to function, then individuation will mean divesting oneself of other people's clothes.

To see how divesting comes about, we looked at the work of four different writers. Central to all of them is the emergence of consciousness. The analytic formulations, although originating in the context of mothers and infants, are also valid in the context of adult relationships. Thus, both Freud and Bion can be taken to describe how, in adulthood too, thought processes operate to help the individual cope with distressing experience and to modify behaviour. As the necessary condition for this to happen, Bion stresses the need for adequate containment. From the standpoint of adult learning, Kolb is perhaps nearer to Freud, in emphasising the need for the postponement of immediate action so that reflection can supervene.

The supervisor divests himself of unconscious identifications and constraining patterns of behaviour within the supervisory relationship, in so far as he is able to arrest the impulse to speak or act out of such overdetermined identifications and constraints. That opens the door to reflection, to extension of consciousness, to increasing freedom of choice and to individuation. For that process to continue and to develop fruitfully, the supervisor himself needs a safe containing space in which to develop the capacity for thought, and it is the provision of such a space that will constitute his best gift to his supervisees.

References

Ekstein, R. and Wallerstein, R. S. (1972) *The Teaching and Learning of Psychotherapy* (2nd edn.) (Madison, CT: International Universities Press.)

Fordham, M. (1957) 'The Origins of the Ego in Childhood', in M. Fordham (ed.), *New Developments in Analytical Psychology* (London: Routledge & Kegan Paul).

Fordham, M. (1995) *Freud, Jung, Klein: The Fenceless Field – Essays in Psychoanalysis and Analytical Psychology* (London: Routledge & Kegan Paul).

Freud, S. (1911) 'Formulations on the Two Principles of Mental Functioning', *Standard Edition XII*.

Gee, H. (1992) 'Supervision – Problems in the Relationship', in *The Practice of Supervision: Some Contributions* (British Association of Psychotherapists, London).

Grinberg, L., Sor, D. and Bianchedi, E.T. (1985) *Introduction to the Work of Bion* (London: Maresfield Library).

Jung, C. G. (1945) 'The Relations between the Ego and the Unconscious', *Collected Works Volume 7*.

Jung, C. G. (1954) 'On the Nature of the Psyche', *Collected Works Volume 8*.

Kolb, D. A. (1993) 'The Process of Experiential Learning', in Thorpe, M., Edwards, R. and Hanson, A. (eds), *Culture and Processes of Adult Learning* (London: Routledge & Kegan Paul/Open University).

Lambert, K. (1981) *Analysis, Repair and Individuation* (London: Academic Press).

Samuels, A. (1985) *Jung and the Post-Jungians* (London: Routledge & Kegan Paul).

2

Reflections on the Therapist–Supervisor Relationship

Jane Knight

Supervision and consultation

Supervision provides a space in which two analysts, one of whom has relatively more experience, reflect together on the work of the one who is less experienced and who may be a student or student analyst. When the less experienced person is a colleague, I prefer to call the process 'consultation'. Within this space there can be room for exploring the content and emotional climate of sessions with a patient, for the sharing of ideas and deepening knowledge of the patient's inner processes. Insights arise from the discussion and these lead to understanding of aspects of the relationship between patient and analyst and the enhancement of listening with a sense of the symbolic meaning of the patient's communications, the development of an analytic attitude. Such an intimate and detailed exploration depends on mutual respect and trust between supervisee and supervisor: the former trusting the supervisor's benign intention and capacity to hold in mind both the patient's and the analyst's needs, the latter respecting the supervisee's integrity and wish to learn. Further, such trust depends on the supervisor's capacity to maintain the boundary of the space, not only by providing the physical area for the work and the frame of regular times and set fees, but also 'through continuous attention on keeping to the primary task of helping the trainee to comprehend the nature of the interaction with his patient' (Szecsody, 1997).

In the world of analysis, psychotherapy and casework, supervision has evolved from its original meanings of over-seeing and controlling, although there is an element of 'watching with authority over a process'. A context of enablement and support and the facilitation of learning from experience has developed with the personal engagement between supervisor and supervisee. It is a co-operative activity between an analyst or a student analyst with a supervisor who can bring to this meeting a view of the work with the patient untrammeled by direct emotional involvement. However, emotional involvement, transference both to the supervisee and to the patient, is inevitably evoked in the supervisor.

The process includes exploring the interaction between patient and analyst and how unconscious forces may affect the work. An important function for the supervisor is responding to, and helping to contain, the analyst's anxiety. This may arise from the patient's anxiety or from the difficulties of working with a particular patient, or anxieties evoked in the analyst by his transference to the patient or to the supervisor. At the same time, anyone who shows his work to another, especially when he needs help, feels some anxiety as this means revealing his personal style, his particular understanding of the case and his uncertainty. Uncertainty is particularly hard to bear for an analyst who has an internal ideal, which may have a persecutory intensity. For trainee analysts there is a very real concern about assessment and reports to committees or other bodies which can grant or withhold qualification. If such fears can be imparted to the supervisor, the working relationship deepens and the student can begin to risk himself and develop his own style of work.

In a training institute a supervisor has multiple responsibilities which may conflict. She has a responsibility to the trainee analyst to make knowledge and experience available, to facilitate learning and also to contain anxiety. There is concern for the student's patient; that he shall have an adequate, good enough experience of analysis. The supervisor also endeavours to ensure that the work is properly bounded and ethically conducted. There is accountability to the training institute and possibly to an employing authority. The supervisor has real power over the future career of a student.

The supervision of a colleague's work is usually free of these conditions. The analyst has been confirmed in his practice. He seeks consultation specifically for his own needs, which may be to seek resolution of a negative collusion of transference and countertransference, or generally to reflect with a senior colleague on his work and to improve his practice. He is not driven by the requirements of a training course or dependent on the supervisor's approval. Relieved of these pressures, discussion can be more open and wide ranging. The analyst can express his personal views and emotional responses, knowing that both he and the consultant-supervisor share the attitude that all thoughts and feelings about the patient are relevant and to be considered as aspects of the analyst's relationship with the patient. The consulting analyst chooses the material that he brings to the supervisor. He holds responsibility for the management of the case. In consultation there is greater freedom within the frame and also the frame itself is more secure, with confidentiality better assured, if there are no demands from an outside authority such as a training institute. Many problems in supervision derive from the stimulation of unconscious conflicts and complexes in the supervisee by the patient's material and the projective force of the transference. It cannot be assumed that the consulting analyst is continuing his personal analysis so that these conflicts may be understood and interpreted. The supervisor needs to convey understanding of the case without becoming the supervisee's analyst.

Which supervisor?

In the choice of a supervisor, it is likely that a number of assumptions and projections are activated. Some people choose a supervisor who resembles themselves, the personal analyst, a parent or a teacher. Others may look for someone who will be kind or who is seen as rigorous, that is, who will be 'good for me'. Unconscious influences affect the choice as inner figures of authority are evoked (see Chapter 3, p. 51). Is the supervisor seen as an expert, critic, judge, friend, teacher or parent (see Chapter 5, p. 92)?

Before the first meeting to discuss the feasibility of supervision, the foundations of the relationship are beginning to form. At that meeting the structure of times, frequency and, if relevant, fees is established: the frame, in Robert Langs' definition (1979). In this preliminary exercise, supervisor and supervisee are consciously and unconsciously registering attitudes, strengths and degrees of openness. Their individual working styles are demonstrated as the supervisee describes something of his work with a patient and the supervisor responds with a comment or observation. Each shows the other a sample of their practice and, if they feel compatible, a working relationship can begin.

The supervisor of a trainee analyst just beginning with the first patient needs to bear in mind the extent to which such work can make a student feel de-skilled. A trainee analyst who has been a senior practitioner in a related profession regresses to some extent and may feel again like a child on the first day at school, so is particularly vulnerable to narcissistic wounding. The skills appropriate in a previous life may be inappropriately applied as he grapples with the emotional demands of the current task. For example, a student who also practises as a social worker, harried by the needs of a patient regarding her difficult children, may seek to assist with this problem and find it very difficult to hear the 'difficult child' in the patient. Often there is an idealisation of analysis so that the 'perfect' analyst is projected on to the supervisor. This can cause a trainee analyst to feel demeaningly incompetent. If the supervisor can engage the student in co-operative work regarding the patient, the disabling fantasy may be gently defused. Some students have to suffer a painful disillusionment.

The choice of supervisor is made from both conscious and unconscious motives. If a third person, such as the Director of Training is required to match the pair, he will need to consider the personality of the supervisor. At first a very anxious student may need a supervisor who will be in alignment with him, but the time may come when constructive opposition is appropriate. In terms of Jung's Theory of Personality Types, an analyst whose predominant function is that of feeling or intuition would need the thinking of the supervisor. If the process of individuation is progressing, the analyst can use the supervisor's thinking to reinforce the development of his own thinking and achieve a new balance. Under stress an individual tends to revert to the predominant function and that is when the complementary function of the supervisor is most needed. An analyst with a conscious thinking function might become disassociated from the patient's feelings, or, if his more conscious function is feeling, he could find it difficult to think about the meaning of the patient's material. When the opposition of functions is too extreme, patient and analyst may have great difficulty in understanding each other and this can lead to impasse. It is the supervisor's task to be aware of such a development and, if possible, to resolve the dilemma.

Recording and reporting

Supervisors have different views about techniques and working practices. One example is the use of the analyst's record of sessions with the patient. The means by which the supervisor comes to know about the progress of the case emerges from the supervisee's reporting, his memory, demeanour, degree of confidence and the state of mind that he brings. It is impossible for any means of reporting to convey the whole process of an interview. There is a discipline in preparing a verbatim record. This, in itself, is educational for the analyst in that it promotes reflection on the material, as does the recounting to a third person, the supervisor (see Chapter 5, pp. 89–90). Therefore, a trainee analyst is frequently required to make a written record of the sessions with the patient, especially during the early phases of the analysis. Some supervisors ask to be given a copy of this record, others leave the control of the report in the hands of the trainee analyst who reads it aloud or refers to it in supervision sessions. In due course, many supervisors prefer that analysts report their work spontaneously, perhaps focusing on a particular passage, a dream or a certain difficulty. All methods have advantages and disadvantages. Full verbatim reporting may enable the supervisor to perceive indications in the detail which have not been significant to the analyst, but it can be deadening and cloak the essential interaction between patient and analyst, thus preventing the participation of the supervisor. Spontaneous reporting gives a lively impression of the emotional interchange and therefore is encouraged by many supervisors, even if some content of the sessions is overlooked for various reasons, including their emotional import to the analyst. By listening with close attention to the case material while allowing thoughts and associations to come into her mind, the supervisor provides a model for a trainee analyst who is building an inner composition of the analyst that he will become, incorporating experiences with his personal analyst, supervisors and others from whom he learns.

Supervisees develop different styles of working and presenting their material. Many speak from brief notes made at the end of each session and are then able to reconstruct it verbally. Sometimes a supervisee briefly describes the bones of a session and then abandons it on the lap of the supervisor, expecting the supervisor to work on his 'text'. Then it is necessary to think about and discuss the meaning of this behaviour as an aspect of the relationship. Is the student intimidated, fearful of exposing his own thoughts and fantasies about a patient to a senior practitioner? He may be confused by feelings of envy, believing that he will get the most out of supervision if he leaves the field to the supervisor. He may be carrying a disabling projection from the patient. So the supervisor tries to engage the analyst in the joint endeavour to understand the patient by observing the interactions between himself and his patient. For a supervisor to express too much knowledge and understanding which goes beyond the student's experience may increase his paralysing feelings of incompetence. When a colleague consults me about his work, I make no condition about the method of reporting. He may refer to notes or speak spontaneously. The communication often reflects the degree of anxiety about the case or the consultation. I endeavour to promote spontaneous reporting within a relationship of trust.

The recording of supervision by supervisors is equally individual. Because of the requirements of training institutes, my own records of work with trainee analysts are more continuous and usually more detailed than the records of work with analysts who consult me. Hence, the case material below derives from work with trainee analysts.

Techniques and working practices

To an extent, the supervisor works from an identification with the analyst, experiencing the doubts, the struggle and the satisfaction, the emotional reactions or the absence of affect. Identification helps the supervisor to realise something of the source of the analyst's response to the patient. At the same time the supervisor needs to take an objective view which is impossible if the alignment with the analyst or with the patient is too complete. It is desirable to foster a spirit of enquiry in which both analyst and supervisor reflect on the work. There may be mistakes but, if they can be perceived as elements in the interaction which can be understood, the analyst can move on from the place at which he has arrived with the patient, rather than try to unpick the mistake. Mistakes arise from various causes, for example, the novice's enthusiasm or anxiety, the wish for results or to please the supervisor. Most frequently they occur because of the analyst's unconscious identification with an aspect of the patient, the analyst's countertransference. Jung (1954, p. 167) emphasised the necessity for the analyst to be open to the patient, to risk engaging in a process in which the therapeutic possibility lies in mutual unconsciousness, the *participation mystique*. In his view both analyst and patient are changed by the process, 'the illness being transferred to the doctor', as the analyst introjects parts of the patient's inner world. This process contributes to, and may determine, the analyst's countertransference. Studies by Heinrich Racker (1953), Michael Fordham (1960) and others developed the understanding of the analyst's countertransference in terms of the analyst's response to the patient's transference. The neurotic (Racker) or illusory (Fordham) countertransference pertain to un-analysed and un-integrated parts of the analyst. With a concordant or a syntonic countertransference the analyst is empathically identified with the patient and able to work without unconscious hindrance. The complementary counter-transference is dominated by the analyst's introjection of inner figures or archetypal images from the patient. These processes are dynamic, they interact and change, and they also are present in the supervisor. The neurotic, illusory and complementary processes lead to misunderstanding and mistakes. They may create conflict between analyst and supervisor.

A problem of technique arises for the supervisor as to how and when to intervene while the analyst is reporting a session. It can be difficult to hold a continuous flow of material and an intervention may be appropriate to highlight a particular issue, although repeated interruptions disrupt the analyst's capacity to bring a living experience to the supervisor. A question or the suggestion that a particular passage in the report needs further attention focuses the supervisee's thinking.

One trainee analyst had difficulty in holding a very disturbed patient who brought a great deal of material about her outer life and work, keeping the analyst at arm's length. She was denigrating of all attempts to understand the unconscious process and greeted interpretations with contempt. The trainee analyst was trying to get alongside, to develop a real contact. One day the patient came saying that she was afraid of becoming just like her mother and she listed all the mother's negative characteristics. The analyst commented that she was not at all like her mother and listed the ways in which she had differentiated herself. She would have continued her report, but the supervisor decided to stop her and wondered why she had said that. Immediately the student could see that her response had been inappropriate and unanalytic. She could then observe how her intention to be with the patient, in contrast to the mother, together with the unconscious introjection of the patient's inner child, had determined her intervention. She had reassured the patient and placated her instead of exploring her fear, self-hatred and envy which could have been linked with the patient's transference to the analyst. It seemed that the analyst had responded as the 'good' mother by reassuring rather than with understanding. This patient's defensive stance infected the analyst by projection of her inner child. The effect was compounded by the patient's often repeated threats to abandon the analysis in her unconscious attempt to pre-empt being herself abandoned by the analyst.

An idealising transference can be as much of an impediment to progress as a negative one. Sometimes the analyst is imbued with the image of an idealised parent and is unable to see anything but his 'child's' achievements, or colludes with a patient's victim position. Both are unconsciously fearful that the analyst, by expressing anything less than approval, will turn into a sadistic aggressor. Again it is the unconscious interaction that the supervisor needs to bring to light, in order to elucidate the meaning of the behaviour.

Consideration of these manifestations of countertransference, determined by the power of the patient's projective identification, questions the extent to which the supervisor comes to understand the supervisee's inner world. It may be apparent that the patient's material has evoked a complex in the analyst. An encapsulated nucleus of repressed or dissociated feelings is activated, causing distress or, possibly, inappropriate action. To acknowledge this is a necessity and a relief and expands the analyst's insight and knowledge of the interaction with the patient. Deeper understanding, interpretation and working through belong with the supervisee's personal analyst. As a result, experience with patients furthers the analyst's understanding of himself.

It is the supervisor's greater psychological distance from the patient that enables her to help the analyst to achieve a space in which to reflect on intrusive affects which can be so disabling to thinking. The analyst may come to supervision in a state which is 'not himself'. For example, he may be confused, unexpectedly angry or anxiously pouring forth questions that demand an answer. This may be confusing to the supervisor until she recognises that the supervisee is effectively *being* his own patient, bringing the patient into the room by his behaviour, the patient who is confused and confusing, angry or demanding answers to questions.

A further manifestation of this process is the supervisor's experience of affect by which the analyst is apparently untouched. It is as if the analyst were a lens through which the patient's feelings are transmitted to the supervisor. For example, the supervisor might become frustrated, angry or sad. She needs to consider the source of these feelings, whether they arise from her own unconscious patterns, that is, from an illusory countertransference, from the analyst, the patient and the relationships between all three. This group of experiences constitutes the *reflection process*, sometimes referred to as the *parallel process*, when the relationship between analyst and supervisor repeats that between patient and analyst. When the analyst remains apparently untouched by the emotions the process more resembles refraction than reflection.

In his paper, 'The Informational Value of the Supervisor's Emotional Experience', Searles states that

> when the supervisor finds himself experiencing some emotion during the supervisory hour, he should be alert not only to the possibility that the source of the emotion may lie chiefly in his own repressed past, in which case he is experiencing a classical countertransference reaction to the therapist; he should be alert to the possibility that the source of this emotion may lie chiefly in the therapist-patient relationship and, basically, chiefly in the patient himself. If the latter is found to be the case, then we may say that the supervisor's emotion is a *reflection* of something which has been going on in the therapist-patient relationship and, in the final analysis, in the patient. (Searles, 1965, p. 159)

The process is also demonstrated as a form of splitting between analyst and supervisor which often originates in the patient. Different aspects of the patient's inner world are projected as overwhelming anxiety causes him to keep inner figures separate. In this way, opposite aspects of the patient's inner world are projected on to analyst and supervisor. It may be that either the analyst or the supervisor takes a concerned, maternal attitude, while the other becomes a strict father. A student analyst may be very distressed by this opposition as his maternal countertransference is interrupted by the supervisor's insisting on orthodox interpretations which seem to aim at separating mother and child. The opposite effect may occur when the analyst sees his role as promoting separation and growth while the supervisor emphasises greater understanding of the patient's baby needs. In many cases each is responding to the projection of one side of the patient's inner parents, at cross purposes because of the patient's fear of separating them and wish to keep them apart. In the supervisory pair, each is identified with an aspect of the parental couple, stereotypically a mother preoccupied with her infant and a jealous father intent on separating mother and child.

If the introjection of the patient's archetypally-determined inner figures resonates with elements of the inner worlds of the analyst and the supervisor, an impasse in the supervisory relationship may develop. In an individual case there may be unconscious envy, jealousy and competition, possibly projected by the patient into the analyst and then conveyed into the supervision, exacerbating shadow aspects of that partnership. There are negative elements in any significant relationship. Envy can block co-operative work. It can also be a spur to development; a student who envies his teacher's knowledge strives to master knowledge himself. A supervisor may suffer jealous pain when she has to bear observing the analyst–patient pair absorbed in each other. Then the question must be asked, 'Is there a denied, excluded child in the case, unconsciously projected from patient to supervisor?' Thus the supervisor has a valuable means of understanding the case through her countertransference. Working with the concept of the reflection process does not exempt both supervisor and analyst from examining their respective conscious and unconscious attitudes to the patient and to the material. Difficulties do not arise only and always from the patient's transference. The projection finds a 'hook' within the analyst and the supervisor. As Stimmel states concerning the supervisor, 'Supervisors' unconscious transferences to the supervisee exist, and the parallel processes in a given supervision process lend themselves, among others, as likely contexts for the enactment of and resistance to the awareness of such transferences' (Stimmel, 1995).

Interruptions in supervision

An unplanned and unexpected break in supervision may be a very disruptive experience for a supervisee, especially for a student. If this happens a trainee analyst, especially one working with a deeply wounded and therefore defensive and aggressive patient, is in danger of falling into collusive reactions or letting the boundaries slide.

During a break in supervision, a patient had reduced, and frequently missed, her sessions. It was very difficult for the trainee analyst to re-establish a consistent continuity. It is hard to know with hindsight to what extent the patient was testing out the analyst, since the patient was convinced that she was not wanted, but then the trainee analyst felt unwanted and abandoned also. She was so sure that she was expected to manage alone that she did not ask for help. Such collusions are difficult to perceive without supervision. Sometimes collusion is a necessary part of the process, but it may be due to the analyst's fear of confronting the patient or to the evocation of a complex in the analyst. An analyst may act out the mother complex by trying to give the patient ideal mothering as a compensation for his own deep sense of deprivation.

A change of supervisor is occasionally necessary. This may be due to incompatibility of personalities, possibly rooted in the mutual provocation of the opposite function type in each other. There may be conflicting theoretical convictions or other extraneous reasons. Whatever the cause of the change, there is a period of readjustment and anxiety which needs to be met with sensitivity by the new supervisor.

One trainee analyst had had a very good experience with her former supervisor who had died. She was grieving when she came to me. She managed the loss and the sense of being uncontained by holding onto, and continuing to apply, everything that the previous supervisor had said. She did not believe that I, who was junior to that supervisor, could have anything useful to add. I was aware that the work had become stereotyped. The analyst was interpreting on the oedipal level, but I felt increasingly in touch with a desolate baby. Was this my own pain at being left out of the interaction? or was it an aspect of the patient? I struggled to bring this experience into our discussions, with little success. The patient came to our rescue. She began to talk about ending the analysis a few months short of two years of treatment. The analyst was bewildered and became angry. She believed that the referrer must have told the patient that the analysis would last for only two years. So I asked the analyst what was happening when the patient was two years old. She discovered that the patient's next sibling had been born when she was aged two years and two months. Then we could understand the patient's unconscious fear that there would be no room for her on the mother-analyst's lap after two years and her defence against this threat of abandonment by leaving the analysis before a repetition of the catastrophic rejection. For the analyst, there was an inner identification with the patient's defence.

Containment

The supervisor's holding function is especially needed for an analyst who is working with a patient with a borderline personality whose characteristic pattern of defence is an extreme form of projective identification. In his situation the patient has fixed ideas about the attitudes and intentions of the analyst and there is a repeated threat of impasse with implications for the breakdown of the analysis. It may be difficult to think in the presence of such a person. The analyst feels attacked from without by the patient and from within by his own persecutory ego ideal. The powerful affect resulting from the unwanted parts of the patient's personality prevents the analyst from understanding what is happening.

One trainee analyst was afraid of a patient who rejected his every move with much hostility. The analyst felt driven to interpret. Consequently his interpre-

tations were stilted and intellectual, fuelled by his unconscious hatred for his persecutor. The patient felt them as blows and returned them as such, with scornful assertions like, 'That came out of a book'. The inner identification was so overwhelming that the analyst could not recognise the patient's fear because of his own, experienced fear. When the countertransference was understood, it could be perceived that the patient needed a response that indicated under-standing of his fear rather than a confrontation of his aggression.

In these cases, the analyst becomes too much enmeshed with the patient to hear his unconscious language. The analyst needs the medi-ation of a receptive supervisor to help him to perceive and listen to the processes at work and the underlying meaning.

There is a difference between helping a trainee analyst to think about the kind of interpretation that is appropriate and suggesting the wording, although at times and in the beginning phase he may need help with the actual words (see Chapter 3, p. 52, and Chapter 5, pp. 90–1). The aim is to enable the analyst to respond from himself in the immediacy of the relationship. In the case of a trainee analyst, the interpretation may be a reproduction of the supervisor's words. This could be a function of the student's identification with the supervi-sor, a sense that he cannot match the supervisor's understanding, or he may not have digested the concept sufficiently to make it his own.

There is so much in the practice of analysis which cannot be taught but may be learned. A supervisor may be essential to recognise that the analyst is bearing a massive projection, but the analyst is the one who is available to receive it and to hold, understand and, in due course, to interpret it. In this process, projected shadow aspects of the patient are integrated. As the analyst relates to the patient's shadow, he enables the patient to do so and to accept disowned parts of himself. Since projections occur when the other has a reciprocal hook or tendency, the process of individuation is furthered not only in the patient but in the analyst also. This is the '*mixtum compositum* of the doctor's mental health and the patient's maladjustment' to which Jung refers (1954, p. 171). He states, that 'the patient, by bringing an active unconscious content to bear upon the doctor, constellates the corre-sponding unconscious material in him . . . Doctor and patient thus find themselves in a relationship of mutual unconsciousness.' (Jung, 1954, p. 176). A supervisor offers a firm point of orientation, experi-encing the storm but with less intensity, so she is more able to think and differentiate the elements of the mixture. There are times when the supervisor needs a capacity to wait in uncertainty, refraining from interference in the patient–analyst bond. If a patient has had traumatic experiences during her early years, she needs to develop confidence in the continuing holding of the analyst. Separations, such as holiday breaks or, especially, unplanned breaks, disrupt this process. A trainee analyst needs the containment of supervision without impingement to re-establish continuity and to repair the consequent disruption of empathy which may follow these inevitable interruptions.

Thinking and feeling

As he becomes more secure in himself, the analyst develops an attitude of reverie and openness to the patient, allowing a flow of feelings, associations and thoughts. Both analyst and supervisor need a capacity to use the two kinds of thinking described by Jung (1956, p. 7), that is, directed, logical thinking, using words, and fantasy thinking, allowing images to emerge. Can they function simultaneously or do they alternate? According to the predominant function type, that is, in Jung's personality type theory, whether the analyst uses thinking, feeling, intuition or sensation predominantly, that function will take precedence. This must influence the analyst's capacity to use the two kinds of thinking. Marion Milner expresses a similar idea in terms of focus of attention, the narrow, centred focus and the 'wide embracing kind of concentration' (Milner, 1950). This attitude cannot be taught but may be discovered when the first anxious concentration is relaxed. Then the whole self is engaged.

Conclusion

Although in this chapter, the examples have concentrated on problems in supervision, the main progress of the work is often an enjoyable, mutual interchange of thought and association. Analyst and supervisor together develop ideas about the relationship between patient and analyst. Sometimes the most cogent insights arise when work becomes play, not an adversarial game but a happy play of ideas, like a duet when themes are exchanged and either partner may take the lead. 'Supervision provides a framework for "bloody serious play" ' (Szecsody, 1997).

In supervision, as in analysis, we work within a paradox, loving and hating, holding and letting go, differentiating and synthesising, giving and receiving. In this unequal partnership the receiving and learning are not all one way. Supervisors learn from supervisees as analysts learn from patients. In effect, the patient is the analyst's best supervisor. As Jung said, 'The analyst must go on learning endlessly' (1954, p. 116), and so must the supervisor.

Summary

This chapter consists of personal reflections on the analyst–supervisor relationship. Some of the influences on the choice of a supervisor and the setting up of supervision have been described. Reference is made to issues of technique and different requirements for the recording and reporting of sessions with the patient. The complexity of the responsibilities of the supervisor is reviewed. The role is considered with regard to meeting the analyst's particular needs in his work, especially the understanding of his relationship with the patient and the projections between the patient, the analyst and the supervisor. The supervisor makes her knowledge and experience available and may be a model for the student to become the analyst that only he or she can be. The practice of analysis can hardly be taught but is learned from experience with the patient and in the spirit of enquiry inculcated in the supervisory relationship. Therefore, particular heed is given to the modes of the analyst's attention to the patient and the parallel processes in analysis and supervision.

References

Fordham, M. (1960) 'Counter Transference', *The Library of Analytical Psychology,* **2,** Techniques in Jungian Analysis (London: Heinemann).

Jung, C. G. (1954) 'The Practice of Psychotherapy', *Collected Works Volume 16.*

Jung, C. G. (1956) 'Symbols of Transformation', *Collected Works Volume 5.*

Langs, R. (1979) *The Supervisory Experience* (New York: Jason Aronson).

Langs, R. (1997) 'The Framework of Supervision in Psychoanalytic Psychotherapy', in B. Martindale, M. Morner, M. E. C. Rodriguez and J.-P. Vidit (eds), *Supervision and its Vicissitudes* (London: Karnac).

Milner, M. (1950) *On Not Being Able to Paint* (London: Heinemann).

Racker, H. (1953) 'The Uses of Countertransference', in *Transference and Countertransference* (London: Hogarth Press).

Searles, H. (1955) 'The Informational Value of the Supervisor's Emotional Experience', in J. D. Sutherland (ed.) (1965) *Collected Papers on Schizophrenia and Related Subjects* (London: Hogarth Press, Chapter 4).

Solomon, H. M., Kalsched, D., Knight, J., Springer, A., and Beebe, J. (1998) 'Supervision' in *Florence '98. Proceedings of the IVth International Congress for Analytical Psychology* (Einsiedeln: Daimon).

Stimmel, B. (1995) 'Resistance to Awareness of the Supervisor's Transferences with Special Reference to the Parallel Process', *International Journal of Psycho-Analysis*, **76,** 609.

Szecsody,I. (1997) '(How) Is Learning Possible in Supervision?', in B. Martindale, M. Morner, M. G. C. Rodriguez and J.-P. Vidit (eds), *Supervision and its Vicissitudes* (London: Karnac).

3

Empathy in the use of Countertransference between Supervisor and Supervisee

James Astor

Introduction

Empathy is a form of identification and as such is a perceptive process. Jung described it as 'a movement of libido towards the object in order to assimilate it' (1971, para. 871). I think of it as an attitude of mind in which the supervisor performs the task of differentiating internally the supervisory from the analytic vertex in the context of the asymmetry of the supervisory relationship. I am borrowing the term vertex from Bion, to refer to 'views with which I am identified. With myself as the vertex all these vertices represent "other-people-as-seen-by-me"' (Bion, 1965, pp. 145–6). So, 'an analytic response' is one vertex, 'some people think' is another, and 'Jungians generally' is yet another. In using the term 'vertex', Bion was getting away from the implicit confusion between the literal and the metaphorical that can result from a term such as 'point of view', with its emphasis on a visual system.

By way of orientation, I will begin with Michael Fordham's observation about analysts and learning how to become an analyst:

> the analyst will know that every single statement he makes is an account of the state of his psyche, whether it be a fragment of understanding, an emotion, or an intellectual insight; all techniques and all learning how to

analyse are built on this principle. It is thus part of the analyst's training experience to realise that he is often going to learn, sometimes more, sometimes less, from each patient, and that in consequence he himself is going to change. (Fordham, 1957, p. 69)

This is my starting point. I have at the back of my mind this principle, stated by Fordham, as well as the hope that both supervisor and supervisee are going to learn something from their work together. This encourages mutuality. The essence of supervision is that it provides a space for thinking (Rustin, 1996). It is therefore both clinical and didactic. It is a space that has a certain quality of attention, not dissimilar to analysis, in that the communications are being considered from the position of multiple vertices (Rustin, 1996). It is like analysis, too, in that supervision leads to the internalisation of a process and a model, which enables us to monitor our sessions. An openness to different ways of thinking about experience, the absence of judgemental attitudes, as well as benevolence and analytic thinking in all its forms, are features which characterise both supervision and analysis. But supervision is unlike analysis, in that the supervisee's transference to the supervisor is not systematically analysed or interpreted.

I acknowledge that as supervisor I am learning from the relationship with my supervisees, and from their relationships with their patients. I proceed on the basis that they *are* learning from their patients and from their relationships with me. I recognise that there exists in their minds my relationship with their patients, and that this can sometimes cause difficulties in their work with their patients. I also demonstrate in my interventions that my relationship with the supervisee is monitored from different vertices, including the supervision itself. I pay attention to w<u>ha</u>t is being reported, the <u>way</u> it is being reported, and what <u>I experie</u>nce while it is being reported. Within this process, I am considering and rejecting hypotheses about the material under consideration. I am thinking about this in the context of what I know about the supervisee, her characteristics, tendencies to understand the material in a particular way, and her residual psychopathology as revealed in relation to me. Technically this means that I often make use of questions, expressed ruminatively or tentatively, because questions allow issues to be raised in an unthreatening way.

Most of us have had the experience of understanding something new about our own material just from discussing it with a colleague.

We can understand this meeting of two minds as a form of parenting in which the thoughts and ideas we have about the supervisee's patient are the children of the process.

Getting to know you

This coming together of supervisor and supervisee does not always produce a creative exchange. Sometimes, usually at the beginning of the relationship, this experience of the supervisor–supervisee couple can re-open in the supervisee old wounds, feelings only partially addressed in her own analysis, including feelings of exclusion, even of envy and hate. This can then be destructive of their work together. More usual, in my own experience, has been an initial struggle to understand whence each of the parties is coming. One supervisee has referred to her early experience of working with me as one of struggling to find a common language, when she felt I was talking mathematics and she was talking intuition and passionate feelings. I was water to her fire. She thought of me as detached, schematic and very English. She needed time to think about her entanglement. She talked about myths and I talked about the quality of the patient's internal objects. Gradually, she came to realise how much I appreciated her engagement with her patients and she, in turn, found her own way to use what I understood and my way of describing it (see Chapter 2, pp. 36–7, and Chapter 5, p. 92).

Another potential complication at the beginning of a supervisory relationship is the added weight of the supervisee's historical relationships to her own internal objects and her need to sort these out. The characterisation of me as mathematical, detached and very English might be plausible superficially, but its significance suggests evidence of residual transferences to internal objects (in her case, her father). If the supervisee is not in analysis, or unable to integrate these experiences through self-analysis, then the supervision process can be derailed. Only occasionally have I found this to be an insurmountable problem.

The supervisory process

The focus: the supervisee or the patient?

If the supervisor focuses too much on the supervisee and not enough on his patient, then the knowledge gained during the supervisory session can take on a persecutory quality through the knowledge of hindsight. It can seem like wisdom after the event if, as in a legal context encased in superiority and contempt, the tone becomes 'if you know that now, why didn't you do something about it then?'. In the context of my quotation from Fordham, however, wisdom after the event is learning from reflection.

On the other hand, if the focus is too much on the patient, then the effect can also be demoralising for the apprentice analyst, but in a different way. When I was training I had a supervisor who had a particularly evocative style emphasising embodied interpretations of infantile fantasies. Those supervised by him would hear him reinterpret their material. His style was to focus on what he, the supervisor, had understood and hardly at all on what the supervisee said (see Chapter 2, p. 45; and Chapter 5, pp. 89–91). This could be inspirational, but it could also promote learning through imitation that, in my view, is a sure way to trample on the individuality of the patient and the supervisee. If the supervisor does not pay attention to the supervisee's own understanding, focusing only on the unconscious of the patient, the supervisee will find himself repeating the supervisor's formulations without being able to follow them up because they have not been integrated. This has been well described by John Fiscalini as 'analysis by ventriloquism' (Fiscalini, 1997, p. 43).

Rhythm in the supervisory exchange

The interactions between supervisor and supervisee have a rhythm to them which is often closely related to the material (Rustin, 1996). When the supervisee is very anxious about what is going on, the supervisor becomes more active in trying to help him contain the experience and makes more proposals and suggested formulations. If the patient is becoming less contained, the supervisor tries to be more containing to his supervisee, perhaps even directive if the supervisee is at a loss. At other times the main function of the supervisor is to be, what Margaret Rustin calls, 'the thinker of interpretative links' (Rustin, 1996).

I was listening recently to material from an experienced analyst who was analysing an experienced patient. The links she was making were close to the material and to the point. The patient was speaking about the difficulty of living in two places, a house in the country and a little flat in town from which her husband went to work and where she stayed three nights a week. She described her behaviour in the language of performance and acting: 'getting my act together' was how the patient described her move from the country (no analysis) to London (analysis).

At first the analyst was interpreting this in terms of the different states of mind in which she lived, relating it to the three sessions a week (analysis and London), and the non-analytic time in the country. Then I began to realise that there was considerable anxiety in the therapist about the falseness of the patient's description of 'getting her act together', and that her efforts to help her patient understand this were failing. The analyst's feeling her failure to get through to her patient was not uncommon in our experience. We had noticed that she had a way of not allowing the truth to touch her. I was aware that I was not being an effective supervisor at this point, and I was thinking about this and the material when I realised what the problem was. 'Getting her act together', performing, and all that this meant, was central to the whole process, especially the analytic endeavour. I suddenly realised that the patient was experiencing the analyst's interventions as just so much performance art. In this example the communication inherent in the patient's performance was its inauthenticity, which matched the analyst's feelings of frustration that she was not getting through to her.

The problem, as I now understood it, was that the analyst was perceived by her patient as playing at being an analyst while she played at being a patient. So the analyst interpreted and the patient 'ummed' along and, from the patient's point of view, this was all that was necessary. Each was in role and the truth remained in the hands of an unseen author who did not need to be consulted. Nothing else had to happen. The analyst spoke and the patient responded, not by letting the words, feelings, and images settle in her mind nor by savouring or digesting, but by tasting and pushing away. The act of serving up the interpretation was the therapy. The patient did not have to make any commitment to what was said, just as she did not have to make any commitment to her own feelings, nor any commitment to the consequences of recognising what the implications of certain truths were. Once I had grasped that, I elaborated it at length, becoming active and descriptive in response to my supervisee's inactivity.

Obstructions to learning in supervision

Supervision provides a space to examine the power and strength of the ideas that are informing our analytic practice (Rustin, 1996). This is valuable at all stages of our professional life but especially so when we become more experienced and realise that we have assumed the significance of certain analytic theories and concepts for so long that we may need to re-examine them, to forge them anew and give them a personal edge. This is important in the context of Jung's statement that we need to make a theory for each patient (Jung, 1946, para. 181) and Fordham's encouragement to us to make a theory for each session. Making theories, like writing papers, makes us think out and find expression for our thoughts and feelings. Sometimes, however, the problem that is brought to us as supervisors reveals that the supervisee does indeed have what he thinks is a theory, but it is in fact a misconception about his patient which is imposed on the material.

Case examples

Example 1   Identifying the supervisee's misconceptions which are not modified by the material

The supervisee was reporting material to me that he had understood as an example of an attack on an enviable object. He basically thought the material was an instance of penis envy. The background situation was that the supervisee and his patient were in and out of the same building, which housed an institute that offered courses, training and treatment. The material brought to me was that the patient had been attacking this analyst (my supervisee) by telling him that she was in the building attending a seminar at the same time as she knew him to be there, and that she had seen him leave a note for someone at the front desk. The patient was angry about this note, which was addressed to someone she knew, and she poured scorn on the small size of the return address information that the analyst had stuck on the envelope. She told him that this small size indicated he was a wimp and a little man, just like her father. The analyst then reported how he interpreted this as if from an identification with the patient's father. He said that he spoke to his patient as if with her father's voice about her denigration and contempt for him. He felt angry with her, he said.

There are two points in question here: the theory, namely that this material is about penis envy, and the style of interpretation, that the way to interpret this is by speaking out of identification with the denigrated object.

I did not agree with the analyst's conception of the material nor with his interpretative style. I thought it was unwise to speak out of identification with the denigrated object, because to do so, suggested that the analyst too was filled with contempt. In my view, he would be experienced by his patient as contemptuous of her intense feelings of hurt and anger. I was concerned rather that the significant other unconscious communication in the material – concerning the analyst's presence in the building, his involvement with others there and the patient's response to this – was not being addressed. I understood her attack as a defence against something. I was interested in the two people in the building who were not meeting (you could understand this as having arisen from my countertransference realisation that my supervisee and I were not in harmony) and what effect I thought this was having on the patient's and the analyst's internal worlds. As a way of monitoring the supervision, I was wondering whether the analyst was feeling at this point in the supervision session that I had an understanding of his patient that he did not have. This might be making him less sensitive to an oedipal interpretation because he felt excluded. At the same time, I was aware that my supervisee was affected by his patient's contemptuousness and that he could easily feel flawed (and floored). I was unclear as to why the analyst was made angry by the patient's contempt.

I began to wonder out loud what the analyst thought the patient's anger was about. My supervisee replied that he did not know. I then suggested my oedipal theory about this session: that the patient was angry with him for being in the building, seeing other people and doing interesting things with them to her exclusion. My supervisee now told me that there was to be a short break in the treatment and this was the session immediately prior to the break. He continued with associations that deepened the understanding of what we were now working on. He remembered that his patient had commented on the two planters on either side of the door when she had come to the Monday session and had expressed her interest in the connections between their contents. Now the supervision session began to take shape. We had reached an impasse; a patient who felt misunderstood, and an analyst who knew something was not right because he had spoken out of his anger. Then we found a way to think about the impasse. The oedipal theory arose out of the material, which was filtered through the knowledge and history of our relationship. A fertile interaction could occur. The supervisee's further reflection was that his identification with the denigrated object (a bit of his own pathology) prevented him from seeing the oedipal dynamic. This I did not comment on as I disagree with those supervisors who tell their supervisees to take such and such a feeling to their analyst. We are analysts, so let us proceed analytically rather than as traffic policemen. Apart from anything else this comment usually indicates some rivalry or unexpressed hostility towards the supervisee's analyst, as if the problem would not have arisen if the analyst had done a better job.

In thinking about the supervisee's contribution to this example, I recognise that by being open and unguarded about the interaction with the patient, he enabled me to feel my way into it. Because he was receptive to thinking about my alternative suggestion and how I had derived it, he both facilitated further associative exploration of the idea and elaborated it. As the supervisor, I needed his response for me to be effective. Once we had started on the oedipal theme, he could quickly see that his previous position was not the significant dynamic of the session we were discussing. It was as if he was employing last week's idea to think about today's material.

A further aspect of the reciprocity inherent in this supervisory relationship concerns the question that has evolved in further work with this supervisee: what is the meaning for his patient of embroiling him in her drama in the way this material demonstrated?

Example 2   Projective identification and countertransference

A colleague with a specific problem asked me for a few sessions of supervision. On the telephone he stated that he had difficulty getting his patients to come more than once a week. In the event, when he arrived he told me first of all something of his own biography and then gave an account of a patient who he felt treated him disdainfully. At the same time, this patient was also having consultations with another therapist, thinking they might be a more suitable choice. He described her as rich and rather grand by marriage, but ill at ease internally with her family of origin.

My internal transference commentary at this point was that this therapist was wondering whether, if he were to have a different analyst for himself, it would improve his work. He was having difficulty thinking about the feelings stirred in him by this patient and was looking elsewhere for the solution to the problem.

My hypothesis at this stage, based on the material he brought about his patient, was that he had become identified with the projective identificatory content of her material and that this was probably due to some personal difficulty he had with envy.

My colleague talked and talked, filling the whole session with material. He was determined to get through everything he had brought, leaving no time for discussion or examination of the material. I indicated that time was up and that we would have to return to this in a fortnight. He said in a somewhat peevish tone of voice, 'Is that all?', meaning 'Was that the best that I could do?'. I was put in the position at that point of the analyst/supervisor who was not able to produce enough, which was exactly his dilemma with his patient and within his practice. I was the recipient of the feelings the supervisee had when he was with his patient, but which he was unable to interpret to her satisfactorily. I said that his comment 'Is that all?' sounded like the sort of thing his patient said to him. This struck a chord with him and he agreed that it did seem to be the nature of the transference.

This pithy little exchange at the end of the session encapsulated the issue and my colleague took it away and worked on it. On his return two weeks later he had digested and internally elaborated it so that he could acknowledge the significance of our exchange, without the boundary of our work being broken and he felt freer of his identification with his patient's projections of inferiority and anger. As a consequence, he was able to process these feelings inside himself and to work with his patient more productively, interpreting his patient's consultations with the other analyst as the potentially better one. It helped him realise that to deepen his own work involved a process of working with his ambivalence as it was constellated in his transference to his patient.

Example 3   The use of empathy within the countertransference of the supervisor as a means of helping to resolving impasse in the supervisee's work with a patient

This supervisee rarely brings process reports. She prepares for the supervision by reading through her material before she arrives and talks out of the re-evoked experience. The supervisee does not have an analytic relationship with me, but the supervision has analytic features. Her material is nearly always about how she finds herself affected by the patient and how often she has struggled to contain her anger, irritation or bewilderment within her professional persona. In other words, she brings a combination of unprocessed countertransference experiences, projective identifications and receptivity to thinking about new ways of understanding them. The supervisions have an observable pattern. First she needs to be settled down, then she describes what is on her mind about her patient.

My colleague began a meeting by saying how desperate she felt about a borderline patient who was screaming at her in the session and that she, the analyst, was evading the big issue about the patient's insistence on knowing whether she fancied her. 'Do you fancy me? You have got to tell me!' the patient shouted. At this point, my colleague told me that the patient had been hospitalised when she was three years old without parental visits. The patient's father had screamed at and physically assaulted her mother, usually when under the influence of alcohol.

At this stage I was proceeding analytically, thinking that my supervisee was having difficulty conveying to her patient that her demand, to know if she was fancied by her analyst, was similar in feeling to her patient wanting to know whether her mother loved her. The obstacle in the way of the patient's understanding was that any reference to her dependency needs was greeted with scorn (perhaps because it was too painful?) and, consequently, any interpretation which was precipitately reductive did not work. She needed an interpretation which would help her overcome rather than defend against her despair. I commented that the patient was screaming at her analyst in a manner similar to the way the patient's father screamed at her mother. I added that the analyst was feeling terrorised, as her patient did as a child, and that the analyst's identification with the screamed-at child was paralysing her.

My colleague continued that the patient beseeched her to tell her that she was special, writing her a letter between sessions that was full of frustration and rage. I commented that the patient's frustration derived from a feeling that she was not exclusively in possession of her analyst, as if her analyst was the mother and she was the child. My colleague now reported that the patient also complained that she could hear other people in the analyst's house and that this was inhibiting. The tone of the complaint was threatening and the analyst commented that she was frightened of her patient's violent feelings. I commented that all of this seemed to be a complicated communication. The patient was anxious about her internal warring parents while at the same time feeling enraged that she was on the outside and left wondering what she had contributed to their fighting. This experience seemed to be evoking feelings in the analyst arising from her identification with her patient as the unwanted, excluded child. What was needed here?

As I was listening to this, I noticed that my colleague was anxious about her patient's insistence that she should be her lover and she attributed this to the erotic transference. I did not think it was principally erotic as there was nothing very erotic in the feelings between these two people. I thought this was the dependent transference masquerading as the erotic so that what seemed erotic was in fact primarily aggressive. I thought this patient was furious that she needed her analysis and the technical issue was to see the attack on the analyst as a defence, to analyse it as a defence and to understand what was being defended against. I wondered how to make use of the patient's intense feelings of injustice that her object had never allowed her the illusion of possessing it?

I was struck by the tyrannical nature of the patient we were discussing and inquired after the imagined age of 'the tyrant' with my colleague. This initiated a discussion between us about the difficulty of thinking when being yelled at. I recalled the experience of containing 'the tyrant', of staying close but not giving in to threats. As I knew this supervisee had brought up children herself, I conceptualised this behaviour as emanating from a childlike part of the self and described what I imagined a three year old would be feeling when left in hospital and not visited by her mother. I described a three year old whose fury threatened to break her up inside. This brought relief to the analyst who could now think about the nature of her patient's insistence that she should become her lover. I had in mind that the analyst's problem with this patient derived from a difficulty which she, the analyst, had as well; namely, a difficulty with acknowledging vulnerable and childlike dependent feelings and the way this expressed itself in her own unresolved oedipal issues. I did not say this to her.

Our discussion brought relief because we had conceptualised the material within the transference. 'Which transference?', you might well ask. In this supervision I was showing my colleague how she would have liked to analyse her patient but also how, instead, she was invaded with the same feelings as her patient. In the process, her complicated feelings became more familiar and less threatening. They were contained. What I had said had stopped the yelling voice in my colleague. We could now consider how to speak to this very unhappy and vulnerable part of her patient. We agreed that the patient's feelings about her object were subject to fierce, ambivalent, regressive pulls of love and hate. We agreed she needed to create in the transference an idealised object as part of her reparation, and I wondered to myself whether my colleague had realised that this was what had happened here with me. We agreed that at some point, her patient's denial of the loving aspects of the parent's intercourse would have to be examined in the context of her insistence that she could supply to her analyst everything she needed. It was also clear to us that this fantasy was a reversal of what she actually wanted. She wished for the exclusive maternal attention of the analyst and this would need to be interpreted at some point.

The problem of the moment, however, was that the patient was feeling frustrated and excluded and this made her feel violent. My colleague and I thought about the quality of this violence. Was it violence as a consequence of the deficiencies of her object or was it violence that had a sadistic relish to it? It seemed on examination to be the former. What enraged her was being excluded from an ideal object.

My colleague and I now began to speculate about how to phrase the thoughts we were having about this patient to her. In doing this it emerged that my colleague was playing a sort of verbal ping-pong with her patient. The patient said, 'Well, you always say you have me in mind but I don't see how you can, as you have all these other patients'. The analyst replied in the same vein, 'Well, I know that makes you angry and we know something about where that anger comes from'. Essentially this was a defensive statement. The patient replied, 'Yes, yes, I know all about that too, but what about now, what about here?'

At this point, I suggested to my colleague that what she was not hearing was the statement the patient was making about the deficiencies in her object; how frightened she was of being left. She was arming herself against the ending of the session by creating a retaliatory atmosphere so that she could storm out and protect herself from feeling bereft. We needed to consider the unconscious assumptions behind the patient's statements. I was trying to mobilise in my colleague a reflective process that would enable her to wonder what it was in her that made working with this patient so difficult. And, as you can probably tell from what I have described, there was an underlying meshing of the patient's and my supervisee's Oedipal dramas. In this description I am following Klein (1928) in hypothesising that there are pregenital components of oedipal fantasies.

I suggested that with the patient in this desperate state, it might be preferable to convey what we had understood, by saying initially something like, 'You want me to understand that you are terrified you might be left, abandoned and rejected'. I continued that, depending on how this was received and assuming that it helped to diminish the yelling, she could gradually add a reference to her rage and frustration and how she felt it broke up her inner world. While in this state of mind, the patient could not receive interpretations until her present emotional state had been acknowledged. You could only say, 'I know you need an answer to your question, but I also know that if I try to talk to you about this in relation to your terrible losses as a child, it will make you even more angry because you feel this is urgent, and this is now and that was then'. This patient needed that fact to be recognised.

That is what I understand Jung (1928, para. 285) to have meant when he wrote of the 'real' relationship that is necessary in analytic relationships. 'Real' means understanding that what you are hearing is a memory in action, which the patient does not as yet realise. She needs to be contained rather than exposed. Feeling exposed can result if a reductive interpretation is made too soon. It can also sound accusatory. What I am trying to demonstrate is that, by responding in this way, the analyst stood a better chance of engaging the patient's imagination and interest in the analytic process.

An interpretation phrased like that recognised the unconscious meaning within the transference of the patient's demands and also the analyst's countertransference. It conveyed that the analyst understood what the patient was feeling. It is another matter whether the patient wanted to understand what her analyst had said. That is why I suggested delaying the additional observations which were directed at the patient's understanding rather than just being understood (Steiner, 1993).

The interpretative style here was aimed at the patient's urgent demand for love and her intolerance of frustration. It was not aimed at making the patient feel guilty for having these feelings. I am particularly keen not to make borderline patients feel that their situation is entirely of their own making; in this instance, that she was put in hospital because she was disliked and not visited because she was so intrinsically dislikeable. Interpretations directed towards these feelings are deeply demoralising, ego-weakening and inhibit development of resources within the patient to cope with living in her own mind. It is difficult enough for all of us to live in our own minds without analysis making it worse!

Reflections on the supervisee's contribution to the supervisory process

Reflecting on this supervisee's contribution to the process of developing this analysis through the supervision, I noted that she brought her feelings and her difficulties in her thinking without inhibition. She also listened and interacted with me. There was a dialogue between us which had the characteristics of an inner dialogue, where

I could articulate what she was preconscious of. Her transference to me reflected the transference in her patient although at times she behaved as if under the dominance of the patient's feelings. Grinberg (1997, pp. 16–17) calls this projective counteridentification to distinguish it from countertransference (see Chapter 5, pp. 88–9). The feelings stirred in the supervisee by her patient are part of the supervisory discourse, whereas her countertransference muddles arising from her own oedipal difficulties, are for her own analysis. This was clearly understood between us. She let me know whether what I was saying was of any use to her and we proceeded from this supervisory vertex. All this helped me, in that I could wait and process the experience she brought, speaking out of my analysis of this experience. I did not have to know. She trusted me and the unconscious and I trusted her and the unconscious and out of this mutual trust something usually happened.

Example 4   Affectivity and the supervisor's role

There are many ways in which a supervisee can use a supervisor, especially when the supervisee's material is very intense and painful. In the following example, the supervisee reported on a patient who was revealing something deeply shameful. The atmosphere of the supervision was very intense. The supervisee was affected by the material and upset by it. What was projected into her was now projected into me. My task was then to describe to her the analytic meaning of the projected material.

The supervisee reported that her patient was talking about how affected she had been when a friend of hers told her that she had locked her little girl into her bedroom at night because she was wandering around. Both the patient and the supervisee were upset by this account. I also found myself affected by the emotional atmosphere in the room. My task was to demonstrate how the horrific nature of this story, which we can easily imagine ourselves into, of a little girl locked into her room at night so that she is not a nuisance to her mother, can distract us from the analytic communication. What I understood from my listening and my distress was that the patient was feeling locked-out, frightened and misunderstood in a vulnerable and childlike part of herself. In addition she wanted her analyst, my supervisee, to know that she was ashamed to think that she may have been a damaging parent herself.

In the context of the transference in the analytic session, I saw it as my job to formulate this and indicate where the supervisee had allowed herself to become so emotionally involved in the horror story of the imprisoned child (projective counteridentifcation) that she had been unable to hear the patient's communication. In my view the patient was telling the analyst of her feelings that she (the patient) could have been a mother who did not understand her child, and that she was frightened the analyst might not understand her (the patient's) own childlike terrors, which were related to her feelings of being locked in and locked out. There was probably some terrifying primal scene fantasy behind this material but, at this stage, this hypothesis awaits more information.

Summary

In this chapter, I have used the concept of empathy to think about the attitude of the supervisor when listening to clinical material presented by supervisees. More specifically, using several detailed clinical examples of sessions with different supervisees, I have endeavoured to distinguish the analytic from the supervisory vertex using empathy as an aspect of countertransference. In essence, I have described emotional experiences between analyst and patient that were felt to be meaningful, were brought to supervision and which then became the basis for further thoughts about the process of supervision. I have tried to think about them in the context of the projective, introjective and counterprojective processes activated within the supervisory relationship.

References

Astor, J. (1995) *Michael Fordham: Innovations in Analytical Psychology* (London: Routledge).

Bion, W. R. (1965) *Transformations* (London: Heinemann Medical Books).

Fiscalini, J. (1997) 'On Supervisory Parataxis and Dialogue', in M. H. Rock (ed.), *Psychodynamic Supervision* (Northvale, NJ and London: Jason Aronson).

Fordham, M. (1957) 'Notes on the Transference', in *New Developments in Analytical Psychology*, (London: Routledge & Kegan Paul) Ch. 4.

Grinberg, L. (1997) 'On Transference and Countertransference and the Technique of Supervision', in B. Martindale *et al.* (eds), *Supervision and its Vicissitudes* (London: Karnac Books).

Jung, C. G. (1928) 'The Therapeutic Value of Abreaction', *Collected Works Volume 16.*

Jung, C. G. (1946) 'Analytical Psychology and Education', *Collected Works Volume 17.*

Jung, C. G. (1971) 'Psychological Types', *Collected Works Volume 6.*

Klein, M. (1928) 'Early Stages of the Oedipus Complex', *Contributions to Psychoanalysis* (London: Hogarth Press).

Rustin, M. (1996) 'Young Minds in the Balance', unpublished conference paper, Tavistock Conference 50 years Celebration.

Steiner, J. (1993) 'Problems of Psychoanalytic Technique: Patient Centred and Analyst Centred Interpretations', in *Psychic Retreats* (London: Routledge).

Note

An earlier version of this chapter was published in *Journal of Analytical Psychology* (2000), **45**(3), 367–85.

Part II

Applications and Settings for Supervision

4

Supervising Work with Children

Elizabeth Urban

Introduction

Supervision is an essential part of the process of becoming and practising as an analyst. It is the primary means by which analytic training
organisations attempt to pass on the art of analysis and it is an important basis for developing an internal consultant to which one
constantly turns in analytic work.

My analytic and supervisory work is with both adults and children,
however in this chapter I shall focus on supervising work with children. Most aspects of this apply equally to supervising work with
adults so work by other contributors to this volume is also of relevance. However, there are areas that are specific to work with children, for instance, matters of management and child abuse or neglect.

'Pure' analytic work with children tends to be rare. It occurs most
frequently in child analytic training, where it is required. It is also
carried out in private practice, but by only a very few clinics. Far
more commonly, supervisors will be working with child analysts and
therapists who see children less intensively in child and family clinics.
In the UK, qualified child analysts become members of the
Association of Child Psychotherapists hold the title and 'child
psychotherapist' in the public service. In child and adolescent mental
health services child analysts will be part of a multidisciplinary team,
which may include child psychiatrists, child psychologists, family
therapists, social workers and art therapists.

Work with children has increasingly spread beyond these clinics to other settings such as schools, hospitals, specialist health units, family doctor practices, various social services settings, and nurseries. Most of this work will be applied, rather than 'pure', psychoanalytic psychotherapy and may be offered by those who have not undertaken formal child analytic training. An analytic supervisor may be working with art, drama and music therapists, as well as teachers, social workers, psychologists, medical students, health visitors, nurses and nursery workers. Supervision of applied work needs to maintain underlying analytic principles, which, like improvisation in jazz, means appreciating the fundamental rules in order to work out its variations (see Chapter 6, pp. 104–5).

The role of supervisor and the aims of supervision

The role of the supervisor and the aims of supervision are, of course, intricately related to the analytic relationship. Fordham studied the analyst–patient relationship and observed that one way the analyst behaves – the way he believed to be the most constructive – is by 'simply listening to and watching the patient, to hear and see what comes out of the self in relation to the patient, and then reacting' (Fordham, 1957, p. 97). He continues:

> This would appear to involve deintegrating; it is as if what is put at the disposal of patients are parts of the analyst which are spontaneously responding to the patient in a way that he [the patient] needs; yet these parts are manifestations of the [analyst's] self.
>   . . . analysis depends upon the relatively greater experience of the analyst in deintegrating so as to meet the patient's disintegration. (Fordham, 1957, p. 98)

The deintegrations and reintegrations of patient and analyst form deintegrates within each. A deintegrate can be thought of as a part of the self that has more or less structure, or dimension (see Chapter 1, pp. 24–6). From the position of the analyst, part or parts of him become connected to, and integrated with, part or parts of the patient, so that he can work on the patient by working on himself in the presence or absence of the patient. By looking into himself, he may discover information about the patient that can be interpreted in order to help the patient claim more of his personality within his sense of himself – what Jung termed individuation.

There is a parallel process in the supervisory relationship. In this relationship the supervisor is expected to be able to deintegrate and reintegrate in areas where the analyst has, for whatever reason, found difficulties. Here the aim of the supervision is to support and facilitate the analyst's capacity for deintegrating and reintegrating in the service of the analyst discovering his own way of working. This will hopefully result in the analyst integrating an internal supervisor that can promote creative self-questioning, give support in excessive self-doubt, provide other perspectives when stuck and, most important of all, stand back and reflect.

Good supervision rests upon careful observation. A model of the supervisor's role in the triangular relationship between supervisor, analyst and patient is that of the observer in an infant observation. The observer's role is not superior to, but different from that of mother or infant. The observer takes in impressions from both the mother and the baby depending on what is happening in the observation, allowing shifts in identifications from one to the other to discover more about each and their relationship.

Astor and Carr consider the role relationships involved in supervision beyond those of supervisor, analyst and patient, and include the institutions in which analytic work is carried out (Carr, 1989; Astor, 1991a). Astor focuses on the analytic training institution, while Carr includes institutions in which analysts and therapists work, such as social services, health services and voluntary organisations. The importance Carr and Astor place on the supervisor's consideration of the impact of the institution on the analytic work applies especially in supervising work with children.

Interpreting in analysis and translating in supervision

There are also important differences between the roles of supervisor and infant observer, and between the analyst–patient and the supervisor–analyst relationships. In regard to the latter, the most obvious difference is that the supervisor does not make interpretations directed to the analyst, but does offer 'translations'. To 'translate' is to transfer meaning from one language or medium to another in a kind of lateral move within the same order of denotation. On the other hand, to 'interpret' implies a value-added dimension, based on the Latin *pretium*, meaning value or price. According to Fordham, the difference between an analytic interpretation and translation is that an interpretation contains a reference to a feeling and aims at personal, emotional understanding, whereas translation aims at making sense on a more cognitive level (personal communication).

A seven-year-old with autistic tendencies arrived at his session excitedly shouting 'Paks! Paks!' His mother translated *his idiosyncratic language to the analyst, saying that he was referring to having recently joined his local Cub Scout pack. During his session the analyst* interpreted *to him his excitement at feeling he belonged to a group of 'normal' boys, something for which he had yearned over the period in his treatment when he went to a special school.*

Much of what a supervisor does is to offer translations in an attempt to bring to light and to contain the patient–analyst relationship. One area in which translations are useful is situations where the analyst may be aware of not understanding a patient's behaviour or what the patient is trying to communicate.

One analyst worked with an emotionally deprived eight-year-old girl, whose mother unexpectedly left home and moved to another part of the country not long after the treatment began. Over the subsequent months the analyst worked closely and sensitively with the girl's pain, anger, fear and guilt about the mother's leaving, and helped her with the intensification of her feelings surrounding visits to her mother. Throughout this time a pattern of play developed in which, toward the end of each session, the girl pretended to be a baby at bedtime to whom her mummy/analyst read until she went to sleep, sometimes actually dropping off. The play was suffused with feelings of closeness and intimacy, quite out of keeping with the girl's more characteristic boisterousness.

After a long holiday break, the pattern of play abruptly changed. There was no more pretend bedtime reading, and instead the girl played at being a bossy teacher, ordering the analyst to do things. Over the following months the analyst occasionally commented in her supervision on the change in the pattern of play, doing so in a way that conveyed a sense of loss. This later became compounded by a sense of giving up, as she began to consider drawing the treatment to a close because little work seemed to be going on.

Rather suddenly, and to the analyst's surprise, the girl once again wanted her analyst to read to her while she pretended to go to bed. When this happened the analyst became quite interested in knowing why and wondered what my thoughts about this were. We then discussed how, when the girl's mother left home, the girl felt despair about ever getting back a good feeling of being-with-mother, just as the analyst had felt like giving up the treatment when what made it feel meaningful seemed to have disappeared. The analyst re-thought her intention to finish, and became committed to continuing. Just as the 'heart' of the treatment seemed to return, there seemed to be a renewal in the analyst's engagement in the supervision, expressed in the question she put to me.

In the above instance the analyst was aware that she did not understand the patient's behaviour. The supervisor also uses translations when the analyst cannot understand her own behaviour in relation to the patient.

One analyst was working with a five-year-old who regularly interrupted his sessions to go to the lavatory. Due to his size, he relied on his analyst to help him turn the tap off when he finished washing his hands. She was extremely careful to keep her responses brief and matter-of-fact. When they returned to the consulting room she interpreted his need to go to the lavatory as an impulse to discharge and eliminate primitive mental and emotional contents and then linked this to his concern over scrubbing his hands.

On one occasion when she had helped him wash his hands, the analyst had called him 'sweetie', something she found embarrassing to mention in supervision because of its inappropriateness to her analytic role. As we considered her 'taboo' behaviour we discussed the boy's intolerance of allowing his parents to be together without him, and how this was undermined at home when he was allowed to sleep in his parents' bed with them. The boy knew he was not supposed to do this, just as he would have known that females are not supposed to go into the men's lavatory. Despite the analyst's care in manoeuvring around his efforts to seduce her, he had succeeded in drawing her into a 'prohibited area'.

Here my translation was aimed at pointing out that the seduction was happening on an unconscious level, experienced by the analyst as using a term of endearment she usually prohibited herself from using. The translation also became the means by which feelings of embarrassment and shame became contained in the supervision.

In both of the preceding examples, the supervisees were conscious of not understanding. However, it happens that the analyst is not aware of failing to understand the patient's communication because of identifying with or defending against it. Astor describes artful management of this in his supervision work, whereby he draws upon empathy in the supervisor–supervisee relationship to enhance the analyst's understanding in such a way that the supervisor avoids direct interpretation (Astor, 2000). To illustrate how translation can be used in these instances I shall describe a child analyst's work with an abused boy who often projected a primitive mindlessness into her, as she and I had often discussed.

Just before a particular session with the boy, the analyst learned from a colleague seeing the mother that the boy's stepfather had become abusive to the boy and consequently the mother had asked the stepfather to leave the family home. During the session the boy was unusually violent toward the analyst and, because most of the analyst's efforts were directed at managing the boy's behaviour, she had been unable to think analytically. At the next session, the boy told his analyst that his stepfather had gone but nothing more, and subsequently the session continued in the same way as before the stepfather left. I was struck that the analyst seemed mindless of the link between the external event of the stepfather's departure, and the violence in the previous session.

When I drew attention to this, the analyst became noticeably defensive. I assumed that there would have been a reason for this and turned my thoughts to the boy and how he may have felt. I told the analyst what I was thinking about the boy and asked how she understood what had happened. She began to describe more fully her reaction to the boy and how all her energies had gone into 'just surviving' the session in which he had been violent. This led to discussion about how he had once again put his mindlessness into her and reflection on whether this had been the boy's way of 'just surviving' his feelings about his stepfather's leaving. His father, who had also abused him, had left the family in similar circumstances. Might the boy have felt responsible for both fathers leaving? If so, his dread of being blamed might be overwhelming. It was with this intolerable feeling of 'doing something wrong' that the analyst seemed unconsciously identified, resulting in her becoming defensive about my comment.

I kept these thoughts to myself, as they were interpretive, while the analyst disidentified with the boy through our joint translation work.

In the previous three situations where translations were used, the analysts experienced varying degrees of identification with their patients that prevented them making use of what was unconsciously known about the patients. Each, however, was able to make use of supervision. Plaut considers reasons why supervisees cannot make use of their supervisors and identifies three areas of fear: the supervisor's power, losing the patient and ignorance (Plaut *et al.*, 1995). It can also happen that identificatory processes and transference to the supervisor are such that the supervision can be rendered useless in some areas of the work.

For over two years an analyst and I discussed his work with a young adolescent girl who was school phobic. She had been involved in a car accident when much younger, which prevented her from going to school for long periods. She had recovered from the accident, although periods of recurrent pain became the basis for her continuing identification with being an invalid. The analyst developed a good relationship with her and gently yet skilfully helped her to understand more about her ambivalence about growing up and separating from her over-involved relationship with her mother. Eventually the girl returned to school and this led on to other considerable changes in her life. She was also becoming pubescent. Although in supervision the analyst commented on noticeable changes in her appearance, in the treatment these were not remarked on, nor considered when I tried to discuss them. In my countertransference I began to feel increasingly excluded from their analytic relationship.

Prior to a summer break, the analyst reported that the girl had briefly referred to a boy in whom she, but not the analyst, seemed interested. I wondered with him whether this may have been a communication to the analyst that she felt left out of a private relationship she imagined he has with his partner, and was a reference to her growing awareness of sexuality. This seemed to be an imposition on the analyst as he later imposed it upon the girl in one of their sessions. Following the summer break the girl gradually began to retreat again into her invalidity, and eventually withdrew from her treatment. When the analyst and I reviewed what had happened, he held that her withdrawal was related to her anxiety about forthcoming exams and was not able to extend that line of thought to cover her anxiety about success or failure in becoming a woman.

In this instance supervision had been rendered ineffective in an area where the analyst was over-identified with his patient in defending against oedipal feelings. He worked competently but exclusively in a maternal transference, focusing on the varying aspects of the girl's attachment to him. He did not seem to allow himself to be a male in the relationship, as doing so created intrusive gender differences that threatened an intimacy for which he himself unconsciously yearned. The exclusiveness of that idealised relationship meant that feelings of being left out could not be contained in the analyst–patient relationship and were instead held by the supervisor. I was unable to affect the analyst's over-identification with his patient via translations, but refrained from giving interpretations, which would have taken me outside my role as supervisor. Instead I tried to work with areas that could be developed. As Fordham puts it, 'a supervisor should not judge the student's capacities, but facilitate the development of what is available' (Plaut *et al.*, 1995, p. 112). He continues, '[h]e may evaluate them afterwards', which was done in this instance when I wrote a reference for the analyst, including both his strengths and the areas in which he needed to develop.

Supervision and management in working with children

Supervision of work with children entails the consideration of good practice in certain management issues that arise, including the support of parents and carers, the child's behaviour, and in a few situations, child abuse.

Working with parents and carers

Any work with children will rely on those upon whom the child is dependent, and analysts should consider what is needed in order for the adults to support the treatment. Fordham felt that child analysts needed to meet with the parents or carers because they develop a transference particular to their child's analyst, although the analyst would not interpret this (Sidoli and Davies, 1988). The aim is to contain a parent's feelings and establish an adult-to-adult partnership in helping the child. This is quite different than offering parents treatment for their own difficulties. If there is a need for this, they should be appropriately referred. Parent–analyst meetings will affect the treatment, and this must be borne in mind.

A child analyst was seeing a boy who was fostered with his grandmother. Social Services, who had referred the boy, expected her to bring him to treatment. Her resentment of this resulted in a number of missed sessions and her refusal to meet with a support worker of her own. The boy's analyst began to make a relationship with the grandmother, although supporting the very needy grandmother and treating the boy was a heavy load for the analyst. Most of the family's complex problems seemed to land on the grandmother's doorstep, and in supervision we discussed how the grandmother's feeling of being over-burdened had been projected into the analyst. Understanding this helped the analyst to be more effective in supporting the grandmother who, in turn, became more committed to the treatment, whereupon the boy started to improve.

In complex situations like this one, it is usual for support to be provided by a colleague of the analyst. In Child and Adolescent Mental Health Services, others in the team may provide support by offering family therapy, or couple or individual therapy to parents.

A child analyst who worked in a child and family clinic treated a nine-year-old boy who had been exposed to pornographic videos as a small child. Because of her ambivalence toward her son, his mother was being seen by another member of the clinic team. Gradually the boy got closer to his experience of abuse and in one session his feelings of anxiety, fear and excitement became attached to the language his analyst had been using, about which she had been quite careful. After the session he complained to his mother that the analyst had used rude words to him and he was never going back. The mother accused him of lying and contacted her therapist, who explained that the boy was not necessarily lying, but was confused and terrified about what had happened to him when he was much younger. This helped the mother to contain her ambivalence and deepened her support for the treatment.

In private practice and non-clinic settings child analysts will need to seek out separate support for parents if it is needed. In whatever setting this happens, attention must given to dynamics within the network of treatments.

Behaviour management

Fordham writes:

> In child analytic therapy the analyst's verbal communications, especially inter-
> pretations, are related to by the child mostly through actions. Many of these
> indicate that the child has taken in the interpretation, and changes in his acts
> reveal that they are being made use of. But sometimes it may become clear
> that the actions are designed to obstruct the analytic process and neutralise
> the impact of the analyst's words. (Fordham, 1988b, p. 131)

In the chapter from which this is taken, 'Acting Out', Fordham describes work with a nine-year-old boy who acted out (or 'acted in' as some analysts prefer to term what happens within sessions) so as to void himself of the impact of Fordham's interpretations. He scratched Fordham's furniture with a knife, ran out of the consulting room, into the garden where he started small fires, and, as Fordham describes it, made it a rule to break Fordham's rules. Although Fordham could remain in touch with him through his interpretations, he was regu-larly faced with the situation where 'instead of analysis, management takes precedence' (Fordham, 1988b, p. 132).

In the course of their work child analysts will face an unlimited variety of thought-defying behaviour. Only some of this can be contained by altering the room, for instance, by adding safety features such as grilles on the windows and simplifying the room as much as possible. Astor writes that 'unlike adult analysts, child analysts need to be physically agile, and they must not mind getting their clothes dirty' (Sidoli and Davies, 1988, p. 10). Most child analysts will agree with this, although the behaviour they experience makes this something of an understatement. Here I have in mind behaviour such as assailing analysts with objects that can – and do – cause injury, kicking, biting, urinating, defecating, performing dangerous acrobatics on couches, climbing on tables, filing cabinets and windowsills, and prodding small objects into electricity outlets. Children may clamber onto the analyst's lap, confiscate the analyst's personal property, such as eyeglasses or jewellery, and try to touch intimate parts of the analyst's body. These events often happen instantaneously and without warning.

Acting out can be an effective attack on thinking, and supervision is a place where the underlying feelings can be mentally processed and contained. As with all communications from the patient, consideration must be given to both the meaning and the motivation for what has happened. For instance, one should ask whether the acting out was intended to be destructive or as a way of preserving something valuable, such as a loving relationship, or essential, like psychic life. Countertransference in the analyst and the supervisor will be important indicators of underlying intention. It is also important to consider the timing of the acknowledgement of the child's wishes to spare and repair if, of course, they are evident.

In the heat of the moment the ultimate concern is for the safety of the child and the analyst, and evaluating this rests to a certain degree with the analyst's threshold of anxiety and tolerance. Sometimes the child's behaviour leads to a session being cut short, while more frequently the analyst is pressed to establish prohibitions and to create rules. These responses tend to arouse a child's primitive fear of retaliation. Within the containment of supervision an analyst can explore ways to manage acting out as well as possible responses to it.

Being attacked can leave an analyst struggling just to preserve his personal safety, while feeling defeated, guilty, demoralised and humiliated. These can be understood as communications from the child, but it is still hard on the analyst, who needs support from the supervisor when this happens.

Child protection

All work with children comes under child protection legislation to which analytic and supervisory work must comply. If a child reports abuse or neglect or otherwise shows evidence that gives grounds for serious concern that he or she has suffered or may suffer harm due to abuse or neglect, then professionals are obliged to act in the interests of the child. This will contravene the usual practice of maintaining confidentiality. If the risk to the child is immediate, prompt action must be taken, and either the police or Social Services asked to issue an Emergency Protection Order, which removes the child from imminent danger. More often abuse and neglect are suspected rather than certain. Where there is any question of abuse or neglect, careful record must be made in writing concerning the material relating to it, separating opinions from facts.

All statutory organisations that have responsibilities for children, such as schools, child and family clinics and Social Services, will have policies for reporting suspected child abuse or neglect. Each organisation's procedures will vary, and some may have a named person whose role it is to work out what is to be done. Social Services hold responsibility for ensuring the child's longer-term well being. When they receive a referral, Social Services will determine whether to investigate the matter and, in most instances, will convene a preliminary 'strategy' meeting of those involved in order to discuss the situation. This will include the child analyst, whose attendance may be required. If the analyst is a trainee or inexperienced in these matters, it may be necessary for the supervisor to accompany the analyst.

An analyst who worked in a primary school for children with mild learning difficulties was treating a nine-year-old girl. From time to time the girl brought highly sexualised material, expressing an awareness of adult sexuality that aroused the anxiety of both the analyst and myself. This seemed to occur when there were changes in the treatment, like holiday breaks, and known changes in the girl's family life, namely the coming and going of her mother's boyfriends. The behaviour was seen in the light of these changes, although we discussed whether the girl's learning difficulties were erected as a defence against knowing about unthinkable experiences.

Thinking analytically continued until evidence emerged that demanded action. Just prior to the last session before a holiday break, the school nurse told the analyst in private that the girl had a vaginal discharge presumed to be thrush. During the session that followed, the girl pretended to call the police and wanted the analyst to do likewise. She then wanted the analyst to guess what had happened. Inhibited by a sense of breaking a taboo, the analyst did not answer but conveyed to the girl that somthing very frightening seemed to be were happening that the girl wanted her analyst to do something about. She then told the girl that she would talk to the head teacher, which after the session she did, thereby following the school's procedure for reporting suspected child abuse. She had made careful notes of the sessions, and on this occasion recorded what had happened in the school records.

Although this occurred just before a holiday break, which may have accounted for the level of anxiety, I supported the analyst's action. I considered that there was evidence both within the session (the girl's wish to call the police and the analyst's anxiety about breaking a taboo) and outside it (what the nurse reported) that provided grounds for reporting suspected abuse. While waiting for child protection procedures to run their course, extreme feelings emerged within the supervision.

The analyst felt weighted down by anxiety-ridden responsibility she felt for the girl and we discussed how she was carrying feelings the girl sought in a protective maternal object. The analyst also became intensely anxious that the girl would be killed, which I too had felt in my countertransference. We discussed how the girl, believing her analyst would be revealing her 'secret', had become terrified that she would be 'killed' for telling it.

These primitive anxieties needed to be processed in supervision in order for them to be contained, and to work out how they could be given back to the girl in the form of thinkable thoughts.

Children who have been neglected or abused require special ways of working adapted to deal with psychotic processes and psychic inadequacies arising from what has happened (see Alvarez, 1992; Sinason, 1992 and Rustin *et al.*, 1997). Those who work with these children need supervision in order to process and contain what these children have experienced (see Crowther, Chapter 6, p. 102).

Assessment

Assessment goes on throughout supervision, mostly informally. However institutional demands, such as those required in training, necessitate a more formal assessment from the supervisor.

In 1961 a symposium of Jungians addressed the question 'How do I assess progress in supervision?' (Plaut *et al.*, 1995). Several writers described qualities they valued and drew upon in assessing an analyst in training. These included flexibility, insight, attunement, and empathy without over-identification with the patient; the development of the analyst's personality and his own way of working; and the capacities to be affected by the patient, to work in the negative transference, to hold opposites, to not know and to show willingness and enjoyment in learning from experience (Plaut *et al.*, 1985; Gee, 1996).

In contrast, Fordham describes the work of two trainees and compared the work of one, who was very good at containing but less gifted in terms of seeing the salience of surface data presented, with the other, who was the reverse. Fordham states that 'lines of development can best be defined from comparative experience rather than from abstract standards' (Plaut *et al.*, 1961, p. 154). However, it is difficult to see how drawing upon abstractions can be avoided. The capacity to contain and the capacity to recognise defences are surely abstract standards that Fordham himself is using here. It is likely that Fordham feels it is not useful to hold up a trainee's work against abstract standards that are readily idealised. As Newton points out, these can become persecutory (Newton, 1961). One can also question the value of comparing one trainee with another, when it seems more relevant to compare a trainee's work at the beginning of supervision with later work.

Little is said about feeding back the supervisor's assessment to the supervisee. Some offer informal feedback at various points in the supervision, for instance Gee's description of his work in developing insight (1996), while others, like Fordham (1995), reserve assessment for a more formal training procedure when the supervisee applies for membership. Fordham remarks that '[i]t is of advantage if [the supervisor] makes clear to the candidate his opinion of the candidate's suitability to analyse patients. This grows inevitably out of his aim of treating the candidate as a colleague' (Fordham, 1961, p. 114). Assessment seems a nonsense unless there is feedback to the supervisee and I question the value of reserving formal assessment for training purposes until the end of a trainee's supervision. By then it is too late for the trainee to make use of the supervisor's thoughts about his work, which most supervisees find helpful.

The Child Analytic Training at the Society of Analytical Psychology has begun a more formal on-going assessment process, in which, once a year, trainees discuss with each of their supervisors the development of their clinical work. I try to work out the procedure with each trainee. For instance, with one trainee, we discussed what guidelines we would use in our assessments of her work with a particular patient. The trainee commented on what she felt she did well, where she found difficulties and in what areas she needed to develop her experience. I thought it important to consider how she made and maintained a relationship with the child, how she experienced his impact upon her and how she integrated her experience of the patient within her emotional and intellectual understanding. In short, I was assessing her capacity for deintegration and reintegration with that particular patient.

My report was in the form of a descriptive account of the treatment, from which the trainee's strengths and vulnerabilities originatede. I examined my judgements for any judgementalism. Judgementalism can be an indicator of primitive defensive operations, such as experiencing the supervisee's way of working to be different than one's own, so that processing is required in order to reach a well-considered assessment. The trainee's response was that my account of the treatment, so familiar to her in her own terms, was quite containing, which I experienced as feedback on the supervision. What is most important is that the assessment process is meaningful, so that both supervisor and supervisee can learn from the experience.

Making a final assessment about the trainee's readiness to apply for membership brings to mind my own experience. When I had met the requisites of the training, I approached Dr Fordham, one of my supervisors, to discuss whether I could submit my application for membership. I detailed the lengths and intensities of the various supervised treatments that had made up my training requirements. We both knew that becoming a member meant that supervision would no longer be required. With a characteristic twist, Dr Fordham said that one is ready to become an analyst when one no longer *needs* a supervisor. I knew immediately that he had shifted the focus from external to internal requirements, and had meant that reaching qualification to be an analyst represents coming to the point where regular external supervision is no longer needed because the trainee has internalised a supervisor (see Chapter 5, pp. 94–7 and Chapter 8, p. 146).

Summary

This chapter has looked at how supervision of work with children differs from that with adults in its concerns with management of the support of parents, acting out in sessions and child protection issues. However, the overall aims and skills of supervision apply equally to work with children and adults. I have described the supervisory role as an aspect of analytic work which draws upon analytic translation skills, in contrast to those of interpretation, aimed at the facilitation of deintegration and reintegration within supervisees in relation to their analytic work. Underlying a supervisor's work is a reliable and well-functioning internal supervisor, which from time to time will advise her to turn to an external supervisor.

In closing, I should like to express my gratitude to those supervisors and supervisees with whom I have shared analytic work, understanding and development. I should like to thank especially those who have graciously given me permission to cite our work together.

References

Alvarez, A. (1992) *Live Company* (London: Routledge).

Astor, J. (1991a) 'Supervision, Training and the Institution as an Internal Pressure', *Journal of Analytical Psychology*, **36**(2). Reprinted in P. Kugler (ed.) (1995), *Jungian Perspectives on Clinical Supervision* (Einsiedeln: Daimon).

Astor, J. (1991b) 'The Emergence of Michael Fordham's Model of Development', in R. Szur and S. Miller (eds), *Extending Horizon* (London: Karnac Books).

Astor, J. (2000) 'Some Reflections on Empathy and Reciprocity in the Use of Countertransference between Supervisor and Supervisee', *Journal of Analytical Psychology*, **45**(3).

Carr, J. (1989) 'A Model of Clinical Supervision', in *Clinical Supervision: Issues and Techniques*, monograph published by the British Association of Psychotherapists. Reprinted in P. Kugler (ed.) (1995) *Jungian Perspectives on Clinical Supervision* (Einsiedeln: Daimon).

Fordham, M. (1957) *New Developments in Analytical Psychology* (London: Routledge & Kegan Paul).

Fordham M. (1961) 'Suggestion towards a Theory of Supervision', *Journal of Analytical Psychology*, **6**(2). Reprinted in P. Kugler (ed.) (1995), *Jungian Perspectives on Clinical Supervision* (Einsiedeln: Daimon).

Fordham, M. (1988a) 'Acting Out', in M. Sidoli and M. Davies (eds), *Jungian Psychotherapy* (London: Karnac).

Gee, H. (1996) 'Developing Insight through Supervision: Relating, then Defining', *Journal of Analytical Psychology*, **41**(4).

Newton, K. (1961) 'Personal Reflections on Training', *Journal of Analytical Psychology*, **6**(2).

Plaut, A., Dreifuss, G., Fordham, M., Henderson, J., Humbert, E., Jacoby, M., Ulanov, A. and Wilke, H.-J. (1961), 'A Symposium: How do I assess Progress in Supervision?' *Journal of Analytical Psychology*, **6**(2). Reprinted in P. Kugler (ed.) (1995), *Jungian Perspectives on Clinical Supervision* (Einsiedeln: Daimon).

Rustin, M., Rhode, M., Dubinsky, A. and Dubinsky, H. (1997) *Psychotic States in Children* (London: Duckworth).

Sidoli, M. and Davies, M. (1988) *Jungian Child Psychotherapy* (London: Karnac).

Sinason V. (1992) *Mental Handicap and the Human Condition* (London: Free Association).

5

Supervision in Analytic Training

Barbara Wharton

Introduction

In this chapter, against a background of my own reflections on the nature and process of supervision, I address some of the issues arising in supervision which are specific to the training situation or are given a particular slant by it.

The historical context – an outline

The point of this historical outline is to show that the problems of how to teach analysis exercised the early pioneers as much as they do training bodies today. Issues, such as maintaining a distinction between analysis and supervision, and the factors which enable a student to learn, are among those to be discussed.

The elements of analytic training as we now know it, that is, the personal analysis, attendance at seminars and supervised analysis of patients, have an interesting, if somewhat fragmentary, history which differs between analytical psychology and psychoanalysis. Although it would probably now be agreed that personal analysis is the most important of these elements, that has not always been the case. Freud's own opinion shifted between 1922, when he dismissed the idea of a 'didactic analysis' as 'nonsense' (Ekstein, 1969, p. 314), and 1925 when he writes:

> [A psycho-analytic training] is best carried out if such a person himself undergoes an analysis and experiences it on himself: theoretical instruction in

analysis fails to penetrate deep enough and carries no conviction. (Freud, 1925, quoted in Ekstein, 1969, p. 315)

He no longer assumed that a novice would learn on the job, discussing with colleagues whatever difficulties arose (Ekstein, 1969, p. 314), a prototype of supervision. Jung had long been convinced, however, that it was essential for a would-be analyst to undergo a personal experience of analysis, and he believed he eventually won Freud over:

Freud himself accepted my suggestion that every doctor should submit to a training analysis before interesting himself in the unconscious of his patients for therapeutic purposes. (Jung, 1951, para. 237)

There continued to be disputes about the timing, duration, and depth of personal analysis, but it came to be seen as therapeutic, not merely a 'training analysis', a term which is still used, in my opinion highly defensively. As early as 1923 Ferenczi was saying that there should be no distinction between the two and, indeed, that the training analysis must, if possible, go deeper (Balint, 1948, p. 165).

Whereas supervision, which as we have seen was initially given more importance by Freud, became a training requirement for psychoanalysts in 1925, for analytical psychologists, the training programme in Zurich in the 1920s and 1930s consisted only of personal analysis and attendance at seminars given by Jung. When the Zurich Institute was established in 1948 supervision was included in the curriculum: at least 250 hours of 'control analysis', as it was then called, were required. Later (by 1962, according to Mattoon), each control case was supervised by a different analyst and control analysis was being distinguished from personal analysis. When a training programme was set up by the Society of Analytical Psychology in London after the Second World War, supervision became a requirement, and the differentiation between analysis and supervision was firmly made. Following the foundation in 1958 of the International Association for Analytical Psychology, minimum guidelines for time spent in 'control analysis' were set down, and have increased over the years (Mattoon, 1995).

By the 1930s, the tasks of the personal analysis and of supervision were being distinguished more firmly: the analysis of the candidate's [neurotic] countertransference to his patient (*Kontrollanalyse*), and teaching the student how to analyse a patient presenting different problems from his own (*Analysenkontrolle*) (Balint, 1948). Arguments abounded about whether or not in principle the analyst was the most suitable person to supervise the student's work. In practice there is still sometimes a question about how far a supervisor should become involved in analysing a student. In pioneering situations a shortage of training analysts often requires that the roles of analyst and supervisor overlap. It can be argued that, with her greater knowledge of the student, an analyst has an advantage in supervising his work. The counter-argument, however, would include the risks of a loss of objectivity on the part of the analyst/supervisor towards the student's patient, and perhaps more importantly, a loss of attentiveness and intensity in the analysis of the student.

The original term, '*Kontrolle*', is still widely used in the German-speaking countries, in France and in the United States, whereas to an English ear it has a connotation of rigidity and authoritarianism, and 'supervision' is favoured. In fact, the German term '*Kontrolle*' means 'inspection', 'supervision', or 'checking' (Mattoon, 1995). 'Supervision' has its own drawbacks: 'seeing over' (looking over some-one's shoulder) can carry an unwelcome sense of interference, although 'overseeing' suggests an element of responsibility and of ensuring safety. But 'seeing', as Zinkin pointed out (1995), is also problematic in this context. What is it that we see, or think we see, in supervision? The supervisee's account of an analytic interaction is at best only a crude representation, however accurate and detailed it is. The difficulties of reporting the multi-layered communications, conscious and unconscious, which take place in an analytic hour have been discussed elsewhere (Wharton, 1998). Zinkin however goes further, suggesting that what happens between two people is unique and ultimately incommunicable. No one else *can* have my experience of another person (Zinkin, 1995, p. 245). Reaching this conclusion divests us of some of the fantasies about supervision, and frees us to think about what does happen in supervision and whether and how it is helpful.

Similarly, there seems to be no fully satisfactory term for the person who is learning to become an analyst (cf. Blomfield, 1985). The connotations of 'training', as in 'bringing [someone] to a desired state or standard of efficiency' (Oxford English Dictionary), suggest a passive attitude of the trainee to the trainer which is particularly unfortunate here. 'Student' at least stresses an active engagement, as well as a seriousness and dedication; its disadvantage lies in its one-sided emphasis on the cognitive, perhaps implying a neglect of the emotional and practical or technical aspects essential to analysis. 'Student' also suggests someone young and inexperienced, whereas an analytic training is essentially suitable for people who already have substantial experience both of living and of professional work. 'Candidate', used commonly in the USA, means 'one who puts himself or is put forward for appointment to an office or honour' (Oxford English Dictionary); despite elitist overtones, it has the sense of someone who assumes a responsibility in assessing his own performance. Several writers have suggested that 'education' is a more fitting term than 'training' in an analytic context; it is both broader and deeper, embracing the whole person, and there is much to be said in favour of it. Even 'education' however underplays the powerful emotional elements of analytic training.

The supervisory relationship

The supervisory relationship, unlike the analytic one, is a relationship between two colleagues at an adult level in which regression is resisted and transferences are not explored (Frijling-Schreuder, 1970). Both participants can benefit: the student develops his skills in the art and craft of analysis and the supervisor has an opportunity to extend and clarify her thinking. The relationship is not symmetrical, however, as one colleague is senior to the other, more experienced and more knowledgeable.

The mere fact that a trainee is *required* to be in supervision, and at a certain frequency (once a week, in the training courses with which I am acquainted), can be a constraint. The question arises of how much the supervisee genuinely wants help, and how much he comes because he has to – an ambivalence which creates difficulties for both partners.

Learning in supervision is experiential and emotional rather than cognitive; it is aimed at enabling the supervisee to progress in his own style of being an analyst. This kind of learning above all requires a benign environment, free from anxiety and suspicion. The supervisor's task of providing such a setting is rendered much more complex by her evaluative role in training: it is difficult for trainees to be honest and open about their work when they feel confused or anxious. Yet they need to be able to question, challenge and disagree, as well as to bring their confusions, lack of understanding and 'mistakes'. The most disheartening statement I have heard from a supervisee was that he was telling me what he thought I wanted to hear – though at least he was then able to tell me *that*!

The supervisor can minimise the inhibiting effect of her power by avoiding dogmatism and being open to the material being presented – admitting the possibility of thinking about it in different ways and emphasising that there are no correct conclusions to be reached, only hypotheses to be tested. It may take time for the trainee to build a sense of trust in the supervisor and for a good 'working alliance' or 'learning alliance' to develop in which the supervisee can critically digest and assimilate what he is learning so that it becomes part of himself.

Although the supervisory relationship differs from the analytic one, it is, in some important ways, analogous. Supervision is a space set apart in which an opportunity is offered for two people to reflect on unconscious processes that are going on, not primarily in this room (as in analysis) but in another room, in the analysis conducted by one of the participants with another person. I see the supervisor as modelling a way of listening and thinking which is informed by the analytic attitude, an enquiring, non-judgemental reflectiveness which presupposes the ability to be in a state of not knowing, of not impos- ing a shape prematurely, of waiting for the unconscious contents to take their own shape. Underlying the waiting is trust that our words and actions have meaning and that their meaning might emerge in time. This modelling is a crucial element in analytic training. Over time, if things go well, it will enable the supervisee, through identifi- cation with the supervisor, to develop his own capacity to read between the lines or to listen with the 'third ear' (Reik, 1948, quoted in Blomfield, 1985). Thus there is a kind of paradox: the supervisee comes for help to the supervisor as to one who is meant to know, only to discover that the help he gets is help not to know. Of course, that is an exaggeration. The supervisor's knowledge and experience are essential for enabling anxiety to be contained and for thinking to take place.

The issue of keeping a firm boundary between analysis and super- vision has already been mentioned. As a supervisor I sometimes feel at a disadvantage when I sense an area of inflexibility in a trainee's emotional response to his patient (Kovacs, 1936). What should I do when I suspect a 'blind spot'? An openly directive approach, such as advice to the trainee to 'take it to his analyst', which is sometimes advocated, is a gross interference in the analysis and contradicts all analytic principles.

It has often been said that it is not the supervisor's task to investi- gate the supervisee's countertransference (cf. Grinberg, 1970, p. 372;

also Lesser, 1983, p. 120). Terms need to be clarified here. Countertransference – the emotional reaction of the analyst to the patient – was originally understood as an entirely neurotic response in the analyst. Since Heimann's 1950 paper, however, countertransference has been recognised as a syntonic response to the patient's transference, in other words as evidence of an unconscious communication from the patient which needs to be understood and, therefore, obviously a highly appropriate focus of attention in supervision. That is not to say that there are not neurotic elements in the analyst's response. It seems important to me that a trainee analyst should be encouraged to consider these different sources of his responses to the patient and to disentangle them as far as possible. Astor has written comprehensively on how the trainee can be helped to recognise his difficulties in projection, without the supervisor getting involved in an analytic process with the student; he gives illuminating clinical examples which highlight the complexities (Astor, 2000) (see Chapter 3).

Identifying a problem, non-intrusively and non-judgementally, is not equivalent to analysing it. The aim is to alert the trainee to an issue that he needs to tackle in himself (see Chapter 13, p. 237). I recall an intuitive trainee who repeatedly took up the patient's negative transference towards him, often in situations where I felt the patient was trying to express positive feeling and, indeed, where the negative side was quite unconscious. His highly developed intuitive function meant that he sensed the underside of the patient's positive feeling, but the patient did not yet seem to me to be ready for interpretations of the negative. I often felt confused at this trainee's responses to the patient, as perhaps the patient did, and I eventually pointed this out to the trainee. He acknowledged, ruefully but with a little humour, that he had difficulty recognising that he might be of positive value to anyone. This minimal acknowledgement was helpful to both of us.

Sometimes a student's difficulties with his patient are unconsciously projected into the supervisory situation. The supervisor may then be faced with countertransferences of her own which have to be understood. Searles named this the 'reflection process' in supervision, and much has been written on it (Searles, 1965). A simple example follows.

During the early weeks of a student's work with a new patient my contributions in the supervision seemed to be dismissed as irrelevant or valueless, and I felt increasingly useless and despondent about how I might help this student.

The fact that he had discussed other patients with me previously, without these effects being apparent, further aroused my curiosity. It then dawned on me that these feelings resonated with the patient's material – her profound lack of self-esteem and her despair about her life and failed relationships. This realisation enabled me to formulate a comment to the student. I said that I felt his patient was expressing a despondency and lack of self-esteem at a more profound level than either he or I had yet appreciated, which it was very painful for him to hear when he was in the room with her. The student seemed relieved, and our work became easier and more productive.

On this occasion I had not needed to suggest that perhaps there was a quality in the patient's low self-esteem which overlapped with a similar dynamic in the student and that this had encouraged his unconscious identification with the patient, which he was then re-projecting into the supervisory relationship. The term 'blind spot' is unfortunate in that it suggests something unalterable, as well as patho-logical. But as Searles points out, perceiving the positive potential in such matters, 'no therapist ever reaches such a high degree of self-awareness as to be consistently free from *important involvements of this kind*' (Searles, 1965, p. 174, my italics). Properly understood, these 'involvements' provide information; as analysts and supervisors we have to work constantly to understand each new situation, and to encourage our students to do the same.

Developing the supervisee's ability to handle the transference situation with his patient is a central issue in his training. When the trainee 'misses' transference projections in the patient's material, as often happens early on, he can feel humiliated and tact is needed. The difficulty in 'hearing' the unconscious communication can lead to a 'flight into action': the trainee focuses on outer-world material, perhaps on 'helping' the patient solve practical problems. His difficulty might be rooted in his fear of being powerless in the face of the unconscious, and it might be appropriate to point out to the trainee his preoccupation with the conscious level in the hope that this will stimulate his own self-questioning.

There are other factors which can mask the recognition of trans-ference. One may be the patient's fear of relating directly to the analyst: the trainee is caught in a projective counteridentification (cf. Grinberg, 1970; Astor, 2000) in which, for a time, there is an uncon-scious agreement that the discourse will be confined to what goes on 'out there' and will not touch on what goes on 'in here' (see Chapter 3, pp. 61–2). A trainee may be afraid of a patient's regression or of recognising how important he is to the patient. He may also be afraid of the patient's anger, and this may lead him to miss negative projections or, alternatively, if he is more afraid of the patient's expressions of love, he may miss the positive ones. A quite different situation arises when a trainee's expectation of entering immediately into a richly transference-based analysis with his patient is disappointed: when his attempts, perhaps somewhat immature, at transference interpretation are met with uncomprehending rebuffs by the patient. He needs help to understand the importance of timing and waiting for the transference situation to 'gel'. It should be acknowledged that the supervisor is in the privileged position of being more distant from the material and hence of having a clearer perspective, although it is the trainee who has firsthand experience of the patient. All these situations need to be handled sensitively in order to minimise the supervisee's discouragement and his envy of the supervisor.

More than once I have felt that a trainee was blocked in the specific area of loss, paying lip service to it, but somehow failing to respond to the patient with an appropriate intensity of feeling. This has led me to reflect further on the trainee's situation. Even when he has been assessed as being ready to take a first patient, he might still be in the relatively early stages of his own analysis and very vulnerable. It may be inherently difficult for a trainee to grasp loss in the early days of working with an analytic patient because, in a sense, his own loss of his 'childhood' is acutely enhanced at this time. Trainees have to grow up overnight, so to speak, from being the sole patient/child in their own analysis, to being an analyst/parent responsible for their own patients. In addition, they have to give up the cosy two-person relationship with their analyst to move into a more complex and stressful three-person relationship which includes their supervisor; painful oedipal anxieties can be reactivated at this stage (cf. Plaut, 1961, p. 100) (see Chapter 2, pp. 36–7; and Chapter 3, pp. 54–6).

Reporting

The supervision hour is based on the report brought by the supervisee of his sessions with the patient. Preferences vary among supervisors as to the kind of reporting they expect from trainees, whether full process notes, random jottings or no notes at all. Since it is generally agreed that note-taking in the patient's presence is inimical to analysis, any record that the supervisee makes is a reconstruction after the event; it belies an appearance of accuracy, having been at best unconsciously shaped, organised and edited (Wharton 1998). Writing up notes is time-consuming, but gives the student an opportunity for reflecting on the material and for self-observation – a kind of self-supervision (Grinberg, 1970, p. 374). The very act of organising the material mentally and verbalising it offers new perspectives. Detailed clinical notes are also an invaluable resource for future writing.

Students may feel discouraged by current political anxieties about confidentiality and legal entitlement of access to records from writing notes. The trainee needs to understand that notes on a patient are primarily about inner world material, based on the analyst's reflections and conceptualisations, and in that sense belong to him more than to the patient.

Notwithstanding the difficulties of recalling and recording analytic interactions accurately, it is vital to encourage the trainee to listen to the words spoken by the patient and to appreciate the resonances and intrinsic images in those words. As Goldsmith said, echoing Pascal, 'Words have meanings which their speakers do not know' (Goldsmith, 2002). To appreciate is to recognise the value of something, not merely in one's head, but to feel it in one's heart, and I want the supervisee to be encouraged (heartened) to listen for the unconscious but rich shades of meaning conveyed by the roots of language. A patient may say dismissively, 'It doesn't matter'. There is a sense that he is saying 'I don't matter'. But how much more we can appreciate his words when we hear the distant echoes reaching back through 'matter' as substance, 'material', 'wood', to '*mater*' = 'mother'. Now we get a sense of this person expressing his grief at the loss or lack of a sense of a mother who could hold him materially, physically, as an infant, and take him into her mind as a unique being who mattered.

A common symptom of a trainee's anxiety is a vague style of reporting: formulations of the patient's feelings or psychological state, or phrases such as 'We talked about . . .'. The trainee often finds it difficult to report precisely what he said himself, perhaps because that seems particularly exposing. But it is important to reflect with the trainee on how his interventions might have affected the patient and to wonder with him about possible alternatives. I try to avoid any impression that the trainee's intervention was wrong because I think rightness/wrongness is a false category here: the issue is the effect of the intervention (cf. Blomfield, 1985, p. 406). In addition, I hope to arouse the trainee's curiosity about any incidents or enactments that took place in the consulting-room. Supervision is a 'space for play', in Winnicott's sense of the term: a rewarding opportunity to ponder on the material together without feeling that a conclusion must be reached, to enjoy the imagery and the sense of discovery.

Discussion of the trainee's responses includes a consideration of interpretation. First, it should be established that an interpretation is not just an explanation, still less a theoretical statement, but a comment that is specifically aimed at making the patient aware of something that is going on in herself just beyond her consciousness: a feeling, fear, wish, attempt at action or avoidance. The question then arises of how to word an interpretation in such a way that the patient will be able to take it in and be *affected* by it. In general, the simpler the words, the more emotional impact they will have; everyday words are usually more powerful than their more learned synonyms; nouns, especially abstract ones, tend to deaden whereas verbs and adjectives bring to life. For example, 'I think you're angry' makes a stronger impact than 'there's anger around'; deciding on the best expression depends on the patient and the circumstances at the time.

Some supervisors see their function as simply helping the trainee to understand the patient: appropriate interventions will automatically follow when the case is understood. Such supervisors disapprove, for example, of suggesting the possible wording of interpretations, on the grounds that this encourages either unthinking imitation by the trainee or idealisation of the supervisor by endowing her with 'magical' powers. Prescribing interpretations is both undermining to the trainee and irrelevant since the precise confluence of events that might once have justified a given interpretation will not occur again. However, the choice of words, and how they are put together, are deeply important and can have profound effects on the analytic interaction and, for that reason, the wording of interpretations needs to be explored in detail. A trainee who tends to intellectualise may need help to value the simpler, more direct, language of feeling and action, and of the body. Simplicity is not the only issue however. The formulation of interpretations is a complex business since interpretations need to be fitted precisely to the state of the patient's defences. An example of this precision is Steiner's differentiation of patient-centred and analyst-centred interpretations (Steiner, 1993). Thus a thorough discussion of the wording of interpretations, including the consideration of alternatives and the various meanings these have for the patient, is an essential aspect of supervision (see Chapter 2, p. 45 and Chapter 3, p. 52).

The timing of interpretations is another important factor. Delaying too long before interpreting the negative transference may result in the patient leaving treatment. On the other hand, as Balint has shown, interpreting too early presents other hazards: premature interpretations, especially of hatred or rage, made before the feelings are fully experienced, can act like inoculations, preventing the patient from ever feeling the emotion in its true intensity. It may also lead to a collusion between patient and analyst that the minor traces of aggression are the real thing, that (borrowing Balint's imagery) the molehills really are the mountains (Balint, 1954, p. 160), a situation which can amount to a *folie à deux*.

Reality issues related to training

A trainee is unlikely to have free choice of a supervisor: the supervisor will have to be a training analyst of the institute or one approved by the institute, and availability and geographical accessibility are also factors to take into account. There needs, however, to be a degree of personal rapport between supervisor and supervisee, and also of matching orientation between the supervisor and the trainee's analyst, especially for the first training case. The trainee inevitably compares the model and style of analysis which his supervisor puts across with his own experience of analysis and, while some divergence is stimulating, wide differences stir up needless confusion and conflict (see Knight, Chapter 2, p. 36; Astor, Chapter 3, p. 51; Mizen, Wiener and Duckham, Chapter 13, pp. 233–5).

A further area of limited choice for the trainee is that of a patient: although in theory he and his supervisor discuss the suitability of a prospective patient on the basis of an assessor's report, the limited supply of even marginally suitable patients is such that an offer of a patient is rarely rejected. The question remains, of course, 'suitable for what'? Ethically, patients must be selected on the basis that they themselves will benefit from an analysis. They should also, ideally, provide the student with a good learning experience. Traditionally, attempts were made to choose patients from the neurotic end of the spectrum in order to give trainees a substantial experience of working with transference. Nowadays, perhaps because of a shortage of patients and also of advances in analytic understanding which extend the possibilities of treatment, patients often exhibit a wider range of disturbances. These more disturbed patients provide invaluable learning experiences in areas of primitive development, but they can also be extremely challenging.

Whether the patient is told that his analyst is in training is a difficult issue. Some writers express strong feelings against such a procedure because it introduces an unanalysable complication into the transference and burdens the patient with the analyst's problems. In the UK it is now a feature of professional ethical practice that the patient must be told. The reduced fee normally paid by a patient in analysis with a trainee, and the request to remain in treatment for at least two years, introduce further transference complications. On the whole, I find these reality factors can be addressed analytically; it is surprising how often they play in with the patient's fantasies and life experiences, and how their analysis can lead eventually to differentiations between past and present, and between reality and fantasy.

The 'time constraint' has numerous repercussions. In the two institutes with which I am most familiar – the Society of Analytical Psychology and the British Association of Psychotherapists, both in London – trainees are required to work with a patient intensively, four times a week and three times a week respectively, over a period of at least two years. Not only is the patient expected to commit himself for this length of time, he is also required to plunge immediately into an intensive treatment, rather than being allowed to 'grow into' a full-blown analysis. This is hard on the patient, but it is also difficult for the trainee who has to handle the patient's anger about the constraints and, in addition, misses out on the experience of facilitating the natural growth of an analysis.

Despite the two-year commitment, it is by no means intended that the treatment should come to an end after two years. Rather it is assumed that it will continue if the patient so wishes, and if it seems therapeutically appropriate, as it usually does. For some patients (and perhaps for some analysts too) the specified commitment becomes distorted into a limitation which can make both partners unconsciously hold back on a full-hearted attachment. The 'analysis' might then, on either side, be more about 'doing time' than about discovering how to relate to another person. The two-year watershed arouses anxieties of various kinds: the patient often has fantasies of being abandoned at the end of it, in spite of analysis of his underlying fears. However, the knowledge that it can continue arouses different fears, of disturbing changes in the analytic relationship, often concretised in a fear of a steep rise in fees or other material alterations. The patient is being challenged to enter into a relationship which has lost its previous 'safety' factors: the analyst will no longer be seeing him because he has to, but because he wants to; the patient will no longer have the 'excuse' of continuing with the analysis for the analyst's benefit: he will have to make his own responsible choice.

The supervisee has matching anxieties and ambivalences: having succeeded in keeping his patient for the prescribed length of time he might feel he has discharged his responsibility. He has worked with the patient for a low fee, or no fee at all, and might well be in constrained financial circumstances himself; and he might be feeling wearily reluctant, as he approaches the end of his training, to undertake more responsibility. At the same time, the supervisor and the trainee both know that the patient's analysis is at a critical point: it could either take off in a new way or it could collapse. The supervisor must try to enable the supervisee to understand and analyse the patient's ambivalence while acknowledging, but not analysing, the trainee's own ambivalent feelings.

One of the trainee's chief anxieties is about losing his training patient. In the training situation the distress at losing a patient is magnified several times over: materially it puts the trainee back in his training; it severely undermines his confidence; and it is public – the training committee and the trainee's colleagues all know about it. He not only feels a sense of failure but also fears judgement. Moreover it arouses infantile fears and experiences of being abandoned. The *fear* of loss, as contrasted with the experience of it, sometimes reaches archetypal proportions and the trainee may need help to bring him back to a more realistic and competent way of functioning. Of course sometimes a patient does leave, either disastrously before the two-year point, or more sadly just after it. The supervisor's task is then to help the supervisee with his 'post-mortem' reflections and recriminations, including self-recriminations, which are part of the mourning process.

Assessment

In an analytic training system there is an inherent tension between the need to preserve and promote the orthodox and traditional, and the seemingly contradictory need to encourage the growth of the individual. Individuation is, after all, the core value of analysis, that of the trainee as well as of the patient. Imposing rigid standards makes no sense. Furthermore we need to encourage the imagination and creativity of students not only for the students' sake, but in the interests of the ongoing development and expansion of analytic thought. The tension exists, however, not only between the individual trainee and the institution but also within the supervisor. A student should not be encouraged to remain in a state of identification, however flat-

tering that may be for the supervisor. The supervisor must be sufficiently grounded in herself to allow the student to differ.

The fact that the supervisor is in a position of authority, evaluating
the trainee in an ongoing way, and passing a final judgement at the
end of the training, can probably never be far from her consciousness.
It is a heavy responsibility in relation to the trainee, to the trainee's
possible future patients, to the institute and to the profession as a
whole. Moreover the very idea of judging runs counter to an analyst's
normal ethical position: we eschew any judgement of our patients.
The supervisor may also feel under public scrutiny and may become
over-anxious about 'standards', ostensibly about keeping up the standards of the institute and of the profession, but also about how her
'standards' are perceived through 'her' trainee. It has been observed
that successive generations of analysts and supervisors seem to make
it more difficult for new entrants to the profession. This might reflect
the shadow side of the analyst's traditionally non-judgemental attitude, as well as the all too human tendency to defend one's patch
against newcomers.

The supervisor's responsibility to the trainee and to the patient can
conflict with her responsibility to the training organisation and she can
find herself drawn into concerns that are beyond her remit. Her main
responsibility, clearly, is to the trainee in his clinical work, but how far
can she ignore what is going on 'outside' when it has repercussions for
the trainee in affecting his confidence and delaying his progress?

Occasionally the trainee's problem is linked to the
transference/countertransference situation between himself and the
patient, and then the supervisor's intervention is appropriate. Of the
trainees I have supervised, who found writing particularly difficult, I
recall at least two for whom the difficulty was connected with the
patient, as in the following example.

*A trainee duly produced his first six-monthly report on his patient and brought
it to me for discussion. I found it incoherent, and said so. The second report,
six months later, was more comprehensible, but he said it had been a struggle.
He then recognised a parallel between his patient's dynamics and his own: the
patient was both fiercely independent and desperately in need of help. The
trainee was caught in a projective identification with her, simultaneously needing help from me and wanting to be independent, which led him, temporarily,
into a paralysis which was enacted in his writing. His recognition of the parallel situation contributed to the eventual resolution of the problem, although the
analysis of it took place elsewhere.*

When doubts are raised about a trainee's progress, whether about his fundamental suitability as a future analyst, or about his competence to manage the pressures of the course, a serious dilemma ensues for everyone involved with the trainee, including the supervisor. In general it seems appropriate that confidence in the initial selection processes of the institute be maintained and that, once the trainee has embarked on the training course, he is given ample time and space to develop. It can seem omnipotent to suggest foreclosing on a student's training. If, sadly, a mistake has been made and it is deemed necessary to end a student's training, the timing of the decision poses an impossible dilemma: there is no good time to do it.

The system of continuous assessment can provide safeguards: it gives an opportunity for difficulties to be perceived early and for help to be offered. A further advantage of regular assessments is that the trainee is encouraged to assess himself. Helping the trainee towards self-observation and self-evaluation is part of the supervisor's task. It is an aspect of continuous assessment which is increasingly a feature of training programmes. Regular assessments and writing reports can be disruptive to the continuity of supervision, keeping the supervisor's evaluative function in focus when it might be better for it to recede; it can be like digging up the plant to see how the roots are growing. At its best, however, the assessment can express the supervisor's responsibility to the trainee to assist him in his individual development whatever direction that takes, either towards becoming a fully-fledged analyst or, just possibly, towards deciding that the profession is not for him (see Chapter 8, p. 146 and Chapter 11, p. 200).

This discussion presupposes that there are criteria by which we assess a student's progress. It has been said that analysts are born, not made. An all-important quality of an analyst is an intuitive understanding of another person's inner world, which is probably a gift; however, as one of the four functions, intuition needs to be differentiated, and balanced by the other functions. Intuition itself can be quite an alarming tool if it is not checked by observation (sensation), by thinking, and by evaluative feeling. However, even when we can identify the qualities we hope to find, they are elusive and it is far from simple to assess how any particular trainee measures up, let alone to convey one's assessment in a report.

The qualities I look for include evidence of movement in the trainee during the course of supervision, especially an increasing emotional flexibility and range in relation to his patients and an improving facility and subtlety in handling symbolism, especially that of the transference; I expect an increasing ability to work independently and without undue anxiety, together with sufficient awareness to recognise the need for help and to seek it. I would hope to see a development and deepening of his judgement and sense of responsibility, and indeed a commitment to and love of analytic work – the beginnings of an ethical attitude (Solomon, 2002). Finally I would look for evidence of a true assimilation and integration of what the trainee has learned – that his analytic persona has become part of himself or, rather, that he is well and truly embarked on what is a continuing process for all of us at any stage, a process to which Goethe refers when he says '*Was du ererbt von deinen Vätern hast, erwirb es, um es zu besitzen*' – 'What thou hast inherited from thy fathers, make not only thine but thee' (quoted in Ekstein, 1969, p. 312) (see Chapter 4, p. 80 and Chapter 8, p. 136).

Summary

I began this chapter by sketching the history of supervision and of how the need for it came to be recognised. I then examined the nature of analytic supervision in general as well as considering some of the specific features of a supervision which takes place within a training context. The development of the concept of supervision reveals that our predecessors faced many of the same problems as we do today about how analysis can be 'taught', and how it is learned, and the extent to which analysis and supervision can or should be differentiated. The various terms used among different groups illuminate the attempts to clarify the nature of psychoanalytic education, and also our ambivalent attitudes to the power that supervisors hold, especially in the training situation where the elements of compulsion and assessment are present. The discomfort we experience about passing judgement may well mask a hidden shadow side of which we need to be aware.

The chapter covered a discussion of basics such as how to facilitate the recognition and handling of transference and countertransference, the nature and purpose of interpretations, and recording and reporting, as well as more specifically training-related problems: the choice of supervisor, the choice of patient, and the potential meanings, for patient and analyst, of the analyst's being in training, of the 'time constraint', and of reduced fee schemes. These factors are unique to the training situation and in some ways provide the trainee with a false or inadequate preparation for his future work.

The question of how a trainee learns is implicit. The supervisor's task is seen as balancing 'teaching', or passing on the benefits of experience to the next generation, with enabling the trainee to find his own course of development. At its best, supervision provides a setting analogous to that of analysis, an uninhibited 'space for play' in which trainee and supervisor can reflect together; the trainee will be enabled, it is hoped, to learn from his own experience, emotionally and intellectually, moving from identification towards assimilation and integration, and becoming in due course the analyst he has it in him to become.

References

Astor, J. (2000) 'Some Reflections on Empathy and Reciprocity in the Use of Countertransference between Supervisor and Supervisee', *Journal of Analytical Psychology*, **45**(3), 367–83.

Balint, M. (1948) 'On the Psycho-analytic Training System', *International Journal of Psycho-Analysis*, **29**, 163–73.

Balint, M. (1954) 'Analytic Training and Training Analysis', *International Journal of Psycho-Analysis*, **35**, 157–62.

Blomfield, O. H. D. (1985) 'Psychoanalytic Supervision – An Overview', *International Review of Psycho-Analysis*, **12**, 401–9.

Ekstein, R. (1969) 'Concerning the Teaching and Learning of Psychoanalysis', *Journal of American Psychoanalysis Association*, **17**, 312–32.

Freud, S. (1925) 'Preface to Aichhorn's Wayward Youth', *Standard Edition 19*. Quoted in R. Ekstein (1969).

Frijling-Schreuder, E. C. M. (1970) 'On Individual Supervision', *International Journal of Psycho-Analysis*, **51**, 363–70.

Goldsmith, G. (2002) 'Teaching Psychoanalysis in the Former Soviet Union', *Journal of Analytical Psychology*, **47**(2), pp. 203–24.

Grinberg, L. (1970) 'The Problems of Supervision in Psychoanalytic Education', *International Journal of Psycho-Analysis*, **51**.

Heimann, P. (first pub. 1950) 'On Counter-transference', in Margret Tonnesmann (ed.) (1989) *Collected Papers 1942–1980. About Children and Children-no-Longer* (London: Routledge).

Jung, C. G. (1951) 'Fundamental Questions of Psychotherapy', *Collected Works Volume 16*.

Kovacs, V. (1936) 'Training- and Control-analysis', *International Journal of Psycho-Analysis*, **17**, 346–54.

Lesser, R. M. (1983) 'Supervision: Illusions, Anxieties and Questions', *Contemporary Psychoanalysis*, **19**, 120–9.

Mattoon, M. A. (1995) 'Historical Notes', in P. Kugler (ed.), *Jungian Perspectives on Clinical Supervision* (Einsiedeln: Daimon).

Plaut, A. (1961) 'A Dynamic Outline of the Training Situation', *Journal of Analytical Psychology*, **6**(2), 98–102.

Reik, T. (1948) *Listening with the Third Ear* (New York: Grove Press).

Searles, H. (1955) 'The Informational Value of the Supervisor's Emotional Experiences', in J. D. Sutherland (ed.) (1965) *Collected Papers on Schizophrenia* (New York: International Universities Press).

Solomon, H. (2002) 'The Ethical Attitude – A Bridge across Analytic Diversity', *Journal of Analytical Psychology*, **47**(2), pp. 279–84.

Steiner, J (1993) 'Problems of Psychoanalytic Technique: Patient-centred and Analyst-centred Interpretations', in *Psychic Retreats* (London: Routledge).

Wharton, B. (1998) 'What Comes out of the Consulting-room? The Reporting of Clinical Material', *Journal of Analytical Psychology*, **43**(2), 205–23.

Zinkin, L. (1995) 'Supervision: The Impossible Profession', in P. Kugler (ed.), *Jungian Perspectives on Clinical Supervision* (Einsiedeln: Daimon).

6

Supervising in Institutions

Catherine Crowther

Introduction

In this chapter I draw on my experience of supervising psychoanalytic psychotherapy and psychodynamic counselling in a number of public and voluntary agencies in the mental health field, sometimes in institutions that are not primarily set up to deliver psychotherapy or with practitioners who are not trained psychotherapists. The different institutional supervisory settings in which I have worked as an analyst include an NHS psychotherapy unit, general practice, a psychodynamic counselling training organisation, a child and adolescent psychiatry department and an institute teaching psychoanalytic psychotherapy in St Petersburg, Russia. As well as group supervision I also supervise individuals, for example a psychodynamic counsellor in an epilepsy service and a senior nurse practitioner, herself running supervision groups. I believe this personal list of organisations is fairly representative of those in which analysts find themselves invited to supervise. It is necessary to make the obvious point that the setting and context in which supervision takes place moulds and influences the nature of the supervision that is appropriate.

Sometimes the analyst-supervisor is a senior member of staff, employed by the institution, with some managerial responsibility for the supervisee and, therefore, identified with the institution. In other circumstances, the supervisor is brought in as a freelance professional, exactly because it is thought desirable to put some reflective distance between the work and the institution. The availability, frequency and quality of supervision represents the value that an agency, group or individual places on securing a protected time and space for reflecting on their patients, their own practice and the dynamics surrounding both. Sometimes supervision is an integral part of the working week. Elsewhere it is hard-won 'time out'.

It is the distinctive contribution of the psychoanalytic tradition to build an attitude towards supervision that it is not only for the untrained and inexperienced, but is a necessary component of our ongoing professional development. Good supervision starts from the top in any organisation. An institution in which supervision is built into the fabric of the organisation encourages a learning culture in which both individuals and the institution itself can develop (Hawkins and Shohet, 1989).

The 'unconscious' of institutions

The particular culture within which psychotherapy is allowed within an institution has far-reaching, but often unacknowledged, effects on all the participants. The essential perspective offered by an analyst-supervisor is the relevance of analytic theories not only to patients but as much to organisations and groups, helping supervisees to understand their role in the conscious and unconscious belief systems, values and purposes of the organisation. Any consideration is coloured by our different unconscious internal representations of the whole edifice of the institution of psychotherapy (Carr, 1988). We all bring institutions in fantasy to the task of supervision, carrying transferences from and to our own training organisations which interact with the fantasies of our supervisees. A strong archetypal field is created around the teacher-student matrix, the attitude towards the supervisor almost always coloured by an archetypal parent projection. Psychotherapy may be idealised and mythologised, sometimes feared and denigrated. A supervisor can be perceived simultaneously as both protective and critical, a parent conferring praise for the child's independent functioning or requiring appeasement because the child has stepped out of line. Supervising in institutions merely exaggerates these parent-child dynamics. Combinations of ego and shadow are received from and projected into the parental institution with which the supervisor is more or less identified. Depending on the level of experience and professional self-confidence of the therapists being supervised, primitive attitudes of power and helplessness, trust and paranoia, idealisation of the supervisor and infantilisation of the worker, can contribute to a collective institutional culture.

Menzies Lyth's (1959) classic study of nursing practices famously showed how nurses were the containers of unconscious personal and institutional projections of terror about the nature of life and death (Menzies Lyth, 1988). The work of any mental health institution inevitably attracts specific projections from a society uneasy with its own victims, misfits, criminals and unfortunates. Doctors, nurses, social workers and psychotherapists are all at risk of identifying with institutional projections and living out archetypally allotted parts. Pietroni (1991) details the antiquity and ubiquity of these archetypal roles: the doctor as hero/warrior/god, the nurse as great mother/container, the social worker as scapegoat/shadow and the psychotherapist as trickster/Mercurius. Moreover, it is well recognised (Britton, 1981) that teams of mental health professionals can become blindly caught up in a parallel process of acting out psychodynamics that echo the 'raw material' of their work. Multidisciplinary teams dealing with families (a child guidance clinic, a primary care team) may structure themselves as if they are a 'family', re-enacting some of the work-related anxieties or, at worst, splitting along stereotyped lines with, say, a (collusive) manager and (controlling) consultant psychiatrist 'pair' of parents. Main's (1957) classic paper, 'The Ailment' (Main, 1989), details how 'special' patients elicit different experiences from different team members, the patient's internal splitting provoking arguments between team members. Teams may also foster entrenched, institutional power and prestige differentials:

> The traditional professional cultures of nursing and medicine socialise their members into automatic, and interlocking, defensive responses – for nurses, giving up power; for doctors, taking it. (Hughes and Pengelly, 1997, p. 123)

It is the job of the supervisor to encourage the recognition of dynamic tension between these archetypal unconscious roles, and to allow multidisciplinary teams some thinking space for processing their anxieties, thus avoiding splitting. It is clear that although the patients are at the core of the system of supervision, their treatment is by no means the sole motivating force in the system.

Different roles and purposes of supervision

There is often difficulty in clarifying the supervisor's responsibility and lines of accountability appropriate to each setting. What is the authority of the supervisor in each institution – is it by role, profession or personal qualities? Zinkin (1988) observes that the implication of the term 'supervisee' is that the object of supervision is the person rather than the work of the therapy. Institutional assumptions about the purposes of supervision express many agendas, overt and covert, which may either dovetail or contradict each other, depending on whether the function of supervision is seen as primarily managerial or developmental. The art and skill of supervision in an institution involves the characteristically Jungian analytic attitude of holding both opposing necessities in creative tension.

Hughes and Pengelly's comprehensive book, *Staff Supervision in a Turbulent Environment* (1997) adapts the concept of the supervisory triangle first developed by Mattinson (1981). Mattinson observed that when a case is being discussed in supervision, there are dynamically not two but three *participants* – supervisor, practitioner and patient – all influencing the proceedings. In an institutional setting the supervisor's responsibility is broader. Hughes and Pengelly's triangle has close connections with Mattinson's triangle of participants, and details three *functions* that are being addressed in institutional supervision:

- focusing on the practitioner's work;
- facilitating the practitioner's professional development;
- managing service-delivery.

As with all triangular dynamics, one corner tends to get excluded, avoided or ignored, usually that which is causing most anxiety. Hughes and Pengelly note that the converse can equally be true – that the most worrying corner can provoke an anxious attachment so that supervisor and supervisee are unable to leave it and pay sufficient attention to the other two, equally important corners.

Institutional and professional agendas for supervision may conflict. There are a growing number of counsellors, employed in primary and secondary health care settings, for whom it is a compulsory requirement of the British Association for Counselling and Psychotherapy (BACP) to maintain supervision throughout their working lives. This contradicts the notion that supervision should be voluntary, sought out, to facilitate the maximum motivation for self-reflection. Sometimes supervision is seen principally as in-service training for novice practitioners. Alternatively, it is regarded as enhancing an experienced practitioner's work and recognised as part of continuing professional development (CPD), a concept increasingly endorsed by all the helping professions.

Supervision is sometimes described as 'support'. Essential though it is to sustain morale, value achievements and attend to the practitioner's emotional stress, support alone cannot be seen as an end in itself, as it tends towards a certain collusive woolliness of thinking about the reasons for the worker's stress. Focusing on the practitioner's needs in supervision should have the overriding purpose of promoting a better service to the patient. This prime function of supervision is open to subversion under the new 'business culture' in the NHS and other welfare services, which emphasises financial and political accountability for public services. Clinical governance, audit, quality assurance and resource management all operate in a climate where the pressure is to 'get more for less'. This raises the question of whether analysts want to supervise in these circumstances. What are we being asked to deliver?

Some analysts believe supervision should maintain a model of psychoanalytic psychotherapy as 'pure', an idea only possible in a designated psychotherapy unit, with patients and practitioners specifically selected. My own belief is that supervision in institutions should attempt the opposite – to see how usefully the psychoanalytic model itself can develop and diversify into contexts other than the analytic consulting room. Some thoughtful adaptation and extension of the usual analytic privileged space can develop a tailor-made service, informed by analytic principles, to suit the particular profile of that agency (for example, a forensic unit, an outreach counselling service for disadvantaged women).

Ambivalent attitudes towards supervision

The ways in which analysts may be invited as supervisors into different health care settings are various. In some institutions, an analyst is requested by practitioners who, without formal psychotherapy training or personal therapy, nevertheless have long experience and expertise in other helping professions and who value the insights and reflective space that an analytic approach brings to their work. However, supervision often evokes ambivalence, well articulated by Streeck (1997), writing about mental health teams and referring to an earlier article by Salvendy:

> Unrealistically high expectations are occasionally attached to supervision, but supervision is also at times regarded as a luxury that is contrary to the essence of psychiatry. Sometimes the prospect of supervision awakens anxiety because

it is associated with control and surveillance. Such fears are especially strong in institutions that operate, as do many psychiatric hospitals, in the force field between therapy and state control – though again, false hopes may be attached to supervision as a means of liberation and self-government . . . One encounters hopeful expectation and fears simultaneously: desire for support and rescue on the one hand, and scepticism and fear of control, exposure, and intrusive surveillance on the other. (Salvendy, 1993, cited in Streeck, 1997, p. 62)

In medical settings, the idea of supervision may be synonymous with 'not coping'. Doctors in general practice, notwithstanding Balint groups, are trained to place a high moral value on their capacity to operate autonomously. Under enormous personal strain from the unrelenting pressure of work, GPs are sometimes confused by the culture of supervision that is introduced into general practice by their counsellor, and may mistakenly take it to indicate a lack of expertise or confidence. At the same time, the doctors sometimes find themselves growing envious of the protected time that the counsellor makes for her own development and learning. This often shows itself in the number of referrals to the counsellor of 'unhelpable' patients, so that she holds the sense of failure, rejection and burn out, without the system as a whole understanding the process. One of the important side effects of the increasing levels of training and self-confidence of counsellors and psychotherapists within general practice may be that medical culture is allowing the idea of seeking discussion and emotional support for one's work to seep in, almost by osmosis. The cell membranes traditionally holding apart GPs, nurses and counsellors in rigidly differentiated structures that limit the flow of psychological-mindedness, seem more porous nowadays.

Supervision as persecution is another hazard. The nursing profession emphasises nurses' capacity to make decisions reliably and function autonomously. The Royal College of Nursing and the Nursing and Midwifery Council (formerly UKCC) recently recommended the wide availability of clinical supervision groups, for experienced nurses to talk about daily issues arising from their work in hospital wards or the community. There is anecdotal evidence that nurses are finding it difficult to use these groups through fear of being seen to make mistakes or expressing negative feelings in a non-trusting atmosphere. The culture of blame attaching to any need for professional support is deeply ingrained, both personally and institutionally.

Traditional patterns of supervision in Social Services departments have changed in recent years. Psychoanalytically-influenced casework supervision used to attend *both* to the implementation of policies *and* to the emotional impact on patients and social workers of high-risk work. The growth of statutory responsibilities and anxious pressure from public accountability now often subverts social work supervision into a defensive, procedural hybrid between support, monitoring and 'covering one's back'.

It is often difficult for an individual worker to go against her institution's culture by seeking an understanding of unconscious, dynamic aspects of therapeutic relationships. Analytic supervisors in this situation may find themselves a piggy-in-the-middle in professional politics. Lloyd-Owen (1997), offering specialist supervision to individuals from different agencies, acknowledges the difficulty of taking a new symbolic understanding back into the worker's home institution, which defends itself against the pain of relating to the patient as a whole (suffering) person.

> In becoming independent of the institutional defences, the worker is seen as rocking the boat, threatening the homeostasis, and he becomes vulnerable to attack by his envious and anxious colleagues. (Lloyd-Owen, 1997, p. 93)

The supervisor's broader systemic thinking hopefully prevents supervisees idealising analytic supervision, and helps them recognise that any integration of psychoanalytic ideas into their workplace can only be effected gradually.

Responsibility and confidentiality within general practice teams

The widespread presence of counsellors in general practice focuses some important issues for institutional supervision. Few psychodynamic training programmes give much thought to issues of multidisciplinary teamwork, communication with non-psychotherapist colleagues or shared files and records. Appropriate internal supervision is often unobtainable and an outside supervisor is used. This can leave line-management issues ill-defined or studiously avoided. To whom is the counsellor accountable? What is the supervisor's responsibility? Who should have a right to know details of the counsellor's work with patients? The hallowed maintenance of boundaries and the establishment of trust, on which counselling and psychoanalytic psychotherapy depend, are influenced, sometimes jarred, by each setting. The future credibility (and funding) of counselling and psychotherapy in the NHS depends in large part on how other colleagues perceive its relevance and usefulness.

It is often in supervision that the ethical implications and practical and emotional effects of confidentiality have to be re-examined on a case by case basis:

> Without initial definition, supervisor and supervisee may act on vague assumptions about maintaining confidentiality until a crisis exposes the severe limits on many aspects of confidentiality in an accountable agency context. (Hughes and Pengelly, 1997, p. 34)

Counsellors and supervisors may try to protect themselves from the anxieties of being involved in taking decisions and responsibility. These parameters should ideally be discussed from the outset in any arrangement for external supervision. It is sometimes forgotten that a supervisor too has an important need to discuss supervisory work with her own supervisor or peer group, so any strict concept of confidentiality has to be redefined. It may be seen as an advantage that institutions bring such issues into sharp focus.

A depressed single mother, Natalie, was referred to the practice counsellor by her GP. The counsellor quickly became concerned for the safety of Natalie's three-year old daughter, who was subjected to her uncontrollable rages. Natalie would leave her clinging, whiny daughter with her own mother for long periods, despite having been neglected and physically abused by her mother in childhood.

Counsellor and supervisor, although anxious about the way the child was being victimised, believed that Natalie's improved understanding of her inner world would reduce her hostile feelings and felt encouraged by Natalie's obvious dismay at her own behaviour. The supervisor did not recommend passing on any concerns to the GP. This lack of communication in the 'actual world' left the counsellor unaware that the health visitor was also visiting. When the three-year old was taken to hospital after a fall, suspicions were raised about the adequacy of the child's care. The GP, health visitor and Social Services, who knew all generations of the family well, felt let down by the counsellor's and supervisor's adherence to principles of confidentiality and the failure to alert them earlier to the recent build-up of explosive tension. Natalie was not the exclusive responsibility of the counsellor and, as far as the GP was concerned, was not the only patient in the family. Subsequently, useful discussions between all the professionals resulted in specialist child care services being offered. The counselling benefited too, as the shared concern allowed Natalie more 'actual' space from guilty anxiety about her daughter to concentrate on the deeper feelings that had generated her rage and anxiety.

This example illustrates the difficulties that occur when, despite employment within the same building, communication between different professional approaches is impeded in both directions, so that ignorance and scepticism about the other's approach is reinforced. The supervisor assumed inappropriately that, as well as the valuable insights that psychoanalysis brings, its techniques and etiquette should also be transposed wholesale into a different professional setting.

Although the supervisor's functions are to help translate patients' material into symbolic meaning and to contain the supervisee's anxiety, it is also essential to be able to recognise a genuine call for action. The need for action around child protection (see Chapter 4, pp. 76–8) or hospital admission is more likely to arise in relation to patients of an agency than within private practice. Supervisors need to be aware of what other services are available for patients and how to gain access to them. Supervisees need help to walk the tightrope of preserving the treatment alliance with patients, while considering the requirements of both their inner and outer worlds. More experienced supervisees are accustomed to pausing for reflection, rather than being jolted into an over-reaction. Very occasionally, a supervisor may have to act by raising a question over a worker's competence to continue working with a patient.

Opportunities for creative adaptation

I believe it is essential that analytic supervisors in public agencies recognise how each unique setting opens the possibility of adapting normative, ideal methods of psychotherapy practice to the benefit of teamwork, while still benefiting patients (see Chapter 4, pp. 74–5). This is as much a careful learning process for the supervisor, as she takes in the constraints of 'reality' in each new supervisory setting, as it is a lesson for the supervisee. What different forms can a meaningful psychotherapy take, without selling short our own values? Is the supervisee encouraging comprehension and interest amongst colleagues? Thoughtful supervision helps supervisees find the flexibility to reconsider over-formal boundaries, even the 50-minute hour, in order to acknowledge and be respected by the culture in which they are working. For time-limited counselling the supervisor may helpfully question the tradition of weekly sessions, spacing them fortnightly, or fixing a review session with the patient a few months after treatment ends, to allow more time for working through. It is only through having a substantial psychodynamic training that supervisees will be confident enough of their internal boundaries and external framework to be able to question them.

Patients' rights to request access to their own notes has to be encompassed. Here the confidentiality that is threatened is professional – that of recording our clinical opinions and private countertransference reactions. Supervisees can helpfully keep separate personal 'jottings' for supervision purposes only. The analytic dimension adds a consideration of process, influencing the manner in which patients are assisted to examine their files – understanding the request as having meaning within the therapeutic relationship, expressing significant anxieties around control, curiosity or mistrust of the transference parents, for example.

Thoughtfulness about race and ethnicity, financial and class differences, alternative cultural assumptions, the risk of violence, all need attention and may result in adjustments or innovative practice. Ethical, analytic judgement is needed to listen, question, challenge and understand, without sacrificing what is fundamental about those professional boundaries and principles that make our analytic attitude distinctive from other helping professions. The boundary can expand to include relevant others in the team, but it is important that personal relations between team members do not become the object of supervision, as this tends to make working relationships more disturbed.

There follows an example of supervision as a creative space for considering ethnic difference and facilitating teamwork within general practice.

A GP and an experienced practice counsellor (both women) brought their work with immigrant and refugee women patients to an external analytic supervisor. Their sessions were conducted with the help of interpreters, appropriately known as advocates, who included in their role both language translation and some interpretation of one culture to the other. This charitably-funded project aimed to understand and ameliorate the women's frequent rate of consultation at the surgery with somatic complaints, such as headache, gynaecological pain or muscular weakness, for which no physical causes were apparent. The GP enjoyed an unprecedented extension of consultation time, from 10 to 45 minutes. For the counsellor it was new to concentrate so closely on bodily as well as psychological 'complaints'.

Both were taken aback by the outpouring of emotion once 'licence' had been given to talk. They witnessed the women's unrelieved grief at the loss of village life in their native country, sometimes hearing stories of traumatic persecution before they left, and their dislocation living in London. Supervision addressed the GP's and counsellor's feelings of helplessness and burden, and their frustration that, despite making symbolic and historical links, the patients' acknowledgement of emotional pain brought only slight change in their somatised pains. The possible psychological meaning of the physical symptoms became many-layered, as the supervisees grappled with cultural difference, language communication barriers and the women's dependent transferences to the surgery. The supervisor needed to restrain the GP and counsellor from setting goals that were too hopeful and ambitious for their time-limited work, at the same time as encouraging the therapeutic endeavour.

Two female advocates later came for some supervision as well, as they were finding it hard to process their own emotional reactions, especially their identification with the women's narratives and depression. The supervisor introduced them to the concept of countertransference and tried to help with its effects.

To quote the counsellor: 'One of the most positive things – facilitated by supervision – was exploring styles of joint working. GPs and counsellors usually work alone. We learnt a great deal about building trust between us, which sometimes involved a blurring of professional boundaries, and this in turn led us to confront difficult material, which was to some extent contained within the supervision.' (Cook, personal communication)

Overall, this example illustrates both loyalty to and adaptation of the analytic model, in unknown territory far removed from the analyst's consulting room (see Chapter 4, p. 68).

Supervising 'beginners' in a psychotherapy unit

The flexibility needed in supervising trained counsellors in general practice contrasts with my experience of more formal supervision of 'beginners' in a psychotherapy unit of an NHS psychiatric hospital – introducing the theories and practice of an analytic model to the uninitiated. The unit offers so-called psychotherapy, delivered by NHS staff or trainees from different professional backgrounds, who often have no experience in psychotherapy. Analytic supervision within the unit is essential to safeguard an acceptable level of care for the patients. I echo the sentiments of Sedlak:

> The unavailability of personal therapy or analysis and of a good training experience does not stop people in the caring professions working in what they consider to be an analytic or dynamic way. Senior practitioners can of course choose to have little to do with this possible diminution of standards; alternatively they can explore in what ways they can help, while maintaining their professional integrity. I have chosen the latter course. (Sedlak, 1997, p. 26)

Supervision groups in the unit consisted of three to four people (from psychiatry, nursing, psychology, social work, counselling) who had approached the unit to learn more about psychoanalytic psychotherapy. They each took one case. As supervisor, I was clinically responsible for their work, while the consultant psychotherapists assessed the patients' suitability for psychotherapy and held medical responsibility. Psychotherapy usually lasted nine months, sometimes extended to 18 months, at once-a-week frequency. Afterwards, some patients would graduate to a psychotherapy group or be referred outside the NHS for longer-term psychotherapy.

Psychotherapy patients are markedly different in institutions from those in private practice – more in poverty and deprivation, suffering from racial discrimination, more survivors of sexual and physical abuse, more drinking, potentially violent or drug-dependent patients. Borderline, personality-disordered, somatising and acting-out patients often avoid the intimacy of a personal consulting room and feel that an institution better contains their fear of envy and madness. The rest of the mental health system has to be reliably in place to allow psychotherapy to take place – psychiatric cover, access to day hospitals and community psychiatric nurses, good psychotherapy assessments. Supervision of psychotherapy with patients who are not 'psychologically minded' must help untrained therapists deal with their countertransference responses to very primitive archetypal projections. Supervisees need to recognise the high level of damage that patients bring into sessions, without destroying their therapeutic optimism. With all their difficulties, such patients provide an extremely rich field for learning about primitive states of mind and defences against catastrophic fears.

It is anomalous that analysts and psychotherapists, used to working with a high frequency of sessions per week with fee-paying patients in therapies of indefinite length, often supervise once-a-week, non-fee-paying, time-limited therapy. Are analysts the best people to undertake the task? Accustomed to the wide ranging style of analytic case discussion groups, some analysts may neglect novice supervisees' need for detailed, 'how to', practical guidance and basic skills teaching. Our own training did not teach us to adapt, and the many supervision courses now being offered are witness to the need to acquaint ourselves with the various contexts in which supervision occurs.

Impingements from the environment

The length of psychotherapy in the unit was dictated partly by the NHS's financial demands for a relatively rapid turnover of patients, but also by the psychiatric training rotation whereby junior doctors regularly move jobs within the hospital. This meant *all* supervisees were expected to do brief psychotherapy. The course of therapy was sometimes interrupted for a few weeks' study leave when the doctors took exams. Sometimes a change of session time was dictated by a timetable change to suit a new job, affecting also doctors' availability for supervision. These are vivid examples of the institution moulding the nature of the work to the demands of another agenda (see Chapter 13, p. 233).

Supervisees often needed help in scheduling and valuing the supervision group as a priority for themselves and their professional development. Lloyd-Owen notes that personal ambivalence coincides with a sort of institutional sabotage:

> Arrangements for regular, at least weekly, supervision are often resisted, perhaps couched in terms of funding and workload or that, somehow, fortnightly supervision is seen as more tolerable. (Lloyd-Owen, 1997, p. 96)

My responsibility as supervisor was to contain anxiety about impingements, to challenge assumptions about answering bleeps during supervision, to stay steady and unflappable about my own routines and model an appropriate balance between the need for firm boundaries and for some accommodation. Hughes and Pengelly (1997) suggest that some discussion beforehand of possibly acceptable grounds for interruption or cancellation of supervision is more useful than attempting to make 'ideal' arrangements that are bound to fail and lead to disillusion.

The hospital's training rotation encouraged a culture of denial surrounding endings and separations. The infantile dimension of frequent separations was covered up by an assumption of adult, professional functioning. Individuals sometimes dealt with their separation feelings by overprotecting 'special' patients for whom unusual arrangements and concessions were made to continue the relationship. The effects of frequent handovers, on patients and professionals alike, were upsetting and largely ignored, but often appeared in the material brought for supervision. Supervision fostered a growing psychological awareness amongst junior professionals that hopefully helped to disseminate some analytic understanding of the damaging disruption throughout the hospital system. This is an instance where analytic integrity dictates not an accommodation but a questioning of the institutional culture and practices.

The NHS has to ration what is available. Supervision therefore has to concentrate on the ending from the outset. We can have only limited expectations of change in time-limited contracts. In effect, supervision presides over a trial of psychotherapy, a prolonged assessment of patients' readiness to adopt a psychodynamic curiosity about themselves. After nine months, patients, hopefully, have acquired a rudimentary new awareness of self in relation to other to carry with them. Supervision of time-limited work can make a virtue of necessity, like the creativity locked up in the 14-line sonnet. The ever-present ending can constellate and amplify familiar themes in psychotherapy, such as separation, trust, idealisation, disillusionment, denigration. Once-weekly sessions carry an extra intensity for patient and supervisee alike. It is important to remind supervisees that the significance of the transference is not diminished by a shorter involvement.

Managing untrained therapists' countertransference

Sedlak (1997) highlights the main feature of supervising untrained therapists – their difficulty with bearing the emotional strain of their countertransference responses, especially in the negative transference. Supervisees who had had some personal psychotherapy showed greater tolerance of external reality and acceptance of their own thoughts and feelings. The pressure in the countertransference to 'do something' rather than reflect is commonly encountered and needs discussion in supervision groups. Sometimes it is difficult for the supervisee to undo his identification with his core profession. Psychiatrists may revert to a mental state examination when they fear a suicide, and social workers feel drawn into anxious responsibility for their patients' external lives. Acting-in is often seen in an anxious change of therapeutic tack – for example, referring patients on. Although 'beginners' are often well-informed about psychodynamic theories, only gradually do they learn to *feel* their own importance as a transference object in a patient's inner world, and realise that their own experiences of despair or anger are largely generated by projective identification. I found it essential to discuss fairly frequently the purpose and importance of formal psychotherapy boundaries and framework. This helped supervisees to conceptualise the psychotherapy relationship as special, taking place in metaphorical as well as real time and space. Instances of countertransference difficulty – the supervisee walking with the patient to the bus stop or bringing tomato seedlings from home because the patient shares an interest in gardening – had to be tactfully explored. They should never be discussed in terms of the supervisee's personal history or personality.

I tend to accept that awkward, inept events will occur between supervisee and patient. These incidents will be explored psychodynamically after the event in supervision, particularly how the supervisee was left feeling in the countertransference. I try to make any didactic explanations of the analytic canon both accessible and interesting in lay language, linked into discussion of case material. Like Sedlak (1997), I tend to use the word 'we' to acknowledge common pressures in the countertransference, and avoid the word 'should', to minimise the operation of the supervisee's primitive superego, which only leads to shame and narcissistic vulnerability about exposing oneself in supervision.

Creative use of countertransference

If this is a supervisee's first taste of psychoanalytic psychotherapy, I feel some responsibility for making the supervision process itself a sort of therapeutic experience, distinct from personal psychotherapy. If psychotherapy within health institutions is to survive, then the experience for beginners has to be, on the whole, a challenging, thoughtful and encouraging episode. Supervisees often talk about the sessions with patients as giving them a personal intensity of experience very different from the rest of their work. Converse feelings also arise: paranoid feelings of self-exposure and sibling rivalry can be activated within a supervision group. Both good and bad experiences in supervision can frequently lead to enquiries from supervisees about starting their own psychotherapy.

As Balint wrote:

> The acquisition of psychotherapeutic skill does not consist only of learning something new: it inevitably also entails a limited, though considerable, change in the doctor's personality. (Balint, 1964, p. 299)

I try to foster a group atmosphere of respect and imaginative enquiry concerning all countertransference difficulties, errors and enactments, in order to help supervisees become intrigued rather than persecuted by what has happened between them and their patients. Hopefully, supervision can give individuals a first hand experience congruent with psychotherapy – their own uncomfortable unconscious processes being understood in a new, eye-opening, symbolic way.

Carol, a supervisee, was disappointed when her patient withdrew from psychotherapy precipitately. She herself withdrew from the supervision group, neither wrote to the patient, nor submitted a closing summary as required by the Unit, nor let me know what was going on. I finally reached her on the phone and persuaded her to come back to the group and talk through her feelings. Her anger at the patient's cavalier dismissal of the psychotherapy was mixed with shame at mishandling the patient through inexperience. The group recognised her identification with the patient's projected sense of failure and self-exposure. We explored how Carol, like her patient, had wanted to flee and deny the pain engendered. Carol saw her reaction in a new, less embarrassing light, allowing her to contain her dismissive anger. The group helped her compose a letter. This elicited a good reply from the patient who expressed some gratitude, acknowledging how hard the sessions had been and saying goodbye. Carol wrote a closing summary incorporating some of this understanding. Both Carol and probably the patient learned something by not discarding the ending but taking it seriously. There is more likelihood that one of them may return to psychotherapy in the future, because the ending left them both with a better taste in the mouth.

Summary

Much of this chapter has been concerned with the inconsistencies, constraints and complexity of institutional supervision. There is an inherent paradox in the supervisor's role of simultaneously ensuring that analytic purpose and framework are valued and guarded and considering how far they can be flexible. Yet it is just this tension between different necessities that gives institutional supervision its imaginative edge and acts as a spur to creativity. I believe this is a manifestation of the transcendent function, hallmark of the Jungian approach. Besides the agency benefiting from the analytic approach we introduce, it is important also to emphasise the beneficial and stimulating effects on the supervisor of being kept on one's toes, and attending to institutional process at many levels. Our abiding analytic values, principles and traditions are brought into sharp focus, not only by encountering various unconscious, often contradictory, institutional assumptions, but also by working in agencies whose clientele, attitudes and contemporary therapeutic methods reflect developments in society as a whole. We are shaping and being shaped by the collective culture in a very Jungian way. Our analytic insights have to be communicated in ways that bring them to useful new life in each context. Institutional supervision helps to train not only the next generation of psychotherapists and counsellors, but also to influence other professionals to value analytic ideas, and thereby disseminate them throughout the health care field.

References

Balint, M. (1964) *The Doctor, His Patient and the Illness* (London: Pitman).

Britton, R. (1981) 'Re-enactment as an Unwitting Response to Family Dynamics', in S. Box, B. Copley, J. Magagna and E. Moustaki (eds), *Psychotherapy with Families: An Analytic Approach* (London: Routledge & Kegan Paul).

Carr, J. (1988) 'A Model of Clinical Supervision. In Clinical Supervision: Issues and Techniques'. Papers from the public conference organised by the Jungian Training Committee of the British Association of Psychotherapists.

Hawkins, P. and Shohet, R. (1989) *Supervision in the Helping Professions* (Buckingham: Open University Press).

Hughes, L. and Pengelly P. (1977) *Staff Supervision in a Turbulent Environment: Managing Process and Task in Front-Line Services,* Tavistock Institute of Medical Psychology (London: Jessica Kingsley Publishers).

Lloyd-Owen, D. (1997) 'From Action to Thought: Supervising Mental Health Workers with Forensic Patients', in B. Martindale, M. Mörner, M. E. C. Rodriguez, J.-P. Vidit (eds), *Supervision and its Vicissitudes* (London: Karnac).

Main, T. (first pub. 1957) 'The Ailment', in T. Main (1989) *The Ailment and Other Psychoanalytic Essays* (London: Free Association Books).

Mattinson, J. (1981) 'The Deadly Equal Triangle', in *Change and Renewal in Psychodynamic Social Work: British and American Developments in Practice and Education for Services to Families and Children* (Massachusetts: Smith College School of Social Work; London: Group for the Advancement of Psychotherapy in Social Work).

Menzies Lyth, I. (first pub. 1959) 'The Functioning of Social Systems as a Defence against Anxiety', in I. Menzies Lyth (1988) *Containing Anxiety in Institutions, Selected Essays, Volume 1* (London: Free Association Books).

Pietroni, P. (1991) 'Archetypes or Stereotypes: The Role of the Psychotherapist in Teamwork'. Public lecture given at the Society of Analytical Psychology. Available as audio-tape, SAP, London.

Salvendy, J. T. (1993) 'Control and Power in Supervision', *International Journal of Group Psychotherapy*, **43**, 363–76.

Sedlak, V. (1997) 'Psychoanalytic Supervision of Untrained Therapists', in B. Martindale, M. Mörner, M. E. C. Rodriguez, J.-P. Vidit (eds), *Supervision and its Vicissitudes* (London: Karnac).

Streeck, U. (1997) 'Supervision in Mental Health Teams and Institutions', in B. Martindale, M. Mörner, M. E. C. Rodriguez, J.-P. Vidit (eds), *Supervision and its Vicissitudes* (London: Karnac).

Zinkin, L. (1988) 'Supervision: The Impossible Profession. In Clinical Supervision: Issues and Techniques'. Papers from the public conference organised by the Jungian Training Committee of the British Association of Psychotherapists.

7

Supervision in Groups

Victoria Graham Fuller

Introduction

The history of psychoanalysis does not record precisely when supervision as a concurrent companion to analysis became an established practice. We know, however, that in the beginning of the last century Freud was seeking theory to advance his fledgling psychoanalytic movement and had established a forum to discuss technique with his colleagues in which he played a parental role.

In 1909, Carl Jung was treating a young schizophrenic patient in the Burgholzli psychiatric clinic, Zurich, and the pair had become intensely attracted to one another. Relatively inexperienced and with no objective mentor to advise him, Jung wrote to Freud explaining that the patient, Sabina Spielrein, was threatening to cause a scandal because he refused to have a child with her.

Freud reassured Jung, 'No lasting harm is done [from such experiences]. They help us to dominate countertransference which is a permanent problem for us.'

When Spielrein herself wrote to Freud for help in the situation he suggested that she control her feelings for Jung and, above all, 'avoid any external action involving third parties'.

Psychotherapy supervision as we know it today, when countertransference has become pivotal to our practice, was simply not an option then. From our contemporary perspective, we can interpret Freud's comments as supervisory. Note his reassurance of Jung and the link to emerging theory. There is irony in his advice to Spielrein, revealing an attitude that prevented him from valuing 'third parties', which is, after all, the place of today's supervisor in the analytic process of the therapeutic couple.

Jung's analysis of Sabina Spielrein was complicated by an absence of formal ethical guidelines for analytic practice. It is not possible in this chapter to explore the professional implications of his dilemma further. (Martin explores the subject in Chapter 8 and, for a full account, refer to Aldo Carotenuto's book *A Secret Symmetry*, 1984.)

The fact that Jung turned to Freud for support exemplifies the analytic practitioner's felt need for theory – in the sense of acquired, documented clinical experience based on observation and modification of the patient's inner world – as a structure on which to base practice and a backbone to support the body of the therapeutic work.

I hypothesise that this need represents a legacy which all clinicians in the field of psychoanalytic supervision have inherited. It is not uncommon for candidates in analytic training to achieve qualification fearing that they do not know enough theory, despite years of intensive study and supervised practice. Some trainees approaching qualification confess in their analyses to feeling fraudulent or fantasise that their training committee will mistakenly judge them fit to practise independently. At the root of such admissions may be complex feelings, including a reluctance to leave the safety of a training institution and those supportive figures who have shepherded them through an arduous learning curve. Even long-qualified analysts express wishes to retrain in another, related discipline.

The end of training can feel frustrating to the newly-qualified candidate. Formal initiation rites into a training organisation are usually perfunctory by comparison with academic and other training schemes and it may take a protracted transition period for the candidate to gain the ultimate approval of his or her superego, not to mention the parental archetype constellated in the training body itself. Peer supervision groups can be especially helpful at these times, serving to prolong contact with fellow trainees which would otherwise end, and offering ex-students an opportunity to flex their analytic muscles free from the pressure to conform to perceived training norms. I suggest that in the process of mourning the loss of trainee status, the quest for theory is regenerated, driven by energies freshly released from the Self, Jung's concept of an archetypal psychic totality with polarised components (Jung, 1971, para. 789) (see Chapter 13).

Mythologically, we are in the realm of Genesis: Adam and Eve's instinctual need to grow in every way available to humans, expressed as rebellious curiosity, led to banishment from Paradise to an earthly world of pain, uncertainty and ignorance. An important element in this developmental process is the presence of a third, an observer of the inner world, commentator on external behaviour and bringer of reality. In the story of Adam and Eve, the third was embodied as a serpent. The archetypal image of the third is ever present within us re-presenting us with moral and psychological conflict, and promoting a potential synthesis of opposites.

The point I am making here is that supervision today, as a practicum affording a range of techniques and models and subject to a myriad of theoretical templates, has arrived at a point where we are keen to advance it as a separate but related skill within the therapeutic panoply, worthy of a distinct training and awaiting an integral theory in its own right (see Chapter 12, p. 216).

Theory

Developing theoretical ideas is a creative act, like recovering dreams or recording therapy sessions. It is a constantly evolving task, like the process of analysis itself. A body of theory, repeatedly sown and painstakingly harvested over a number of years, can provide the seasoned analyst with a sense of inner authority, an autobiographical reservoir from which to draw support for others, in a supervisory role.

Freud acknowledged the role of the analyst's unconscious fantasies in constructing theory. These included the clinician's unresolved conflicts which influence how he assembles interpersonal reality into theory consistent with his experience and observations.

Internal psychic conflict, as Jung pointed out (Jung, 1959, para. 174), is an essential condition of psychological life. The principle of two equal opposing forces at work in our psyches is at the root of many of his hypotheses about the human condition. Whether we are aware of it or not, many of our present day explanations for human behaviour rely upon his theory. An awareness of tension from opposition inside ourselves is the hallmark of consciousness and can be discovered through the projections we make onto others.

Jung's 1909 appeal to Freud highlights the paradox inherent in the therapeutic endeavour. What is meant to be a strictly confidential relationship conducted symbolically within a 'sealed vessel,' as sacrosanct as that between a priest and a penitent, seeks to transcend the boundary of the dyad. In fact, as Jung discovered, the relationship often requires the presence of a third element to resolve a situation that has become polarised. Jung believed that the clash of unconscious opposites could never be finally resolved, but that it was possible to achieve a synthesis of conscious and unconscious elements in the personality, resulting in a tension which could be held creatively. This principle will be useful in considering the tensions inherent in supervision groups.

Relevance of group analytic theory to supervision

Members of groups, large or small, institutional or not, share ideals and common goals, especially at an unconscious level. In psychoanalytic training institutions and the committees responsible for training seminars or other events in which dissemination of concepts and principles are implied, members ascribe great importance to maintaining a cohesive view, at least in these immediate settings, as a way of protecting revered founders and promoting their ideas.

At times of crisis or transition, such as the death of an institutional founder, we are inclined to experience others who hold divergent views from our own as rebellious or 'nonconformist', although we may not express this overtly. Under pressure to contain the anxieties engendered in institutional life, it is hardly surprising that theories can be transformed intra-psychically into self-sustaining belief systems that can ossify into an in-group ideology. If we happen to be included in this dominant structure, our narcissistic needs for recognition are gratified and doubt and confusion are alleviated temporarily. If we happen to land outside a particular theoretical fold, however, we can feel abandoned and excluded from the centre, exciting rivalry and oedipal desires to belong. Despite the fact that rivalry and competitive pressures are essential prerequisites for the growth of a healthy community, as Redfearn (1992) points out, it will be difficult to sustain creative tension between conflicting elements in such a climate. I will return to a consideration of these dynamics in relation to supervision groups.

The collective level of group life

A year after Jung's death, S. H. Foulkes proposed a dimension of group life he called the *primordial level*, in which images from the collective unconscious arise in a group spontaneously (Usandivaras, 1986). As Jung (1959) had hypothesised, the collective manifests in the form of archetypal images – universal symbols found in myths and fairy tales such as the Hero or the Witch. They may also appear in dreams or fantasies, films or art, and are constellated in human relationships as they correspond to human life-stages – birth, death, marriage, separation, to name but a few. Hopcke helpfully makes the distinction between the content of the archetype and the archetype itself:

> The archetype itself is neither an inherited idea nor a common image. A better description is that the archetype is like a psychic mould into which individual and collective experiences are poured and where they take shape, yet it is distinct from the symbols and images themselves. (Hopcke, 1989, p. 15)

Much has been written about the archetypal roles that may arise in supervisory relationships, (see Chapter 1, pp. 20–2; also Usandivaras, 1986, p. 119; Brookes, 1995, p. 125; Speicher, 1995, p. 197). These authors stress the importance of recognising archetypal manifestations in groups, collaborating with their development without resorting to interpretation prematurely, and emphasising their usefulness in promoting the functioning of the group.

Corbett (1995) states, 'it is time for us to characterise a specifically Jungian approach to training, which requires that we discern the workings of the Self and its archetypal constituents in this process.'

While archetypal themes may be named and elucidated, they cannot be manipulated or evoked, even in the interests of the maturational needs of supervisees. Nonetheless, some supervisors, in recommending a mentor model, claim that they can influence the constellation of specific archetypes. This optimistic view arrogates an omniscient degree of control over the contents of the collective unconscious, while underestimating the potential contribution of the supervisees to the supervision project. As Jung emphasised, archetypes are not entities at our disposal, to be evoked at will – they emerge in relationships, generating our emotional responses just as a magnet will organise shards of metal around negative and positive poles; *they* live *us* (Jung, 1959, para. 57).

Oppositional forces in supervision

In supervision groups, members are aware of the (ideal) conscious wish to achieve learning and mastery of their art through mutual co-operation. In parallel however there is an alternative group wish, based on shared *unconscious* fantasy, that opposes participation. It resists development and learning from experience, and persists in pursuing avoidant, dependent or rescue fantasies in typical Bion defensive postures such as flight, fighting, pairing, as well as Hopper's massing (Hopper, 1997).

Filtered through previous experiences, supervision group members have fantasies about what situations feel threatening or dangerous. For example, supervisees openly dread the colloquial 'cathedral hush' response to their presentations. Alternatively, the fellow-supervisee who states 'I have a patient like yours' is felt to be encouraging.

Just as individuals live in a constant state of internal opposition, groups tend paradoxically toward variance once a sense of cohesion is established. Members express internal opposition by splitting into subgroups organised around polarised archetypal configurations. Supervision group members may align themselves around aspects of the group's task: timing, consideration of clinical detail, conditions for learning. Supervisees may disagree about presentation time and how to share it, whether content takes precedence over process or what topics may be employed to distract the group from the prime task appropriately or defensively.

Within a supervision group, each subgroup will unconsciously aim to create conditions that favour its own development (Berger, 1964). Thus one subgroup may believe that it will be unable to risk disagreement until the norm of dependence is established in the group as a whole. This subgroup may conflate disagreement with discord, rejection or disapproval and may react by being withdrawn, reluctant to participate fully and fearful about risk-taking and competition.

The opposing subgroup will share an unconscious belief that, when group members can differentiate in a spirit of independence, there will be space to risk attachment. Until the threat of being smothered or engulfed is neutralised, this subgroup may also restrict participation until dependence can be risked or, alternatively, may persist in an over-determined independence.

In fact, both subgroups are linked collectively by a preoccupation with the same issue: dependence – upon the group, the supervisor and the training institution.

Furthermore, supervisees' unconscious identification with dynamics in a patient's material may activate the energy of oppositional forces. The group as a whole may not be capable of seeing why the group is not working optimally, and an individual may only be vaguely aware in an isolated way that the climate for him or her is uncomfortable.

Redfearn has made the salient point that subgroups in human communities behave as subpersonalities of the Self:

> We know that an individual may be crippled if his neurosis, or a neurotic family or cultural upbringing, prevent him from living out all the diverse parts of himself. Habit, rigid social roles, and neurosis can all bring about these rigid boundaries [which] may produce an explosive situation in an individual. (Redfearn, 1992, p. 7)

Because supervision, especially in training, is exposing and induces vulnerable feelings, individuals may conclude that they are alone in feeling stressed. Actual performance in supervision may appear to be going well with supervisees contributing and responding according to pre-arranged group norms. Only gradually may signs emerge that the group is identifying with strong anti-developmental forces which ultimately can disrupt creativity. One supervisee may bring a case where he remains 'stuck' with his 'intractable' training patient week after week. Another may miss supervision sessions without alerting the group or the supervisor; or the group as a whole may resort to distractions, such as complaining about training regulations which 'interfere' with their work, thus projecting their opposition into the larger group of the training institute.

An attentive supervisor will be aware of her own inner divisions in the context of the group. She may rely on one supervisee more than others and feel adrift if that person is absent. Intense irritation can be aroused by another supervisee who openly challenges her authority. Alternatively, she may depend on trainees for interventions, particularly if they are confronting other members, as this can allow her to remain ostensibly benevolent and uncritical. Such inner signals require the supervisor to investigate the possibility that communications, including the non-verbal, from the group are equally comments about the group and could refer to process as well as to individuals' practice. In other words, the astute supervisor, and indeed group members, will be alert to parallel process, depending upon various factors, including individual temperaments, the supervisor's capacity to remember her own supervision and her relationship to the training institute. It is all too easy for group members to seek to alleviate the group tension by resorting to reinforcing 'rules' or criticising the behaviour of the group. If the supervisor addresses a supervisee's unexplained absences in a critical way, the subgroup that values independence will feel that their right to autonomy is compromised. On the other hand, if the group passes lightly over a supervisee's missed sessions, the dependent subgroup will suspect a collusion with the supervisee's unreliability, which they will experience unconsciously as a neglect of their need for a firm boundary. Added to this is the dimension of identification, by which supervisees may pass on unprocessed material from their supervision groups to their clinical work with patients. It is important, therefore, for supervisors to contain tension and to resolve disruptions. Their success will depend upon their skill in recognising signals from the group and devoting time to their discussion. A supervisor's denial or avoidance of real anxiety on the part of a group about their dynamics can leave members vulnerable to acting out in an unconscious attempt to bring oppositional forces into the open.

A group consisted of one supervisor and four supervisees in training (Karl, Mel, Anna and Don). Karl had been absent from the previous meeting without notifying the group. On a previous occasion of Karl's absence the supervisor had not contacted him and had discovered subsequently that he had been in hospital. This time the supervisor called and left a message at his home. The group is relieved that he has attended today as he and Anna are due to present. Anna negotiates to go first, describing a session revealing her young female patient's emerging pattern of lateness and absence: she is afraid of travelling by bus. Anna has accepted this explanation without question, but now she is concerned about a boundary intervention on her part which, she acknowledges to the group, reflects her patient's boundary breaks. Anna wishes to cancel a session at short notice in order to accompany her young daughter on a school outing and she asks the group for help in composing a letter to her patient. She seems anxious and guilty, and admits that she fears the group's disapproval. Anna wishes that the supervision group could come with her on the outing. The group observes that Anna's feelings for her daughter mirror her unquestioning approach to her patient's travel phobia. The group enquires whether Anna can trust both the child and the patient to be responsible for themselves without sacrificing either one? Anna realises that she is in danger of acting out countertransference feelings for her patient and that she may need to have both the daughter and the patient dependent upon her.

As yet Karl has not had a chance to negotiate his presentation time. He is annoyed that only half an hour remains for his material about his patient, a depressed, middle-aged novelist whom he has introduced to the group before. Karl now says that he doesn't want to 'crush' his material by 'squashing it into too little time'. When the supervisor observes that one of the powerful themes of the session today has been apparent fragility, he replies with intense irritation that this supervision group is 'doing his head in'. The other group members are visibly shaken by his outburst, which is met with an awkward frozen silence.

In archetypal terms, this group is demonstrating a preoccupation with a universal theme: dependence, expressed as rivalrous bids for attention – not only in Anna's clinical material but also in her own and Karl's consuming personal concerns and spontaneous reactions. Group members in the grip of archetypal influences tend to display heightened levels of emotionality – fear, guilt, anxiety, fascination, irritation – which they may attribute to pressure from the social system, that is, the group itself, as Karl does.

In terms of group development, the fact that archetypal influences are present does not prevent members from working at the supervision task. However it is noticeable that the dependency issue – note Anna's wish to take the whole group, undifferentiated, on her daughter's school outing – grips the group *en masse*, while the independent counterbalance, represented by Karl, is quietly – but palpably – ignored. That is, until Karl himself, feeling annihilated, says so forcefully, awakening powerful feelings of guilt in the group for having 'denied' him time, just as Anna felt at fault for wanting to take a session away from her patient. There is now a choice to make which will affect the group's potential growth.

In the remaining session time, the group chooses to postpone Karl's clinical report and confronts him, respectfully, about his absence from the group. They reveal his need for care that he has taken outside the group to the hospital, just as Anna's patient was attempting self-care at home. It will take more than this single effort for the group to restabilise. However, now the whole group, including the supervisor, who has moved from a position of noncommittal tolerance of Karl's absence to one of attentive concern, has an opportunity to wrestle more consciously with the issue of dependence/independence both intra-psychically as well as in the group itself.

Another phenomenon apparent in this session is that Karl has unconsciously established a particular role for himself in the group. I will explore this in the next section.

Supervision groups in institutional settings

Ever since Menzies Lyth's (1959) important research on defences against anxiety in institutional life broke new ground in the psychotherapy field (Menzies Lyth, 1988), numerous papers have confirmed, supplemented and built upon her findings. As a result, conductors of staff supervision groups are able to anticipate a wide range of transference–countertransference responses arising from tensions between patients and staff, management and staff, as well as within a staff team itself, and to the institution as a whole. In a recent review, Fagin (2001) outlines these dynamics comprehensively. The following example of a multidisciplinary team supervision reveals institutional and inter-staff transferences and countertransferences which will be familiar to supervisors who work with such groups. While these aspects could be fruitfully explored, I would like to emphasise a different set of phenomena evident in the group's dynamics.

Understanding group transformation: the focal person concept

I will elaborate two aspects of archetypal theory subsumed in the Jungian concept of individuation: the focal person concept and group disequilibrium. The focal person, as described by Dirkx (1991), is a member who focuses the group's attention on unconscious attitudes influencing the group's behaviour. This individual provides the means by which other members can unconsciously satisfy undesirable drives common to the group, and can intensify group emotion through 'initiating behaviour.' In the same way that the archetypal figure of the Hero instigates a new direction by achieving liberation from enthralment to the unconscious, the focal person in a group challenges the status quo in existing organisational structures and points the way toward the new:

> Theoretically, the concept is grounded specifically in Neumann's (1954) work on the development of consciousness and, specifically, in his notion of the Great Individual . . . the temporary leader of a group who has no relationship to the permanent leadership but who contributes something unique and valuable for the group within a specific situation. (Dirkx, 1991, p. 82)

Even though he or she may not otherwise exert great personal influence in the group, the focal person serves multiple functions: to activate a discerning attitude in the group, to energise a group toward a critique of the system and even possibly to promote reform of the prevailing order. One of these functions is illustrated in the following example.

The staff of a day service in a city hospital meets twice a month for supervision. Although the staff group has a rapid turnover, the patient population tends to remain on the service's books, resulting in their therapeutic groups becoming severely overcrowded. The service functions as the point of discharge for psychiatric patients, but this is difficult to achieve. Patients are reluctant to leave the congenial atmosphere of the day service and, in the absence of criteria for discharge, staff feel guilty about releasing them, fearing they will feel rejected. Consultants adopt a noncommittal attitude, using the service to monitor the progress of patients without terminating their contact entirely.

At this supervision meeting, the service manager excuses herself with the announcement that she has to chair the hospital's daily community meeting. The art therapist expresses irritation that the day service is yet again expected to cover for consultants, who are supposed to chair the community meeting. The yoga teacher remarks that other departments in the hospital turn to the day service and 'we always say yes'.

With the backing of the supervisor, the manager had explained to the consultants that the group was being overwhelmed by demands from other hospital departments to perform tasks that were outside the service's remit. The group feels that the hospital wants more and more from the day service that it cannot provide, yet when staff acquiesce they are not given credit. They can't understand how arrangements with consultants repeatedly break down, leaving them feeling powerless and undervalued.

At this point a member of the catering staff enters the room, noisily collects a tray by the door and departs without a word. The music therapist puts her head in her hands in helpless embarrassment. The art therapist is furious. The group marvels at how the intrusion was so swift that there was no chance to react. The supervisor is aware of the possible transference feelings to her fortnightly appearance at the hospital, but she chooses to observe that the demands of the hospital upon the service feel like an unwarranted intrusion that leaves the group feeling furious and helpless. The art therapist concurs: only yesterday a consultant had spoken to her rudely, ordering her not to discuss this issue in the community meeting. She had therefore refused to go into the meeting with him. It emerges that the art therapist's refusal to be bullied into silence, as she sees it, has caused great inconvenience to the team and has whipped up irritation and unspoken criticism of her behaviour. In the minutes before the group ends, members realise they will be unable to resolve this issue today and table it for a future meeting.

These events can be interpreted from varying perspectives: as displacement acts reflecting transference issues with the consultant and/or the institution as well as the supervisor; as conflict between staff subgroups based on unconscious rivalry and envy; as boundary transgressions signalling a need for clearer individual role definitions; even the fact that there is insufficient time for the group to reflect on the meaning of the various interactions is significant.

However, I wish to focus on the archetypal manifestations in the group, which is acting as a collective entity. Note the group's struggle to assert itself in terms of its boundary, role and function within the institution. At a collective level, this group is caught up in an archetypal experience of separation from parental influences – expressed generally as the institution's regulations and by the consultant's assertion of leadership, which the group experiences as controlling and oppressive. Indications of archetypal influences operating in the group are the intense levels of emotionality and the division of the membership into subgroups. (One feels helpless and compliant while the other clamours for redress of grievances.)

From an analytic perspective, it is apparent that the focal person – in this case the art therapist – is activating processes of projective identification. She is a 'phenomenon of collectivity which manifests in an individual' (Dirkx, 1991) and her voice is one of anguish, anger and outrage. When she challenges the consultant's instruction she voices the frustration and tension in the group about its relations with authority. Although she succeeds in instigating a critique of the prevailing culture, as Karl did in his group, she has also alienated members of her team with a challenge to their prevailing group image, which is characterised by a spirit of co-operation and helpfulness. Just as Karl's supervision group unconsciously reduced his allotted presentation time, this group is not appreciative of the art therapist's efforts, and she has excluded herself from the venue where she could be instrumental in inspiring change in the wider system.

Dirkx notes:

> Typically the social system is increasingly faced with the decision to either move forward in the direction called for by the focal person or retreat further into deeper entrenchment . . . The second function that the focal person serves is to critique the status quo and to challenge the members to a new way of seeing . . . [Out] of apparent opposition springs the possibility for new life and energy. (Dirkx, 1991, p. 91)

This was the serpent's role in the Garden of Eden, and I suggest that a supervisor is in a position to promote or hinder this opportunity for a group. In the above case, this is yet to be realised. The example exposes the struggle that individuals face in bringing about growth in themselves as well as their organisations, and highlights the need for patience, persistence and faith on the part of supervisors and their groups if appropriate, effective learning is to be achieved.

Summary

In this chapter I have examined ways in which the archetypal phenomena of *subgrouping* and the *focal person* contribute to a theory of supervision. The concept of the archetypes of the collective unconscious represents a prime co-ordinate on the Jungian theoretical map. Archetypes can be recognised by their universality and the powerful affects they induce in individuals and groups who become gripped in all-encompassing, polarised, experiences. Because archetypes are inherently bipolar in nature, the emergence of themes or images in a group can split members into subgroups organised around opposing ideas or positions. As a result, members may feel intensely uncomfortable and destabilised, although archetypal influences in the form of a focal person can also herald imaginative alternatives to current group functioning.

Spontaneous seismic commotions such as the ones observed in the above clinical examples occur routinely in groups although they may not be recognised as archetypal constellations, perhaps precisely because they are commonplace and stereotypical, not to mention extremely uncomfortable and even frightening to endure. I concur with Gordon's (1993) view that *the* archetypal process that is rarely recognised as such, and incidentally is seldom welcomed in a group context, is that of splitting. While splitting in supervision groups may be perceived, accurately, as defensive over-identification with patient material or even destructive to group process, its recognition by a supervisor as an archetypal dimension of group life can ultimately promote supervisees' greater understanding of their own and their patients' psychodynamics.

Archetypal activity in groups typically arouses intense feelings in the members and, especially, profound anxiety. Particularly susceptible are those supervisors who feel responsible for maintaining firm boundaries. A supervisor may not wish to draw attention to the disruptive function in a specific supervisee for fear of scapegoating or inflating him or her, but if the supervisor can refrain from reaching for premature consensus in a group that seems grossly divergent, the group's potential for learning about the human condition is enhanced.

References

Berger, I. (1964) 'Group Psychotherapy Training Institutes: Group Process, Therapy, or Resistance to Learning?', *International Journal of Group Psychotherapy,* **17**, 503–12.

Brookes, C. E. (1995) 'On Supervision in Jungian Continuous Case Seminars', in P. Kugler (ed.), *Jungian Perspectives on Clinical Supervision* (Einsiedeln: Daimon).

Carotenuto, A.(1984) *A Secret Symmetry. Sabina Spielrein between Jung and Freud* (London: Routledge & Kegan Paul).

Corbett, L. (1995) 'Supervision and the Mentor Archetype', in P. Kugler (ed), *Jungian Perspectives on Clinical Supervision* (Einsiedeln: Daimon).

Dirkx, R. (1991) 'Understanding Group Transformation through the Focal Person Concept', in R. Boyd (ed.), *Personal Transformations in Small Groups* (London: Routledge), Chapter 3.

Fagin, L. (2001) 'Therapeutic and Counter-therapeutic Factors in Acute Ward Settings', *Psychoanalytic Psychotherapy,* **15**(2).

Gordon, R. (1993) *Bridges: Metaphor for Psychic Processes* (London: Karnac).

Hopcke, R. H. (1989) *A Guided Tour of the Collected Works of C.G. Jung* (Boston: Shambhala).

Hopper, E. (1997) 'Traumatic Experience in the Unconscious Life of Groups: A Fourth Basic Assumption', *Group Analysis,* **30**, 439–70.

Jung, C. G. (1959) 'The Archetypes and the Collective Unconscious', *Collected Works Volume 9i.*

Jung, C. G. (1971) 'Psychological Types', *Collected Works Volume 6.*

Menzies Lyth, I. (first pub. 1959) 'The Function of Social Systems as a Defence against Anxiety', in I. Menzies Lyth, (1988) *Containing Anxiety in Institutions* (London: Free Association).

Redfearn, J. (1992) *The Exploding Self* (Wilmette, Ill.: Chiron Books).

Speicher, M. (1995) 'The Education of the Supervisor', in P. Kugler (ed.), *Jungian Perspectives on Clinical Supervision* (Einsiedeln: Daimon).

Usandivaras, R. (1986) 'Foulkes' Primordial Level in Clinical Practice', *Group Analysis,* **19**, 113–24.

PART III

Problems in Practice

8

Problems and Ethical Issues in Supervision

Edward Martin

Introduction

The charge that supervision is a practice looking both for a theoretical and an ethical foundation is hardly surprising since the energies of the longest established training organisations were devoted to training therapists. Supervision was merely an adjunct to the training process. This is a position from which it has had to fight hard to escape. Within training organisations there is a hierarchy of membership that has at its apex 'training analysts', often chosen for their clinical and theoretical skills rather than their supervisory abilities. In the past, their shared task, in concert with the trainee's own analyst and seminar leaders, was to nurture the trainee analyst's theoretical and clinical skills by supervising their 'control cases'.

For many years supervision was more or less confined to work with trainees and much of the published work on supervision reflects this. Recently, the position of supervision in the UK has been enhanced by the requirements of some registration bodies. The British Association for Counselling and Psychotherapy, for example, mandated that BACP-accredited therapists must remain in appropriate supervision for the whole of their professional lives. This had a roll-on effect. Agencies using volunteer or salaried therapists began to employ supervisors, partly to assure their users that the agency was *bona fide* and partly to support the therapists it employed. This in turn led therapists in private practice to recognise that regular supervision of their work was becoming the professional norm. The role of the supervisor then evolved from a main pillar of training to becoming in addition, a mainstay for qualified therapists. 'Supervisee' was a term that was no longer synonymous with 'trainee'.

Whether a qualification as an analyst is also a qualification to supervise another's work has not been resolved. The general consensus seems to be that supervision requires additional skills to that of being an analyst, not least because, while analysis is a dyadic relationship, supervision is triadic. There are now a growing number of courses that are aimed at enabling practitioners to acquire supervisory skills. However, while there is general agreement about the requirements for training analysts (personal therapy, theoretical teaching and supervision of control cases), the same has not been agreed for training analysts as supervisors and the standards and rigour of the training courses currently on offer reflect this. Today, it would be considered unethical to practise as a therapist without training, but not unethical to practise as a supervisor without training.

Traditionally the supervisor's task was confined to a focus on the trainee's professional development, trainees' analysts concentrating on their affective inner worlds. However the experience of trainees suggested that a refusal or inability of a supervisor to address the transference relationship that inevitably exists between supervisor and supervisee not infrequently caused painful and intractable situations to develop. Many supervisors now supervise qualified practitioners who are no longer in analysis and look to their supervisors to maintain their connection to their unconscious. Perhaps the supervisors of practising therapists need to be prepared to embrace the affective inner world of their supervisees as well as keeping the triadic relationship in focus? This would mean that the regression all experience in supervision has to be more directly taken into consideration by supervisors (see Chapter 13, p. 229). To address the transference relationship while ensuring that the patient's needs are being addressed would seem to require, at the very least, an expansion of analytic technique. It would also mean that an ethical base that directly speaks to issues of regression and vulnerability in supervisees is required.

Ethical analytic practice is about addressing and protecting the internal world of the patient, which obviously includes protecting a vulnerable person from abuse. Ethical supervision practice has the same objective in mind by addressing the inner world of the patient through the internal world of the supervisee and simultaneously the unconscious conflicts that arise in the supervisee through his work with his patients. The hypothesis central to this chapter is that supervision should in itself be therapeutic both for the supervisee and patient and therefore conducted in a way that is congruent with analysis. This chapter addresses some of the issues that may impair that endeavour.

Confidentiality

All who have experienced a personal analysis will understand how important it is that the discussions, the disclosures and the confessions made to the analyst are kept confidential. Yet it is well known that this does not always happen. Little Hans, Dora and Freud's other recorded cases all evidence this reality. Was permission to publish sought from those patients or was it assumed? If assumed, then the 'Breaching (of) the Confessional' (Bollas and Sundelson, 1995, p. 3) occurred early in the profession's history.

Jung drew his rationale for confidentiality not from the Hippocratic Oath but from another, no less prestigious source, the Confessional:

> Nothing makes people more lonely and more cut off from the fellowship of others, than the possession of an anxiously hidden and jealously guarded personal secret . . . here confession has a truly redeeming effect. (Jung, 1954, para. 432)

In his later years Jung pioneered the idea that therapists should use ongoing supervision to underpin their professional practice. In so doing, he again used the concept of the confessional to illustrate his idea:

> Every therapist ought to have a control by some third person, so that he remains open to another point of view. Even the Pope has a confessor. I always advise analysts: – 'Have a father confessor or a mother confessor!' Women are particularly gifted for playing such a part. They often have excellent intuition and a trenchant critical insight and can see what men have up their sleeves, at times see also into men's intrigues. They see aspects the man does not see. That is why no woman has ever been convinced her husband is a superman. (Jung, 1963, p. 156)

Jung's correspondence with Freud over a patient Jung called 'difficult' was probably the genesis of his link between confession and therapy and supervision. Jung, faced with an erotic transference that was not being contained within the therapy, found a need to confide, to *confess* to Freud the difficulties he was having with his patient, Sabina Spielrien (Kerr, 1994), who, in turn, had confessed her love for him. Perhaps it was this experience that suggested to Jung, a Protestant parson's son who was drawn to Catholicism, the idea that therapy and supervision shared the characteristics of a subjective confession?

These two distinct but ancient sources, the Confession and the Hippocratic Oath both support the ideal of patient/therapist confidentiality. Psychoanalytic therapy is a relationship of great intimacy. The degree of intimacy will vary, but it has been likened to the conversation of lovers or of mothers and babies. It is as invasive in terms of personal psychic boundaries as a physician is invasive in his physical contact with a patient. It signifies trust and dependency which, if breached, will cause great distress; an intimate relationship which is unique in that it is conducted only through language and has one aim, namely that succinctly defined by Money-Kyrle (1978) as to 'help the patient understand, and so overcome, emotional impediments to his discovering what he innately already knows'.

It would seem logical that, in the interests of congruency, the objective of supervision must be intricately linked with the analytic process. However, once a supervisor or a supervision group becomes connected with patient material, an ethical conflict is established because absolute patient/analyst confidentiality has then been breached. Henderson, an American Jungian analyst, illustrates this matter with the following vignette. He tells of his supervision of a student psychotherapist who did not tell his (training) patient that he was taking the case for supervision. At some point the patient was present at a public event at which the supervisor was also present. Henderson reports:

> He exclaimed: 'Who is that man? I must know him!' My student then realised that an unconscious form of recognition had been awakened and the patient's question should have been put the other way round – not 'I must know him' but 'he must know me!' (Henderson, 1982, p. 113)

Henderson's account is of a patient discovering through attending a lecture that someone other than his analyst 'knows him', not 'knows his appendix' but knows '*him*'. Supervisors and supervisees may also be aware that another way in which a patient discovers that someone other than his analyst knows him is through the change that can take place in analysis following a supervision session. The supervisor may have facilitated a new way of understanding the patient's material and enabling the supervisee to free him or herself from an entanglement in the patient's internal world. The patient may let the analyst know that something has changed. Is it a difference of emphasis, of approach or direction? What has got into my therapist? In fact, the patient has been discussed with another and this may not be clear to the patient consciously.

While a case can be made that there should be a place where one person can talk to another in *absolute* confidence, an equally persuasive case can be made for the place for benign revelations in the name of scientific advancement (Wiener, 2001 pp. 434–5). Ethical decisions have to be made about whether or not patient consent is obtained before presenting case material for supervision, just as when considering publication of clinical material. One attempt to minimise the ambiguity posed by supervision on patient/analyst confidentiality is to tell patients at the beginning of the treatment that their work will (or may) be taken to supervision. At least the analyst will have made things clear and the patient will initially have been made conscious that the contents of sessions may be reported to a third party. What effect this may have on the patient's ability to use analysis remains an open question. Some would say that, when a patient is actively engaged in analysis, the subject of supervision ceases to be important. This must remain speculative because of the lack of any supporting evidence. A decision to 'tell' or 'not to tell' would have to take its place alongside an account of the effect that *any* extra transferential contact was having on the transference relationship.

For the supervisee approaching a supervisor, a decision has to be made whether or not to disguise the material. A decision to disguise is not a simple solution to the problem. A change of name, for example, is a change of identity. Simply renaming Carl as Sigmund cannot but make supervisee and supervisor (or author and reader) confused! Trust on the other hand is not enhanced if confidentiality transmutes into secrecy. A *modus vivendi* needs to be found using the ethical guidelines that are available, bearing in mind the notion that 'to do no harm' is part of the Hippocratic oath and gossip is not part of the confessional.

An all-persuasive argument is that without supervision, therapists could not be trained. However to argue that trained analysts need supervision to protect their patients is less easily sustained. Supervisors are not responsible for overseeing all supervisees' work even if such a task were logistically possible. Supervisees choose which patients to present in supervision and there is little evidence that supervision actually prevents abusive analysts abusing their clients. The most it can claim is that it might place a steadying hand on a few. Supervision, in the same way as analysis, is most effective where there is a strong working alliance between supervisee and supervisor and a wish to change and grow. Psychodynamic supervision, which relies on the sharing of fantasies between supervisee and supervisor, will only have limited value as a source of quality control. What actually happens inside a consulting room tends to arrive at supervision in an edited format, and lazy or abusive supervisees can easily remain just that. A strong case can be made that ethical practice requires practitioners to ensure that their skills are constantly honed and their knowledge base updated. Perhaps supervision, with all its limitations and difficulties, forms the optimum container in which this can happen?

My present supervision practice consists of experienced therapists using supervision as professional support and some who are engaged in higher professional training. To use a musical analogy, neither group needs to be reminded of the position of middle C on the keyboard. Most of the supervision work is akin to exploring the many different ways a phrase can be shaped, like the myriad ways in which a pianist chooses to colour the opening of Beethoven's fourth or Rachmaninov's second concerto. My hope is that subtle shading engages our joint unconscious processes which enables supervision to be a therapeutic venture for the supervisee, whilst at the same time keeping the patient firmly in view.

Searles (1965, p. 157), in particular, has been credited with the recognition of a connection between *parallel process* and countertransference; a phenomenon arising in supervision when the supervisee's presentation registers a strong affect in the supervisor and/or members of the supervision group. Psychodynamic supervision, essentially an oedipal relationship (Mattinson, 1981), is one in which one party in the triangle, the patient, is always absent. One of the fascinations of supervision is the differing ways in which the absent patient becomes present through the mutual reflection process and the countertransference of supervisor and supervisee. The following vignette illustrates how this process can be a source of fruitful insights into the patient's unconscious.

A female supervisee is presenting to a male supervisor. The supervisee works as a counsellor in a university. She presents a new female patient whom she describes as 'stroppy'. The supervisee feels bullied by this patient and can say nothing useful. The supervisor realises that his responses are becoming dictato- rial. He finds himself feeling critical about what the supervisee is not doing and begins to give her 'good advice' about how to handle the next session. The supervisee becomes increasingly defensive, silent, and feels de-skilled; there is a feeling of deadness in the room. The supervisor, aware of this, reflects and, using his internal supervisor (Casement, 1985, p. 7), considers whether this coun- tertransference is complementary or concordant (Lambert, 1981, pp. 147–50). He comes to recognise that his remarks are like an absent father visiting an estranged wife. In dialogue with the supervisee, he suggests that the work concerns the absence of father. The supervisee is able to recall that the patient's parents divorced acrimoniously fairly recently and the supervision work begins to feel alive again, as the supervisee regains her skills once more.

The effective use of parallel process requires a highly developed abil- ity to use a variety of modes of identification and countertransfer- ence, and the capacity to offer the supervisee a triangular rather than dyadic interpretation.

Boundaries, frames and countertransference

Langs' (1994) polemic on shoddy supervision argues that, to be ethi- cal as well as useful, supervision should be conducted in an identical manner to a therapy session. To achieve this Langs proposes adherence to a number of simple ground rules, closely aligned to basic thera- peutic techniques such as neutrality, anonymity, properly negotiated fees, a suitable setting with regular meeting times. This includes an examination of the frequency of supervision sessions and whether good supervision of individual work could be given in a group setting (despite the economic and other attractions of this model). Langs suggests that whilst our conscious mind is primarily defensive and built for survival, unconsciously our use of encoded communications confirms that we are alert and concerned with boundary issues in our significant relationships. By maintaining a secure frame, the analyst enables the patient and the supervisor enables the supervisee to expe- rience intense feelings of the vulnerability connected to the 'recogni- tion of the inevitability of time and ultimately death' (Money-Kyrle, 1978). There is inevitably an intense attack waged on secure frames and a strong wish to modify these as a defence against separation and death anxieties. Langs suggests that the supervisor is required to secure the frame of supervision because any ambiguities in the supervisor's encounter with the supervisee are likely to sanction unconsciously alterations in the supervisee's encounter with the patient.

The following historical vignette illustrates the importance that needs to be given to the setting of supervision. In her biography, the analyst Esther Menaker (1989) recalls how, in the thirties as a young newly-married woman, she travelled with her husband from the USA to Vienna for them both to embark on an analytic training. Menaker paints an amusing, insightful, if at times rather disturbing, picture of their endeavours. In contrast to contemporary practice, trainees engaged in two training analyses and these events take place as she makes an appointment for an initial interview for her second analysis.

On the appointed day I was ushered into a simple, almost bare, waiting room decorated in the Bauhaus style that was fashionable among the younger analysts of that time. After a few moments the maid reappeared and indicated that the doctor was now ready to see me. She ushered me into the dining room, where there were two place settings at the table, a large silver bowl of straw-berries (it was June, the season in Vienna for the most luscious and plentiful strawberries), and another bowl filled with whipped cream. Dr. Hoffer gestured toward a place at the table, inviting me to sit down. I was embarrassed and confused. Had he misunderstood my visit? I didn't want to be there under false pretences, and so I explained that I had come to talk about going into analy-sis with him, adding that of course patients were not supposed to enjoy straw-berries and cream with their analyst. 'Why not?' said Willi Hoffer. 'What's wrong with eating strawberries and cream with one's analyst?' He then explained that he had thought I was coming to consult with him about arrang-ing for supervision, but that he had available time for analysis and would be glad to work with me. We proceeded with the strawberries while Dr. Hoffer talked on about his feelings in regard to working analytically with a younger colleague. (Menaker 1989 p. 127)

In this vignette, a classic scene is presented. A junior female supervisee and a senior male analyst (supervisor) eat strawberries and cream, symbolising the beginning of some sort of relationship, analytic, supervisory or social. Before anyone is tempted to a knee jerk criti-cism towards Hoffer's methods, it is worth remembering that coffee, admittedly not as seductive as strawberries, is still made available to patients by some analysts. Some supervisors also offer refreshment to supervisees because they claim coffee helps differentiate between an analytic relationship and supervision. Others would argue that coffee or strawberries are only appropriate in a social setting, which makes Menaker's embarrassment and confusion understandable. She was there as Hoffer's prospective patient; had she been there as his prospective supervisee should that have made a difference?

Fordham (1982, p. 110) suggests it could make a difference. He writes about training supervision for trainees of the London School and how this was modelled on the Viennese model, separating analysis from supervision. Fordham's point of view is that 'supervision, in contrast to analysis, should be directed to the student's performance with his case and not to the student's affective inner world'. For Fordham, supervision is an adult-to-adult relationship (see Introduction, p. 7). While I doubt whether he, or others who subscribe to this point of view, would endorse Hoffer's indulgence, they do seem to claim that supervision is a relationship in which the transference is not to be acknowledged, let alone interpreted. As many analysts will have discovered when emotionally entangled with a supervisor, this does not always work out in practice. For if the aphorism that supervision is 'more than teaching, less than therapy' holds any truth we might, with Menaker, feign surprise and embarrassment, for those six words imply that supervision is *both* a didactic and an emotional exercise, not merely a discussion about technical matters. The work 'didactic' implies an imbalance of power where the supervisor is a more experienced if not hierarchically senior therapist. 'Emotional' implies that one of the parties may be more regressed than the other. It is perhaps not surprising that anecdotal information suggests that there is a greater tendency for relationships between supervisor and supervisee to become socialised and sexualised than those between analyst and patient. Socialising with a supervisee may be easier but it is still as ethically problematic as socialising with a patient.

Institutional issues

Traditionally, supervision has been described using a boxing (or fencing) metaphor of 'seconding', where the supervisor is 'outside the ring' and sequentially (and hopefully) emotionally behind the supervisee. Such idealism might be hard to work with, particularly if the supervision is being carried out within an institutional setting. Ekstein and Wallerstein (1972, p. 11) remind us of the delicacy involved in trying to maintain a good framework even in the most favourable of institutional settings. Their concept of the 'clinical rhombus', which illustrates the complexity of the institutional setting, is well known and useful. However its one weakness is that it seems to assume that 'administration' (the executive or management) consists only of one person and such administration is the epitome of sanity. Most people will have had experience of the opposite, where administration consists of more than one person, frequently engaged in internal battles and experienced as quite psychotic. It is obviously essential that the contract made between supervisor and supervisee and the employing institution is very carefully considered if boundaries and effective supervision are to be maintained. The following vignette illustrates the problems that ensue when suitable contracts are not drawn up. This rather dramatic example is set within a general hospital some years ago and unfortunately bears some resemblance to Fawlty Towers.

A nurse went on a counselling training course and, enthused by the experience, persuaded her management to establish a counselling service for female patients suffering from breast cancer. The person who agreed to supervise her work, who had no other contact with the hospital in any capacity, was well-intentioned rather than well-advised, a feature which permeated the whole exercise. The nurse and the supervisor negotiated the supervision contract. Nursing management, who agreed that the hospital would pay the supervisor's fee on a monthly basis, approved the arrangement.

At first all seemed to go smoothly. A clientele was established fairly easily and the work was regularly presented for supervision. However, some months into the work a charity independently established a research post for a psychiatrist and two counsellors to work with the same group of patients. The early frictions caused by this were settled over morning coffee breaks when it was agreed that the counsellor would deal with out-patients and the research team counsellors with in-patients. The patients were not, of course, consulted about this and appeared not to co-operate; out-patients becoming in-patients and vice versa. The edifice really tumbled when an out-patient spent a hour raging at the counsellor about a junior doctor who, she claimed, had treated her 'like shit'. What happened afterwards is somewhat confused. It seems that the patient left the counsellor, sought out the doctor and laid into him verbally, implying that her counsellor had told her to say what a shit he was. The doctor went post haste to the consultant who immediately informed nursing management that the nurse (that is, the counsellor) was no longer to work on his ward. Nursing management either capitulated or colluded. The upset supervisee told her supervisor at the next supervision session, realising that she too had been effectively sacked. The supervisor did what she could to rescue the situation but the nurse, who felt humiliated, had little energy for this and therefore the supervisor was rendered impotent. Ironically, the most difficult task for the nurse, after giving in her notice and leaving supervision, was to stop the finance department sending the supervisor her monthly fees!

It is easy to scapegoat a number of people involved. Obviously the organisational dynamics around the counselling were complex. The administration was in conflict and split and, as so often happens, the patients were forgotten. As well as interdepartmental rivalry, important differences in the aims of patient treatment were not considered. However, although the outcome was disastrous and a number of ethical conflicts were observable, there were no clear breaches of ethics by individuals.

Hindsight exposed an insufficiently experienced therapist initiating and running the counselling service as a single-handed enterprise. Faults in the initial contract between supervisor, therapist and organisation were evident. The supervisor, tried to remain in role but her link with the organisation was too weak for her to intervene effectively.

Even agencies dedicated to counselling do not escape from causing supervisors difficulties. Such centres are usually set up by a local concerned group and are often under-capitalised. They tend to function with a lot of good-will, and staff may work on a part-time basis. There is a provision of a good and useful service to the community, but administrative structures may be weak or fragmented. An agency that has no clear policy regarding the range of people it treats is an obvious case in point. Contracts for therapists often omit to set clear lines of accountability, including the frequency and nature of performance reviews for therapists, criteria used for evaluation and who is responsible for undertaking the review procedure. Some organisations fail to set a clear retirement age for employed therapists and, sometimes, supervisors will have therapists in their supervision groups who have other roles, such as the treasurer or chair, in the agency. People holding responsible administrative posts can cause difficulty in supervision groups if they are not functioning well as therapists.

A supervisor took over a supervision group of volunteer therapists at a small, but well-established agency. The group consisted of women only, with varying degrees of experience. One saw herself, with the collusion of the group, as being 'senior' because she was the longest-serving member and one of the founder members of the agency. The supervisor became aware of her need both to dominate the group and to challenge comments made by the supervisor. The supervisor also began to be aware that this therapist's response to patient's material was often inappropriate. For instance when a male patient made a disparaging remark about women, the supervisee's response was 'You can't say that, it's not politically correct!'. A patient on a high dose of anti-depressants talked of

suicide just before a break, without apparently affecting the supervisee at all.
She dismissed him as 'attention seeking'. After the break, however, the super-
visee drew the attention of the group to an agency notice about suicidal patients
suggesting that the group might have a problem with this matter!

There are implications for administrators and supervisors in this
situation. For instance in this agency no assessment or review procedures for the supervisees were in place. Administration had long
ignored anxiety expressed about this supervisee by other agency
supervisors, presumably hoping that the difficulties would go away.
There seemed to be no effective line management. In such a situation, the extent to which the supervisor is a colleague, mentor or
supporter of the supervisee is confusing, and it was likely that the
supervisee's line manager had become an administrative watchdog.
The effects on patient/therapist confidentiality are considerable.

Assessment issues

One important issue that marks out the difference in role between
analyst and supervisor is that supervisors are often asked to make
value judgements on their supervisee's work. This is perhaps most
marked in institutional work where the supervisor's contract includes
some form of specific quality control, but supervisors in private practice do not escape either. For example, if a supervisor is presented
with a number of superficial presentations from a supervisee, does this
suggest evidence of burn out? Is the inability of the analyst to engage
in a particular way with a patient evidence of lack of clinical skill or
a blind spot and a manifestation of the reflection process? A severely
depressed supervisee would obviously give cause for concern, likewise
one who admitted missing appointments or who became sexually
involved with a patient. The issue is further clouded when age or
incapacity are taken into consideration. When is it time to manage
rather than supervise? A supervisor may worry when a trainee is
struggling to make the grade, but the same supervisor has the task
making out the report that may cause the trainee's training to be
ended or extended. Either of these courses of action will affect the
work with the patient and the quality of the relationship between
supervisor and supervisee, where trust and the establishment of a
good working alliance will be severely tested (see Chapter 4, p. 80 and
Chapter 5, pp. 94–7).

Supervisors can easily defend themselves against confronting such difficulties, not only because of the subjective nature of the judgements made, but because it raises sadistic fantasies and fears of revenge attacks. If supervisor *A* judges supervisee *B* harshly and causes *B*'s training or contract to be terminated, how might others judge supervisor *A*'s own ability as an analyst? Who hires, who fires? Is it the administrator or the supervisor? The support supervisors receive from administrators raises practical and ethical issues. Supervision can be a lonely task (see Chapter 11, p. 200).

It usually falls to the supervisors, especially in agency settings, to *assess the suitability of patients for psychotherapy*, the ability of a supervisee to deal with a particular patient, and to attempt to make a match which optimises the possibility of a good therapeutic fit. The supervisee may be accredited for once-weekly work while the patient seen is making clear clinical signals that once a week is insufficient. Should the supervisee be encouraged to see this patient more frequently or should the therapy be terminated and a referral made to another therapist? Among other considerations to be borne in mind, apart from the effect of changing the supervisee's training parameters, is the quality of the therapeutic alliance, the standard of the supervisee's work and whether the supervisee had matured since finishing training. The conflict, of course, can be encountered in reverse when supervising a trainee whose patient is required by the training agency to be in more frequent therapy than the clinical material indicates is appropriate. The patient may need to reduce the frequency of her sessions but the supervisee needs the patient not to reduce in order to qualify. The number of anecdotal references to patients who constantly attack the therapy with threats to leave during the trainee's training period and then uncannily seem to know when the trainee's training hours have been completed evidences the effect that the stress of training has on the therapeutic work.

The conflict of a female supervisee working as a therapist in an agency that was not particularly sympathetic (but with a sympathetic non-therapist manager) illustrates some of the themes introduced above. The supervisee worked as a solitary appointee in a general hospital. Her job description required her to see any member of staff who wished to use the service. Patients either self-referred or were referred by a manager or colleague. One referral from a colleague was a staff member who worked literally as well as metaphorically in the bowels of the hospital. The work was potentially stomach turning.

The patient, (A), was male, borderline, sexually provocative, immature and abused alcohol. He presented in a bullying, sexualized manner, frequently going into unnecessary detail about the more gruesome details of his work. He appeared to want to frighten, shock or intimidate the therapist. The covert reason for the referral gradually revealed itself through the patient's material. The patient's retirement was a few months away and administration were concerned about how he would handle this. Fortnightly supportive therapy was established with this patient up to the date of his retirement.

Soon after therapy was established, a female colleague of patient A, (Patient B), encouraged by A, self-referred. She presented with depression, a history of a very disturbed childhood and could also be described as 'borderline'. This supervisee and supervisor were faced with a clinical and ethical difficulty. Should the supervisee work with both? As she was the only therapist in the institution the answer seemed to be 'Yes'. Should then the same contract be offered to both? Clinically it felt wrong to do this. After carefully considering the matter with the supervisor, Patient B was also offered once weekly therapy but for a longer period than patient A. Patient B then produced complaints about patient A's bullying behaviour as well as criticisms of his failure to follow proper hygiene procedures, putting her at risk of serious infection. It was a work marriage made in hell.

The ethical dilemmas presented to both supervisee and supervisor were essentially management rather than clinical issues. There is a role for supervisors (or umbrella organisations) to provide information to administrators who employ and manage therapists, which addresses boundary issues and a need to ensure that proper psychiatric backup is available for therapists? Holding both these patients in meaningful therapy required skill and firm internal boundaries on the part of the supervisee.

Ethics and society

Over time, the Christian church has had to face external interference in its practice of confessional confidentiality. Parallels can be drawn between the history and politics of the church and the psychoanalytic profession. Codes of ethics in the UK have so far been fairly benign, drawn up by experienced practitioners without undue influence from third parties. While analysts in private practice are more or less free of state or third party interference, Bollas and Sundelson (1995) have written a timely warning based on their experience in the USA where codes of ethics are influenced by statutory registration and are less benign. It is too early to know whether experience in the USA will translate into UK practice. The price for statutory registration of psychotherapy in an increasingly litigious society may be high. Overall, regulating the profession has been beneficial in the UK and most therapists are now registered with one of three umbrella bodies. Complaints procedures are available and registered therapists must be professionally insured. Other organisational requirements are more controversial, for example, requiring therapists to reveal details about patients with specific psychopathology to third parties. The future role of the supervisor is uncertain. However, the cosy relationship of supervisor–supervisee is becoming increasingly accountable to the views and requirements of bodies representing the general public. Psychotherapists and analysts need to be seen to work ethically but they also need to protect the inner worlds of patients and supervisees. Supervisors may be obliged to impose their active influence over trends in public policy on psychotherapy and analysis. Bollas and Sundelson's (1995, p. 191) concerns are still pertinent:

> To a considerable degree the passivity of the psychoanalytic profession, in particular of its professional organisations, is largely to blame for the failure to respond adequately to a public misconception that led to legislative and regulatory actions that have unintentionally but seriously harmed psychoanalysis.'

Conclusion

Money-Kyrle (1978, p. 144) considers there to be three supremely important facts: aspects of reality that are particularly difficult to accept, but without which no adequate acceptance of other aspects of reality are possible. These are 'the recognition of the breast as a supremely good object; the recognition of the parent's intercourse as a supremely creative act; the recognition of time and the inevitability of death. Supervision can help analysts and, indirectly, their patients to remain engaged with this life-long, difficult struggle. In their support for the work with their supervisees, supervisors contribute to patients' search for a means to overcome the impediments to discovering these primal facts of life. All three – patient, supervisee and supervisor – are engaged in this search within themselves and with each other. Supervision is a complex activity and the supervisor's capacity to cherish the inner space of supervisee and patient can sometimes be severely tested.

Psychoanalytic supervision is a multifaceted concept. There has been, and hopefully will continue to be, a place for consultative supervision with an experienced colleague about a difficult case.

There is a place for guru supervisors who will entice their own disciples, although the mainstay of supervision work (which might claim to be truest to the original concept) is the ongoing weekly interplay of the minor gods.

If supervisors are tempted to offer 'strawberries and cream', symbolically or literally (coffee and biscuits, a chance to gossip), or, alternatively, 'sour cream' (changes of room, time, a different fee structure, the establishment of a relationship that is more than a working alliance) then, while these are not necessarily mortal sins that need to be confessed elsewhere, they may be warning signals that ethical boundaries are in danger of being breached.

References

Bollas, C. and Sundelson, D. (1995) *The New Informants* (London: Karnac).

Casement, P. (1985) *On Learning from the Patient* (London: Tavistock).

Driver, C. and Martin, E. (eds) (2002) *Supervising Psychotherapy* (London: Sage).

Ekstein, R. and Wallerstein, R. (1972) *The Teaching and Learning of Psychotherapy* (Madison, Conn.: International Universities Press).

Fordham, M. (1982) 'How do I Assess Progress in Supervision?', *Journal of Analytical Psychology*, 27(2) 110–12.

Freud, S. (1913) 'On Beginning the Treatment', *Standard Edition XII*.

Henderson, J. (1982) 'How do I Assess Progress in Supervision?', *Journal of Analytical Psychology* 27(2) 113–17.

Jung, C. G. (1954) 'The Theory of Psychoanalysis', *Collected Works Volume 4*.

Jung, C. G. (1963) 'Psychiatric Activities', *Memories Dreams Reflections*. (London: Routledge & Kegan Paul).

Kerr, J. (1994) *A Most Dangerous Method*, (London: Sinclair-Stevenson).

Lambert, K. (1981) *Analysis, Repair and Individuation* (London: Academic Press).

Langs, R. (1994) *Doing Supervision and Being Supervised* (London: Karnac).

Mattinson, J. (1975) *The Reflection Process in Casework Supervision* (London Institute of Marital Studies).

Mattinson, J. (1981) *The Deadly Equal Triangle* (Northampton, MA: Smith College School of Social Work and Gaps).

Menaker, E. (1989) *Appointment in Vienna* (London: Martin's Press).

Money-Kyrle, R. (1978) *The Aim of Psychoanalysis: The Collected Papers of Roger Money-Kyrle*, D. Meltzer and F. O'Shaugnnessy ed. (Perth, Scotland: Clunie Press).

Searles, H. F. (1965) *Collected Papers on Schizophrenia and Related Subjects* (London: Maresfield Press).

Wiener, J. (2001) 'Confidentiality and Paradox: The Location of Ethical Space', *Journal of Analytical Psychology*, **46**(3) 415–563.

9

Boundaries in Supervision

Hugh Gee

Introduction

The concept of boundaries belongs to the development of the ego. Hartmann (1964) states that the development of the ego comes from the increasing conscious perception of the internal and external worlds. Similarly, Jung (1913, para. 757), in describing the concept of individuation, talks of the process of differentiation. It is this capacity to differentiate between perceptions that enables us to establish boundaries. The phenomenon of differentiation is dynamic which is why we refer to it as a 'process'. However, as perceptions and boundaries become established, the ego slowly develops a sense of constancy, and the defensiveness of this identity is likely to depend on whether it can adapt to new perceptions, enabling existing boundaries to be challenged. In the first part of this chapter I shall look at some of the more obvious boundary problems in supervision. I shall then explore how, for those who have a good sense of their boundaries, it is both inevitable and creative to lose the sense of boundaries in order to bring about further differentiations and the establishment of less defensive boundaries. Wharton (1985) thinks that the development of the ego and the capacity to make boundaries is dependent on the child's good enough relationship with its mother. Similarly, the relationship between analyst and patient and also between supervisor and supervisee can provide the containment necessary for the boundaries to be challenged by the psyche using what Jung (1916, para. 519) described as the process of unconscious identity. I end the chapter by suggesting that the process of unconscious identity is an inevitable component of the supervisory relationship and a troublesome but creative aspect of supervision.

Clinical boundaries

The provision of a professional container by the supervisor shows the supervisee how the supervisor functions as an analyst. The professional persona of the supervisor will be conveyed by the quality of the container that he provides for the supervisee and also by the supervisor's attitude towards the supervisee's patients. Part of the provision of a safe container is to show respect and concern for the patient by adopting good standards of practice. The provision of a consulting room offering a high degree of privacy that is reasonably quiet, suitably furnished, not over-stimulating, with a waiting room and toilet, all contribute towards the containing aspects of a professional relationship. The container needs to facilitate a focus on the patient's inner world, but also, in my view, to provide a pleasant and comfortable environment. The analytic attitude of the supervisor is perhaps the most important message that can be communicated to the supervisee. He demonstrates this by the way he listens in a non-judgemental way; observes and describes his detailed observations; ponders aloud on the possible meaning and purpose of the material; states that we may not yet know what is going on; makes clear the distinction between interpreting within the transference and other forms of interpretation; and most important of all, shows how interpretations are offered as hypotheses and evaluated in terms of their meaningfulness to the patient.

Management and therapy

It is helpful to supervisees for the supervisor to differentiate between management and therapy, including clarity about the need to discuss practical issues such as fees, session times, holidays and so on, at a noninterpretative level. Analysts may become so involved with the analysis of the patient's psyche that they 'forget' to deal with practical issues in a straightforward way. All of these issues concerning the frame may of course become part of the analytic process, but they should be clearly stated and arranged by the supervisee with the patient. On one occasion when I was in a discussion group of analysts, a member of the group described how he was attempting to treat a child but was hampered because the child's mother was reluctant to leave the consulting room. The analyst described how he had made a number of ineffectual interpretations to the mother. Michael Fordham, who was present, asked the analyst, 'Why didn't you just ask the mother to leave?'. The analyst had not thought of this. I think that this example shows how we may neglect management issues because of our strong wish to engage the patient in the analysis. In this example the mother had not been asked to remain outside the consulting room while the analyst interviewed her child and the analyst had made a false assumption that the mother would realise for herself.

It is helpful for the supervisor to make clear differentiations between those people who come to see him for 'consultation' and those who come because supervision is a component of analytic 'training'. Consultations generally involve supervisees who tend to be qualified therapists and who have a greater freedom of choice when it comes to using what the supervisor says in relation to their patients. When supervising trainees the supervisor actually shares the clinical responsibility for the patient and the supervisee may be obliged to follow the guidance provided by the supervisor. A trainee's supervisor could be cited in a case of professional negligence, and the clinical responsibility for the trainee's patient is shared between the supervisor and the training institution that has accepted the trainee. This is not the case with qualified supervisees who consult a supervisor. The supervisor still carries some responsibility, but their relationship is more collegial and the supervisor's more limited clinical responsibilities could be relevant in a case of professional negligence.

Boundaries between the supervisor and the agency

In my experience there are confidential matters between the supervisee and supervisor that do not concern the agency while at the same time, confidentialities between the supervisor and the agency that are not the concern of the supervisee. For example, the supervisor may have a degree of concern about a trainee's level of competence, wishing to share this concern with the supervisee but preferring to wait to see how things develop before sharing the issue with the training body. On the other hand, there may be occasions when the supervisor observes that the trainee is in difficulty because of her relative lack of experience. In such cases the supervisor may be happy to discuss this with the training body but not with the trainee. In this way the supervisor can avoid causing trainees to behave in compliant ways by doing what is seen to be desirable, instead of developing in their own authentic style. However, if the supervisee's satisfactory progress is in doubt, then the supervisor will do well to enter into discussion with a representative of the training body. If there is no available provision for such discussions, the supervisor may be left feeling alone with his concerns. Should this happen, the problem is best handled if the supervisor is a member of a discussion group for supervisors. I have found such groups to be extremely valuable when processing problems that arise in supervision.

Confidentiality

The issue of when or whether to break confidentiality is a difficult one. There are many possible ways in which boundaries can be tested or broken by patient or therapist and space does not permit an adequate exploration of this subject (see Wiener, 2001). Difficulties can arise when a supervisee becomes involved in a collusive arrangement with her patient and to protect the right to privacy of a patient, the supervisee may not feel able to take action if the patient threatens to commit suicide or to cause physical harm to someone. The Society of Analytical Psychology's Code of Ethics makes it clear that if a patient becomes a potential danger to himself or herself or others then the member must take whatever action is necessary in the patient's best interests. This may involve the breaking of confidentiality. In any extreme situation, such as a threat of physical violence, the supervisor, together with the trainee, should ensure that after discussion with the patient, the training body is informed and, if necessary, the police. The cited victim of any threatened attack may also need to be warned.

It would be impossible to make a list of all potential ethical problems that may arise or the psychological attitudes that underlie them. A supervisor will need to remain alert to individual ethical issues as they arise in the supervisee's work. In my experience, when a Code of Ethics is violated, it frequently means that the analyst has become involved in an enactment of a state of partial unconscious identity with his patient.

Supervision and analysis

All supervisees will be, or will have been, in analysis (see Chapter 6, p. 113). I value Jung's original insistence to Freud that people wishing to become analysts must first receive analysis for themselves as an essential part of their training. In supervision, the main focus is on the supervisee–patient relationship rather than the here-and-now relationship between the supervisor and the supervisee. The only exception is when problems emerge in the supervisory process which need to be examined at a special meeting, such as a six-monthly review. Some supervisees will try to use the supervisor as their analyst and in the past it was common professional practice for analysts to supervise their patients who were trainees. Eventually, the functions of analysis and supervision were separated (see Chapter 13, p. 225). Michael Fordham had strong views on the subject: 'I wish to propose dogmatically that it is the supervisor's role, together with that of the seminar leaders, to treat the candidate actively as a junior colleague, and not as a patient, right from the beginning' (Fordham, 1961). From my own experience, supervisees try to turn their supervisors into analysts when they are reluctant to talk about a patient, preferring instead to talk about their own feelings in relation to a particular area of psychopathology (see Chapter 13, p. 227).

It is inevitably the case that when discussing the supervisee's countertransference, the supervisor is in danger of analysing the supervisee's personal psychology. However, at times, interpreting the countertransference can be a valuable part of supervision, providing the focus of the interpretation remains on the relationship between the supervisee and her patient rather than on the supervisee's personal psychology. My understanding of the sentiment behind Fordham's quotation to be the need for the supervisor to keep in mind the supervisee's infantile and neurotic material but to avoid interpreting it solely in terms of the supervisee's psychology. If, however, such material comes into the supervisee's relationship with the patient, I have found it helpful to emphasise that the supervisee's countertransference is *counter* to the patient's *transference* and, in this way, the focus can remain on the patient's transference. There are, of course, occasions when the supervisor will observe that the material indicates the supervisee's transference towards the patient; for example, patients sometimes represent parent figures for the supervisee and this may be handled by focusing on how the patient is activating such a transference.

Supervisees may have a problem dealing with the patient's pathology because they have not yet resolved this piece of pathology in themselves within their own analysis. The supervisor can easily enact a 'superego' attitude and refuse to look at the pathology in the patient on the grounds that the supervisee should first deal with the problem in their analysis. I think that this rigid attitude can stem from feelings of rivalry experienced by the supervisor towards the supervisee's analyst. A supervisor who sees himself as having superior insight to the supervisee's analyst may use this to justify such rivalry and contempt. Such situations are particularly likely to arise when the supervisor has been trained in a different institute from that of the supervisee's analyst, but they can also occur when there are unexpressed disagreements between analysts within the same organisation. Sometimes a supervisor may have problems of rivalry and contempt due to the amount of anxiety they are holding in relation to the supervisee's repeated failure to pick up the transference, often because of their own psychopathology. After many months of trying to deal with this difficulty, the supervisor may come to feel frustrated at the supervisee's slow progress in this area. It is then that the supervisor may begin to think that the supervisee's analyst is not doing his work properly. A supervisor under such strain can easily lose sight of the fact that it is the identification of the transference that is of the most difficult areas for the supervisee to learn. Such learning often takes a long time.

Related to this can be the way some analysts openly influence their patient's choice of supervisor. The analyst's attitude, including non-verbal responses, will inevitably reveal itself when the patient is discussing her choice of supervisor and it is also true that a trainee may use her choice of supervisor as a way of attacking her own analyst. However, analysts may move away from their function if such advice is forthcoming. Inevitably, trainees will hear about the relationships between their analysts and other members of the training organisation, and this 'knowledge' is frequently saturated with fantasies, which need analysis. Some trainees may bring these dynamics into the supervisory relationship and, on occasion, the supervisor has no choice but to address them.

Criticisms that a supervisor may make of a supervisee

Let me introduce this subject with an example.

While listening to a supervisee's description of her work with her patient, I began to feel swamped by the amount of material that she was presenting. At first I switched off as a way of protecting myself against the barrage of material. Then I became more consciously aware and started to think about why the supervisee could not contain herself, when presenting. I did not voice these crit-

ical thoughts but continued to feel slightly overwhelmed. Then I became aware that the patient was flooding the supervisee with material, and I realised that the patient was doing this as a way of protecting himself against the feared contents of his unconscious life. At that point I shared with the supervisee my thoughts about what the patient was doing to her. She seemed to feel relieved and I too felt similarly relieved and no longer overwhelmed.

In this example, I became unconsciously identified with the supervisee, wanting her to relieve me of the burden of my confusion by providing me with a clearer presentation. When achieved, the constant monitoring of our feelings and thoughts about the effects that supervisees have on us is potentially fruitful. It is obviously important to consider very carefully the criticisms that we make about a supervisee. They may stem from an unconscious identification with the relationship between the supervisee and the patient. Searles (1962) called this *parallel process*. He talks of a *reflection process*, but since the word 'reflection' means to bend back as with a mirror, I prefer to use the word *resonance*. Chambers Dictionary defines the word 'resonance' as 'the complex of bodily responses to an emotional state, or of emotional responses to a situation'. I think that a supervisor needs to *reflect* on his thoughts and feelings because these feelings are likely to *resonate* with the processes involved in the supervisee/patient relationship.

Discussing theory in supervision

Many think that intellectual educative endeavours should *not* be part of individual supervision, preferring to leave them to the supervisee's general reading. I would agree that displays of theoretical understanding are not the most important constituent of individual supervision, but relating relevant theoretical concepts to a patient's material can be valuable, especially if this does not interfere with the main focus of the supervisee's relationship to her patient. However, both supervisor and supervisee can use such discussions to defend against the patient's material, or as part of a counter-resistance. Here is a simple example of this problem.

One day the supervisee arrived for supervision saying that she felt bored with her patient. She then went on to ask me a number of questions about various training institutions. She was aware that I have a strong interest in training courses and methods, and so I was easily distracted. Our general discussion on training lasted for about six minutes before I became aware that we were avoiding the patient. We then came round to talking about how the patient manages to get us to ignore her in exactly the same way in which her mother ignored her.

Theoretical discussions with colleagues look at the past from the comfortable position of the present and tend to view psychological issues as if they were static absolutes. They are often used as a way of avoiding having to become involved with the difficult dynamics of the 'here-and-now' exchanges. Here and now exchanges are uncomfortable mostly because we may be exposed to what we do not necessarily understand, challenging existing formulations and even our existing identity. For the same reason, dynamic interactions are the lifeblood of growth. As Jung (1938) remarked, 'theories in psychology are the very devil. It is true that we need certain points of view for their orienting and heuristic value; but they should always be regarded as mere auxiliary concepts that can be laid aside at any time.'

On one occasion I tape-recorded a series of my supervision sessions and timed my interventions. I found that, in a fifty-minute interview, the average total time of my intervention was seven minutes. During a supervision session when my interventions took up a longer period of time than usual, I was discussing theoretical concepts. My supervisee insisted that she found these discussions helpful, but I continue to believe that they were mostly defensive (Gee, 1996).

Supervising the supervisee-patient relationship

It will be obvious that, when the supervisor interprets the patient's material, it tends to encourage the idea that the supervisor will sooner or later give his views on what 'should' have been said to the patient by way of interpretations. I think that this function was at one time considered the most important activity of the supervisor. It was thought that through modelling, the supervisee would identify with the supervisor's way of working, as might an apprentice working with a master tradesman. However, in my view it is not desirable for the supervisor to analyse the patient. I have found that when I analyse the patient's psychology the supervisee tends to find the supervision demoralising. When I focus on the supervisee-patient relationship, my supervision has been experienced by the supervisee as more facilitating. I am not saying that the supervisor should never analyse the patient presented by the supervisee. However, this focus should be kept to a minimum and most supervisory time needs to focus on the relationship between the supervisee and his patient. It is important to remember that whilst the supervisor is analysing the patient, the supervisee–patient relationship can be neglected.

I have found that I am most likely to make patient-orientated interpretations when one of three different dynamics operates. First, when the supervisee is feeling angry with the patient as a result of a countertransference of which the supervisee and I are as yet unconscious. The supervisee is asking me to rescue him from a state of confusion about the patient's 'irritating disturbance'. In my heroic position of wanting to 'help' the supervisee I will then make a clarifying reconstructive interpretation. The second most common occasion when I make interpretations about the patient's material is when I over-identify with the patient's anger towards the analyst, which causes me to want to show the supervisee 'how it should be done' and even how ineffective the work has been'. My identification with the patient's unconscious attack upon the analyst is strengthened but also my irritation that the analyst has not taken up the patient's attack within the transference. In my irritation I provide insight, which leaves out the transference.

The third main stimulus for making such interpretations is when I am feeling inferior or depressed outside of the supervisory relationship. At such times, I try to repair my narcissistic damage by displaying my 'superior' degrees of insight. The 'eureka' response to an insight reveals, as Jung observed, that insights can have an inflating effect, and their antidepressant action is as effective for the supervisor as for the supervisee. In other words there is a wish to 'get high' on insights.

Professional practice and social behaviour

In some cases, the relationship between supervisor and supervisee may well border on the social, for example, providing drinks for a supervisee or discussing holidays. While this is the concern of the individual supervisor, it should be kept in mind that this kind of social contact may give supervisees inappropriate messages about how to relate to their patients.

Although the supervisor is essentially relating to a colleague, the relationship is an asymmetrical one in that the supervisor may have more experience than the supervisee. More relevantly, the supervisor has the advantage of greater objectivity as he is less emotionally

ed with the patient. Potential problems are generally avoidable
supervisor remains task-orientated. The task of supervision is
u. rent from that of analysing a patient, as clinical analysis is a professional relationship formed in order to analyse the patient's psyche. The
joint enterprise of the supervisor and supervisee is one of co-work-
ers trying to facilitate the supervisee's capacity to analyse the patient
through the analytic relationship.

Unconscious identity

The main area of difficulty activated in relation to boundaries is the
process of unconscious identity as part of the process of gaining
insights. Jung (1916, para. 519) defined unconscious identity clearly as
follows:

> all projections provoke counter-projections when the object is unconscious
> of the quality projected upon it by the subject, in the same way that a trans-
> ference is answered by a counter-transference from the analyst when it
> projects a content of which he is unconscious but which nevertheless exists
> in him . . . Like the transference, the counter-transference is compulsive, a
> forcible tie, because it creates a 'mystical' or *unconscious identity* with the
> object'. [emphasis added]

Jung wrote this in 1916 and his concept is similar in many ways to
Klein's later concept of 'projective identification', which she did not
introduce until 1946. When Klein first introduced her concept of
projective identification, she defined it as relating to one projection of
parts of the ego, 'so far as the ego is concerned, excessive splitting off
of parts of itself and expelling these into the outer world considerably
weaken it, . . . I have referred to the weakening and impoverishment
of the ego resulting from excessive splitting and projective identification'. (Klein, 1946) In states of unconscious identity however, it is the
self that takes possession by projection. It is also the case that unconscious identity includes the characteristics of the archetypal world and
therefore describes states of deeper unconsciousness than those
conveyed by Klein's concept. Jung's concept of unconscious identity
describes *mutual* unconsciousness and, unlike Klein's concept, does
not emphasise pathology.

Jung did not differentiate between 'participation mystique', a term
first used by Lévy-Bruhl, and 'unconscious identity'. In fact, Jung
sometimes uses the two terms in the same sentence. Personally I

prefer the term 'unconscious identity'. By extending Jung's concept of unconscious identity, it seems to me that there are two types of insight: 'ego insights' and insights that arise from the self, 'self insights'. These are not watertight distinctions but indicate a pattern in the way insights come into being. By 'ego insights' I am describing the process whereby we make conscious links between aspects of the patient's material. These may include comparisons between her present behaviour and past experience. 'Self insights', on the other hand, describe a *process* by which patient and analyst first lose their sense of boundaries so that they are in a state of 'unconscious identity'. An image may emerge from which the analyst or the patient may then come to find symbolic meaning. Ordinarily, this process can help the analyst to separate or differentiate out of the state of unconscious identity with the patient, leading to the possibility of formulating an interpretation.

This may foster a change in the patient's relationship between ego and self, which will give rise to a new identity. If there is a defence, or some other blockage to this process of separation in the patient, it sets up a tension in the analyst. These defensive states in the patient are clearly seen in the 'repetition compulsions' that resist change and therefore growth. The patient brings the state of 'being in a vicious circle' to the analyst and the analyst who is unconsciously identified with the patient has to allow a process of separation to occur within himself in order to find insight.

Both types of insight can be operationally defined as the end product of the process of separation or differentiation within the individual and between individuals. An analyst's interpretation is based on an insight occurring on the basis of separation within the analyst, but its well-timed delivery results in the separation process occurring *between* the patient and analyst, which, in turn, results in a differentiation taking place *within* the patient. What I am describing here is part of Jung's concept of 'individuation': 'Individuation is practically the same as the development of consciousness out of the original state of identity' (Jung, 1921, para. 762).

In my experience 'self insights' tend to have a greater transforming effect than 'ego insights'. 'Ego insights' are frequently influenced by intuitions and 'self insights' involve the ego in the latter stages of the insight. It is my belief that these same processes take place in supervision, because the supervisee brings to supervision similar defences and resistances to differentiation, actively involving the supervisor in the work of the separation process. Mutative insights can similarly occur between supervisor and supervisee; insights gained through these processes include becoming aware of the transference/counter-transference involvements. It is also the state of unconscious identity and the process of differentiation that provide the supervisor with eventual understanding of what is happening between the supervisee and her patient.

Problems arising from states of unconscious identity

I had discussed a male patient with a female supervisee and we had jointly agreed that the central problem for the patient was that he was over-identified with the hero archetype. He was insisting on competing with his driven friend and thought that what mattered in life was being successful. He admired his friend who saw people as things to be used. Because he did not see himself as capable of such a ruthless attitude towards people, he concluded that he was a failure. This, of course, came into the transference because, although he found his analysis helpful, he saw it as a failure to need analysis at all.

During the supervision of this case, we had come to realise that the patient's friend was very similar to the patient's parents and that there was a need for the patient to separate from his parents and friend in order to gain a greater degree of autonomy. The main focus of our work had been on analysing the way the patient underestimated his abilities and also how he frequently behaved in ways that were not in his best interests. He resisted looking after himself because he was still looking for the external ideal parent to come and rescue him.

Some time later I became increasing aware that my supervisee was getting more anxious about her patient and I was left feeling that this was because she was unable to cope with the patient's resistance to growing up. During one of our supervision sessions, I suddenly realised that the patient's identifications with his parents and friend were part of his idealised persona. With this new formulation I came to see that the main need of the patient was to make contact with his authentic self by way of an appropriate regression within his analysis. In other words, I became aware of the resistance and counter-resistance within the analytic relationship. When I put this to the supervisee, she showed an immediate state of relief.

This example shows that because I was unconsciously identified with the supervisee, and because she was unconsciously identified with her patient, we had both colluded with the patient's inner conflicts that he ought to be more adult than he could authentically be. Only after I had slowly differentiated myself from the state of unconscious identity with the supervisee were we both able to re-establish the boundaries between the patient and supervisee.

Another simpler example occurred recently.

During a supervision session I asked the supervisee what she u... *patient may have meant by a certain communication. The supervisee gave me a clear explanation that seemed to me to be very appropriate. She had not, however, made any comment to the patient. The supervisee said that she now thought it might have been desirable to have made an interpretation about this issue. Later when completing her six-monthly report, I wrote that the supervisee was hesitant to use her understanding in order to make interpretations. Two weeks later the supervisee described how she saw the patient as being 'hesitant' to use his abilities that then led me to make the link with the supervisee's hesitance in relation to her patient. We came to see how the patient was afraid of expressing his feelings in case they drove people away, and that the supervisee had identified with this fear; her fear that her interpretations might drive him away.*

With hindsight, it could be said that my inability to recognise the supervisee's undifferentiated involvement with the patient had caused me to see the problem as solely related to the supervisee's attitude rather than the nature of the therapeutic process.

While these examples illustrate a number of difficulties in supervision, I hope that I have made it clear that the loss of boundaries is both inevitable and desirable because it is an essential part of primitive relationship without which one of the most important therapeutic processes could not take place. An analogy that I sometimes use with supervisees is that in order to understand the patient's neurotic 'pits' it is necessary for the analyst to get into the pit with the patient and together find the way out. It is no use thinking that you can remain on the rim of the pit shouting instruction down to the patient!

There is a significant danger that comes with unconscious identity. I have observed that when an ethical problem arises in the analytic relationship, it often relates to the analyst's tendency to become caught up with the patient's desire to meet their primitive needs. In a state of unconscious identity when there is a dovetailing of pathology, the analyst tries to meet a need in a concrete way rather than coming to an understanding of the nature of the need by analysing. By 'dovetailing of pathology' I mean a situation in which a patient is possessed by a particular psychological dynamic, which is met with a similar dynamic in the analyst. A simple example would be one in which the patient's masochism is met by the analyst's sadism. When in a state of unconscious identity with the patient, the analyst's ego is considerably weakened and it is while we are in these states that powerful enact-ments, or acting out, are likely to occur. Here supervision plays a vital role in helping the supervisee to maintain their boundaries.

Although supervisor and supervisee are working towards a well-integrated understanding of the dynamics of the patient–analyst rela-tionship, there is a good case for giving the supervisee a reminder of the 'rules'. Integrating the contents of a relevant Code of Ethics and an understanding of the 'analytic attitude' can provide the analyst with 'intellectual handrails' during the periods of emotional blindness engendered by the ego-weakening experience of unconscious iden-tity. The content of such a code is likely to include:

- do not have sex with your patient;
- do not hit your patient;
- do not get involved in your patient's finances apart from collecting fees;
- try not to shout at your patient, and so on.

These may seem obvious but by emphasising them, the supervisor is providing the supervisee with simple and clear containing statements. While we are in an ego-orientated state, these rules may seem almost puerile but we should never underestimate the power of the uncon-scious and, when we are in its grip, even the simplest of rules may provide the essential ingredient to help the supervisee maintain an ethical position. Supervisors should not adopt a 'holier-than-thou' superego attitude to supervisees' muddle but with an understanding of the power of unconscious identity, an understanding of the shadow side of their relationships with their patients can emerge in supervi-sion. It is worth noting that the superego aims to suppress the prim-itive rather than integrate the contents of the primitive psyche. Rules will only be of help if the supervisee has a strong professional ego, based on a sound personal analysis, but it also helps when supervision is positively reinforcing and is supportive of ego states. Then the supervisee can gradually develop the many aspects of an analytic atti-tude, manifested in the form of a professional ego. Once sufficiently established, the professional ego is strong enough to permit forays into areas of unconscious identity because it has sufficient confidence that it will be able to reestablish itself.

Summary

In this chapter, I have focused on a number of different boundary issues arising in supervision. I have emphasised how analysts require an analytic attitude in order to orientate themselves to functioning as analysts and how it is helpful for supervisors to clarify the boundary between management and analysis. Supervisors have greater responsibility for supervisees who are trainees than for those who are qualified colleagues and this can be a helpful internal boundary for supervisors to keep in mind. It is also important to think about what is confidential to the relationship between the supervisor and trainee and what the supervisor can report to the trainee's training body. It is desirable for supervisors to help their supervisees clarify the boundary between ethical and unethical behaviour. I have emphasised how supervisees require their own personal analysis and the delicate boundary that can be crossed inappropriately if supervisors analyse their supervisees.

I have also explored the processes involved when supervisors discover how feelings towards their supervisees can resonate with the supervisees' relationships with their patients. Many difficulties with boundaries in supervision can be avoided if the supervisor is orientated towards supervising the relationship between supervisees and their patients rather than focusing on analysing the supervisees' patients. Finally I have emphasised the links between boundary issues and the process of unconscious identity. Discussions between supervisors are likely to play a very important part in improving states of consciousness and enhancing professional identity.

Unfortunately, some psychotherapists in training find it difficult to become deeply involved in relationships because of the degree of damage to their own personalities. I am convinced that the personal analysis of the supervisee has done its work when the future analyst is sufficiently undefended to accept the states of unconscious identity that are an essential part of the therapeutic process as well as a hopeful sign that they are able to integrate these confusing experiences and thereby continue to individuate.

References

Fordham, M. (1961) 'Suggestions towards a Theory of Supervision', *Journal of Analytical Psychology,* **6**(2).

Gee, H. (1996) 'Developing Insight through Supervision: Relating, then Defining'. *Journal of Analytical Psychology,* **41**(4).

Hartmann, H. (1964) *Essays on Ego Psychology* (London: Hogarth Press).

Jung, C. G. (1913) 'Psychological Types', *Collected Works Volume 6*, paras 757–62.

Jung, C. G. (1916) *Collected Works Volume 8*, para. 519.

Jung, C. G. (1921) *Collected Works Volume 6*, para. 762.

Jung, C. G. (1938) 'Psychic Conflicts in a Child', *Collected Works Volume 17*, Foreword to the third edition.

Klein, M. (1946) 'Notes on Some Schizoid Mechanisms', *International Journal of Psycho-Analysis*, **27**, 99–110.

Searles, H. (1965) 'Problems of Psycho-Analytic Supervision' and 'The Informational Value of The Supervisor's Emotional Experiences', in *Collected Papers on Schizophrenia and Related Subjects* (New York: International Universities Press). Chapter 20 and Chapter 4

Wharton, B. (1985) 'Show me Another Reality!: The Need for a Containing Ego', *Journal of Analytical Psychology*, **30**(3).

Wiener, J. (2001) 'Confidentiality and Paradox: The Location of Ethical Space', *Journal of Analytical Psychology*, **46**(3), 431–43.

10

Supervising the Erotic Transference and Countertransference

Joy Schaverien

Introduction

In this chapter I will consider the frame of analysis in relation to the frame, form and structure of the supervisory relationship. It is not in question that the erotic transference is central in analysis. However problems sometimes arise because the erotic transference and the associated countertransference may confront the analyst with the limits of the analytic frame. The erotic reveals much about the patient's way of being in the world but it may be difficult to introduce into supervision. This may be because it engages the analyst-as-person and so may, at times, challenge the analyst's self concept and sense of professional identity. The supervisor's countertransference may be a way of accessing such material when it might otherwise be missed. This too is complex as it emphasises issues of gender and sexuality within the supervisory relationship. However, in a time of threats of litigation and awareness of ethical dilemmas, confronting this topic within supervisory practice is essential. I will give vignettes from supervision where the erotic was either very evident or notably absent. Rather than addressing the analytic material in depth, as I have done elsewhere (Schaverien, 1995, 1997, 2002), I will consider the supervisory relationship.

The erotic transference in analysis

Transference is at the very centre of the analytic enterprise. It was Freud who came to understand transference as a repetition of past patterns of relating when he noticed that his patients frequently seemed to fall in love with their psychoanalyst (Freud, 1912, 1915). It was the case of Anna O, who was the patient of his colleague Breuer, that led him to realise that, in psychoanalysis, the undivided attention of the analyst, the confidentiality of the setting and its bounded nature, led to the re-experiencing of past patterns of relating (Jones, 1953). The patient unconsciously related to the analyst as if he were a parent or authority figure and so the transference was very often characterised by affect originating in childhood (Freud, 1905). Freud (1912) wrote that the pattern for conducting erotic life is laid down in the early years of life and 'if the need for love has not been satisfied the person is bound to approach every new person he meets with libidinal anticipatory ideas' (Freud, 1912, p. 100). Therefore he considered that neurosis could be traced back to infantile sexuality.

Jung's view was rather different from that of Freud and this disagreement was one facet of the break that eventually occurred between them (McGuire, 1974). Jung considered Freud's view to be reductive. He proposed that incest fantasy had a meaning and purpose beyond regression to infantile sexuality. He agreed with Freud that regression in the transference was a return to an earlier state of being but he thought that its purpose was in order to grow forward anew (Jung, 1956). Incest symbolism engaged the patient, and sometimes analyst, in an intense process, which drew the analyst into an atmosphere of familial intimacy (Jung, 1946 para. 56). Jung writes: 'The patient, by bringing an activated unconscious content to bear upon the doctor, constellates the corresponding unconscious material in him' (Jung, 1946, para. 12). Thus the analyst may become temporarily affected by the patient's material (Jung, 1946). This involvement offers understanding that is beyond cognition and which, over time, facilitates the patient's separation from the initial undifferentiated state. The analyst is at once a participant and observer in this process.

Supervision helps to maintain the ability to observe and to think when the analyst is immersed in such intense material. The purpose of supervision is to focus on the patient and not the analyst and yet attention to the bodily responses, emotions and images experienced by the analyst is very often a key to understanding the transference. This 'counter'-transference is an analytic tool that needs to be honed and all experiences of the analyst, when with the patient, are potential material for supervision. However the erotic transference, and the associated countertransference, can be a sensitive area that the analyst may be reticent to discuss as it brings the analyst-as-person into the material of supervision. Awareness of bodily arousals, or lack of them, in the analyst may indicate the level of functioning of the patient at any particular time. For example, regression to an infantile state may evoke a maternal response or, conversely, a rejecting repulsion, whilst oedipal demands may arouse a genital response in the analyst. This may be additionally confusing as such arousals may occur irrespective of the gender or conscious, sexual orientation of the analyst or patient. These are not fixed and perceptions of them may alter, taking different priorities during the course of an analysis. Eros is central in the individuation process but it is not merely one thing. The meaning of its insistent presence or persistent absence in any particular therapeutic relationship may reveal much about the patient's way of being in the world. Attention to the countertransference is often the key to the level of functioning of this particular patient at this particular time. There are many other countertransference responses that are less obviously demanding but this area needs to be given particular attention, as it can be embarrassing to approach in supervision.

Framing supervision

Like analysis, supervision is framed. The analytic vessel is metaphorically considered to be a sealed container. Jung likened it to the alchemist's alembic within which opposing elements are first attracted, come together and mix, and from the intense chemical reaction something new is produced (Jung, 1928). In analysis, unconscious elements from patient and analyst come together in the transference in a similar way. Like the chemical elements there may be an attraction or repulsion, then a mixing, and finally a separating of the diverse elements and a new, conscious attitude is born (Jung, 1928). The frame of the analytic vessel needs to be strong in order to withstand the pressure from the powerful reactions that take place within it.

Supervision might be viewed as contributing to this frame but to report material from such a sealed container might be considered a breach of the sacrosanct nature of analysis. However supervision too offers a sealed vessel that, at its best, is an extension of the frame of the analytic vessel. In considering this I turn to the wider culture of society and to one of the many framed spaces set apart from everyday life for a particular purpose (Schaverien, 1989, 1991; Wiener, 2001). The theatre is a well-known metaphor for the psyche (McDougall, 1986; Gordon, 1989; Jenkyns, 1996) but I will consider it in terms of its form and structure.

In the traditional theatre the proscenium arch frames the drama. The audience is admitted to the auditorium, the outer frame, but not to the stage, the inner frame. Actor and audience play their part in this imaginal enterprise; both know the rules. It is a cultural given that, on entering the theatre, the spectator is required to suspend disbelief. This is a symbolic enactment and to interpret it concretely would be to confuse the frames of reference. The action is imaginary, however, if the performance is good, both player and spectator experience real emotions. Therefore tragedy may move the spectator to tears, whilst aggression may induce fear; the effect may be cathartic, evoked by empathy, or identification with the protagonist. There may be vicarious enjoyment in witnessing an intimate drama whilst also removed from it (Aristotle, 1965). Psychologically, members of the audience make a split that enables them to suspend disbelief.

There is a parallel here with the frames of analysis and supervision. Analysis is a drama that takes place between two people, the patient and the analyst (or in group work the group and the analyst). As if from the privileged position of the audience, the supervisor witnesses the drama, sometimes moved by what is observed. There is an attempt to help one of the actors de-role and to join the supervisor/spectator in observing the action from a critical distance. In order to do this the actor/analyst makes a psychological split that permits her simultaneously to stand beside the supervisor, as a spectator of this drama, and to play a part in it (see Chapter 11, p. 192).

The therapeutic relationship

In order to examine these different psychological positions I turn first to Greenson (1967). Following Freud, Greenson separates the facets of the therapeutic relationship into three parts.

- The **real relationship** is the *real* experience of patient and analyst together. This is like entering the theatre. It takes account of practicalities such as the setting up of the frame, financial arrangements, breaks and the limits of analysis (see Chapter 13, pp. 231–2).
- The **therapeutic alliance** begins in the assessment session whereby the analyst assesses whether the patient has the capacity to

think symbolically. Like the viewer in the theatre a psychological split is required whereby a part of the patient maintains an alliance with the analyst to observe the drama of the transference. This therapeutic alliance mediates between the real and the imaginal and requires a symbolic mental attitude. A patient who thinks too concretely, such as someone who is in a psychotic state, would be unable to understand the symbolic nature of the transference.

- The **transference** is an imaginal enterprise whereby past patterns of relating become live in the present. Although it may feel very real, the transference is *symbolic*. In the moment it may seem '*as if*' the analyst is the parent but a part of the patient knows that this is not the case. Psychological transformation gradually develops as this re-experiencing of past patterns of relating brings insight that is gradually integrated (Freud, 1912, 1915; Greenson, 1967). Transference is present, although usually unconscious, in all relationships but in analysis it is given attention. There is not always an intense transference, as Peters (1991) has graphically demonstrated, and so a distinction needs to be made between the milder forms of transference and the intense forms of it. Intense transference engagements evoke powerful countertransference responses.

The supervisory relationship

If we extend Greenson's categories into the supervisory relationship we see that the same categories apply but with altered priority:

- The **real relationship in supervision** is a comparison of what is real between analyst and supervisor.
- **Transference in supervision** is treated differently from transference in analysis. The imaginal drama that is transference is enacted on the analytic stage and not the supervisory one. Transference will develop between analyst and supervisor, as it does in all relationships, but it is not interpreted here unless it is inhibiting the process of supervision. This is because interpretation of the transference between analyst and supervisor would be a breach of the supervisory frame; it would place the analyst in the position of patient. However, if the drama that develops between analyst and supervisor is monitored, it may be understood as parallel process; that is a reflection of the therapeutic relationship that is being discussed (Langs, 1994).
- The **supervisory alliance** is central but it is a different form of

alliance from that of the therapeutic alliance. It is an agreement, usually implicit, to observe the analysis as presented by the analyst. Like the actor, who de-roles and stands beside the spectator to consider his performance, the analyst stands beside the supervisor to observe the patient–analyst interactions. For this to be effective there are certain requirements of the analyst:

1. Giving an account of the patient's history;
2. Writing up and reporting the facts of the interaction;
3. Observing the transference;
4. Observing the emotional impact of the interaction;
5. Observing the countertransference including, at times, emotional and bodily sensations, images and fantasies generated in the analyst by the therapeutic relationship.

The supervisor's role will include:

1. the **supervisory countertransference**, takes account of the whole supervisory relationship, its feeling tone and the attitude of the analyst, as well as the material presented.
2. the **supervisor as witness.** The witnessing function of the supervisor is significant given the confidential and sealed nature of the analytic vessel. For the analyst it may be a relief to have someone with whom it is permissible to discuss confidential material and express the feelings evoked within the analytic frame. This is important because it helps the analyst to process and think about the analytic material.
3. **Reflections on the transference**, dreams and imaginal material.
4. **Listening to the unconscious** or underlying implications of the patient's communication as reported by the analyst.
5. **Practical help**, for example discussion of boundary issues and decisions regarding assessment, fees and termination.

Thus in supervision the central framed area, the stage on which the drama is enacted, is the analysis. Supervision is like the auditorium in which analyst and supervisor together observe the images shaped by the feeling tone and content of the sessions. Rather than a breach of the sacrosanct nature of the analytic vessel, supervision is an extension of the frame and it benefits the patient by helping the analyst to think objectively.

The erotic transference in supervision

The erotic transference is sometimes difficult to access in supervision because, as already stated, the associated countertransference brings the analyst-as-person to the fore. The analyst may be reluctant to report erotic countertransference experiences, for fear of disapprobation. Yet observation of such countertransferences may be significant in unlocking areas that most distress the patient. Open discussion is often liberating, overriding the taboo on speaking of sexual feelings, whilst avoidance may repeat the secrecy of the incestuous dynamic of the patient's family. A distinction in the mind of the analyst, as well as patient, needs to be made between incest fantasy and acts of incest. It is incest fantasy that is evoked within the analytic frame. However, if there has been sexual abuse in the past, there may be an unconscious expectation that analysis will repeat this experience. This is a confusion of frames and so a distinction is needed, within analysis, between the symbolic, the '*as if*', and the concrete. Like anger, the erotic, sometimes takes the analyst to the borders of the analytic frame but it may not be immediately evident in the reported material. In the following examples I will consider some of the many manifestations of the erotic transference with attention to gender and sexual orientation. The focus is the supervisory relationship and so the patient's material is not discussed in depth.

The erotic countertransference

Daisy had heard me speak about the erotic transference and countertransference at a clinical meeting of her society and soon afterwards she made an appointment to consult me. She was working privately and, a year earlier, a professional man in a high-powered job had contacted her asking for analysis. She admitted that, because of his social status, she had been slightly in awe of him even before she met him. On meeting him face-to-face she had been immediately attracted to him; the analyst-as-person was then in conflict with the analyst-as-professional. Pope et al. (1993) discuss this type of situation and suggest that at this point there is a choice to be made; in acceptng the person for therapy, the analyst makes the decision to forego any personal or sexual encounter. Daisy agreed to see this man as a patient. She was curious about this attraction and what it might mean. As the therapy developed, his appeal became stronger and it became fairly evident, from his material, that the attraction was mutual. In analysis the task is to interpret any material that arises. Therefore understanding of the type of appeal of this patient would have been helpful (Samuels, 1985; Rutter, 1989).

However, because Daisy felt guilty about her own feelings she found it diffi-cult to take this to supervision. After a few months, aware that she was confused, she plucked up courage to raise this sensitive topic with her supervi-sor. The supervisor seemed to ignore it and so Daisy did not mention it again. Soon after this, as part of a planned move unrelated to this incident, she changed supervisors. This offered her the opportunity to approach the subject afresh. Daisy waited a while before raising the topic with the second supervi-sor. This supervisor took the matter very seriously, advising Daisy to terminate the analysis as soon as possible. This response confirmed Daisy's doubts about her own practice; she felt humiliated, incompetent and guilty of some misde-meanour. Ashamed of her feelings, she ended the therapy without disclosing the reason to the patient. Now she came to consult me because she realised that perhaps there could have been another way. Indeed I do consider that there was another way and that this had been a lost opportunity for both patient and analyst.

First let us consider the analyst: Daisy's story is far from unique, as such arousals are a rather ordinary aspect of the work. The important point is the confusion of frames here; the transference and the real relationship had become mixed up. The feelings in Daisy arose out of a two-person relationship but she felt responsible for them. In such situations it is common for women analysts to blame themselves for causing the arousal in the man (Guttman, 1984; Schaverien, 1995, 1997). This was compounded in supervision when the feelings were not treated as part of the symbolic enactment of the drama that is transference, but as real and inappropriate. In order to differentiate her own personal feelings from those of the patient, some discussion of Daisy's personal state was needed in supervision but this did not happen. As we discussed this now, a year later, it emerged that Daisy had been personally vulnerable, as her marriage had recently broken up. This does not necessary indicate a need for further analysis but the analyst's personal support network might be discussed and, if the supervisor does consider that some unanalysed element in the analyst is a problem, this too might be offered for consideration. This is all a part of supervision because it is only when the problems that are inhibiting the analyst's work have been discussed that the patient's material can be fully addressed.

If we knew more about this patient it is likely that his part in this dynamic would become clear. I would have wanted to know more about the nature of the attraction? Did she want to go to bed with him? What were her fantasies? Was this appeal for maternal holding or sexual contact? Was this similar to other dynamics in the patient's life? It would be important to consider what it was about this patient that was so irresistible and what purpose the attraction served. Reflection on his history and the presenting problem might have revealed much about the patient as it is likely that this was a reflection of similar problems elsewhere in his life. The premature termination of analysis is the patient's loss and he may feel confirmed in the sense that he is dangerous, too much for others, or that he is unlovable.

The supervisors should be considered, as it would be too easy for them to be split off as bad object/supervisors. It is likely that many of us have been in the position of these supervisors: the first seemingly hoping that, if the topic were not discussed, it would go away; the second possibly worried about sexual acting-out and consequent litigation. Concerned about the extent or limits of their responsibility, the supervisor may be tempted to cling too rigidly to the perceived rules. Neither of these supervisors held to their witnessing role. The first appeared not to have heard and so behaved like the 'other' parent in cases of sexual abuse who, when told, is unable to accept the truth and turns away; thus refusing to be a witness. The second supervisor relinquished the witnessing role by advising termination of the analysis. There may be good reason for doing this in certain rare cases. There are other possible reasons for turning away from the erotic transference. For example, it can be pleasurable to work with someone to whom one is attracted, and this can induce guilt in the analyst and envy in the supervisor. As witness to this particular type of human drama, the supervisor may fear being gratified in a voyeuristic manner. This merits attention as part of the supervisory countertransference, as it is likely that this too is a reflection of the therapeutic interaction under discussion, indicating a need for thought and discussion rather than action.

This analyst seemed to be faced with two options, both of which involved action that would breach the analytic frame. To go to bed with the patient, even if the patient seems to want it, would be an abuse of the analyst's power and so unethical. However, to terminate the analysis with no valid explanation to the patient is also potentially damaging and this too might be considered to be unethical. Instead of action, the aim would be to permit full expression of the feelings; firstly in supervision, where it would be possible to reflect on their potential meaning in the context of this therapeutic relationship, then in analysis, where, if the topic were opened out, it is likely that the patient would contribute to understanding of the meaning and purpose of the arousal. I am not suggesting disclosing to the patient, but rather finding a way of listening to his material and questioning it in such a way that the topic is permitted. The problem is that it is personally exposing to present this type of material in analysis and in supervision. In supervision it confronts the supervisor with her own sexuality and this may contribute to the difficulty in openly discussing the material. It takes the analysis to the edge of the frame and exposes the analyst-as-person. In order to re-instate the frame, the boundaries between analysis and supervision need to be clearly delineated in the supervisor's mind, with the patient as the central focus of supervision.

The hidden erotic transference – the gift

The reality of the gender and sexual orientation of the dyad in super-vision, as well as analysis, may influence the erotic transference. Gender and sexual orientation are central to our ways of being in the world. Unconscious allegiances or differences may be evoked around issues of gender and inhibit discussion of sensitive material. In the case I will now discuss the analyst and supervisor were both women and the patient a man. This may have contributed to the fact that the erotic transference was initially unnoticed. However there are times when the erotic transference is impossible to detect until some comment or action of the patient takes the analyst by surprise. The presentation of a gift to the analyst is such an act and one that reveals much about frames. The patient may confuse the therapeutic rela-tionship with a potential love affair. This can be especially confusing for the male patient working with a female analyst, as he may be trou-bled by his arousal in relation to a female authority figure, and so find it impossible to broach the subject. It may be difficult for the analyst to pick up signals that would indicate the emergence of an erotic transference and, if it remains hidden, the analyst may miss the erotic until it is too late (Schaverien, 1997).

Jess, an analyst in her mid-thirties, had been seeing Trevor, a man of a similar age, weekly for a year and a half. Trevor had discussed his early life experiences with a belittling father and a dominant but loving mother who died when he was in his early twenties. His feelings of inadequacy with women came to the fore when, soon after beginning analysis, his relationship with his woman friend broke up. His failed relationships with women then dominated the sessions. He knew that women found him attractive but this present rejection evoked the memory of his first girl friend and he wondered why she had left him. *Frequently Trevor would recount how he had fallen in love with both these women, throwing all of himself into the relationship. He was devastated when in each case the woman had found it too much and withdrawn; he felt hopeless but as he recounted this there was apparently little real emotion. Jess tried to help him to understand the link between these losses and his mother's death. She interpreted his feelings of inadequacy in relation to earlier elements of his history. She attempted to make links with his dependency and the infantile elements of the transference. It seemed that, throughout this time, she was treated as a convenient listener but Trevor did not seem to relate to her as a person.*

In supervision each week Jess would report the latest session or two and we would discuss the material in terms of Trevor's early experiences. I usually ask for a written account of the sessions but I do not always insist on a verbatim report, except when the analyst is in training. Writing up sessions is an important discipline, it keeps the actual material of the session and, hence the patient, in focus. It also distances the supervisor from the analyst and maintains the focus on the patient; this is a non-verbal statement of boundaries and it reiterates the purpose of the work. Reflecting on my own experience in this supervision, the supervisory countertransference, I realised I was getting little sense of the transference, and so I asked Jess to record the sessions in detail. The most evident manifestation of the transference was the way that Jess seemed to be treated rather like the mother who provided for him but who knew best; it seemed that he was in awe of her perceived power.

Jess described Trevor's appearance as designed to appeal to women but there seemed to be very little fire in this therapeutic relationship and so I asked Jess whether she found him attractive. She thought about this and then said that he was attractive, in a 'medallion man' sort of way, but despite his rather confident, macho presentation he left her unmoved. This seemed quite odd considering the amount of material he presented about women who were apparently attracted to him. It seemed that either Jess was denying his appeal, or Trevor was splitting off his sexuality in the analytic context. He was not appealing to her as a man but neither was he drawing her into his world at an infantile erotic level. This suggests that there might be a secret split-off aspect to his sexuality that was played out in masturbatory fantasy but did not translate into the reality of interpersonal relating.

It was when Trevor went alone on a two week summer holiday to a European resort, returning with a suntan and a gift of a necklace for his analyst that the erotic transference became available to be understood. The necklace was a simple beaded one, of the sort quite typical of the resort; it was not expensive, but pretty. Jess had accepted it despite feeling uncomfortable and rather embarrassed about it. She wanted to discuss this as she felt that the gift was inappropriate. When questioned she said that she had accepted it because she did not want to hurt Trevor's feelings but now she had a problem. As she reflected on what to do with it, she realised that she could not wear it, and that taking it home would be quite wrong. It would be taking something into her personal life that did not belong there. It became clear that she could not accept it because it was not meant for her, personally. This gift was for Trevor's analyst/lover, a part-fantasy figure evoked by the transference, with little real relationship to who Jess really was. Clearly it would be inappropriate to wear the necklace.

Until this time the erotic transference had been hidden. Jess had been unclear about what Trevor's feelings for her might be and so had been unable to interpret them. The effect of this lack of comment on the nature of the relationship was that Trevor's expectations had been raised. The presentation of the gift brought all this out into the open. The problem was its substantial existence. The symbolic had been misinterpreted as real and the necklace was a concrete manifestation of the confusion of frames. Even though he had given no prior cues to this, it was now evident that Trevor was thinking of Jess as a potential lover. Denying the reality of the limits of their relationship he had convinced himself this might be possible without checking it out. It became clear that Jess could now relate to her task; it was now imperative to interpret the multiple levels of the transference.

After discussing, in supervision, how she might return the gift in a manner that would help Trevor, she took the necklace back to him. In supervision this was an instance where, as well as considering the transference, practical help was necessary in thinking about how to approach this. Returning the gift was a tough thing to do but it was also a form of kindness. It brought out into the light that which was previously hidden in the shadow. Jess explained to Trevor that she recognised his feelings for her but that the task in the analysis was to develop an understanding of how his relationships went wrong. At first he was understandably angry, then hurt but, gradually over several sessions, he came to understand that this was typical of the way in which he related to women. Trevor admitted that he was attracted to his analyst and came to realise that this was neither something to be denied nor ashamed of. Moreover he realised that this sort of thing often happened in his relationships with women. He did not check out their feelings first, but went ahead and fell for them, only later realising that they did not reciprocate. By making it possible for him to discuss the meaning of the gift and interpreting his desire for her to be his woman, a whole area of past sadness became available to him. At last he could truly grieve for his losses rather than, as before, repeating them but in a split-off manner. He became sad and the inflated macho image gave way to a much younger, rejected child aspect of his personality. Once its meaning had been understood it became possible for him to take the gift back.

This supervision was characterised by my knowledge of Jess, an analyst who was well able to use her own feelings in relation to her patients. Thus, as her supervisor, I knew that this case was different from others she had brought in the past. The supervisory counter-transference takes account of the aliveness of the presentation as well as the material that is presented. In this case I sensed that there was something unstated but neither Jess nor I could pinpoint it until the presentation of this gift. Once the necklace appeared, the main thread of the drama that is analysis was exposed. The analysis was, like the action on the stage, the inner frame of this process; it was the central action. Supervision was at one remove, the outer frame, with analyst and supervisor like the audience observing the action; this is the supervisory alliance. The protagonists in this drama were Trevor and Jess. However the emotional responses of the supervisor, like those of the audience of a theatrical production, are significant. At first as witness to this drama I was not engaged because it was not engaging Jess. This changed when the erotic became live within the analysis, the relationship was then available for mediation, and the unconscious could begin to become conscious. The point is that a variety of emotional and intellectual responses are demanded of the supervisor as spectator and attention to these very often reveals the parallel process. However it also raises the question of whether a male super-visor might have picked up the erotic transference earlier than I did? A man might have been more able to sense intuitively the sexuality in the relationship. Did the fact that Jess and her supervisor were both women mean that there was an unconscious collusion in discussing this male patient's rather macho presentation? There are no clear answers to such a retrospective question but in terms of supervisory practice it merits consideration.

Sexual orientation and erotic transference

The final point in this chapter is the way in which fixed ideas of the sexual orientation of analyst or patient can limit the progress of analy-sis and prevent the deepening of the transference. This leads to an implicit question regarding the influence of gender and sexuality in supervision. Problems of the erotic transference, arising in same-sex pairings, may inhibit the full emergence of the meaning of homosex-ual material.

Holly was working with a woman, Carol, who had been married for ten years. Initially the patient appeared to be quite happy in her marriage. Her presenting problem related to other areas in her life. However several months into the analysis she began to speculate about whether or not she might after all be lesbian. As far as Holly knew, her patient did not know that Holly was herself lesbian. The patient had become aware of her feelings about other women and reported fantasies about their bodies. This puzzled her and she was worried that it might affect her marriage.

In supervision Holly discussed her concern that the analysis was evoking something that was not previously there in her patient. When asked she said that she was not aware of being attracted to her patient but was worried that she might be unconsciously influencing her. Thus the analyst-as-person was inhibiting the performance of analyst-as-professional. Concerned that, if Carol explored this she would be taking on something that would radically affect her life, Holly veered away from discussion of the topic. In supervision she suggested that perhaps it was time to end the therapy before it damaged this patient's marriage. In this situation the supervisor needs to listen carefully to the reports of the sessions to attempt to elicit what is really going on.

I asked Holly to recount the previous two sessions, in detail, reading from the written reports. This is where writing-up is so important. I listened to the material without commenting and a pattern seemed to emerge. Beneath the overt dialogue, were oblique references to the body of the analyst. Carol talked of leaving her session and seeing a woman walking along the street. The idea came into her mind that she felt attracted to this stranger. It seemed that this was linked with the material of the session that she had just left. In the next session the nature of the erotic fantasies were developed and it became evident that she had been drawn to the woman's breasts. We speculated that it was possible that indeed Carol's interest in other women's bodies related to her desire for closeness with her analyst's body, but perhaps this was primarily a desire for maternal closeness.

The problem here was that the analyst's ideas of her own and the patient's sexual orientation were too fixed. Holly's anxiety about influencing Carol, and so affecting her life adversely, meant that she avoided the material that would deepen the transference. The nature of any desire needs to be fully explored and after that the patient may need to deal with any potential consequences in the outer world. This arousal may or may not have led to a lesbian lifestyle but, at the time, it was merely the erotic aspect of the therapeutic relationship that was being aroused by the deep, intimate, relating of the analysis. Here again is a confusion of frames; this time the analyst was confusing the real and the imaginal. The imaginal enterprise that is transference needed to be fully explored before its affects in the outer world were addressed. It is also possible that Carol may have sensed, in some unconscious way, that her analyst was lesbian. However what is important for the case analysis was that Carol's own homosexuality was now coming to the fore and that was part of the material she needed to explore.

Analyst and supervisor were both women and so were the patient and analyst. It is possible that in a same-sex pair unconscious identification may inhibit awareness of the erotic transference. In the example that follows the patient and analyst were both men. This may contribute to an unconscious perception in the female supervisor of otherness, which may inhibit confrontation of the erotic transference.

Erotic transference as defence

Philip, a rather formally attired doctor, came for weekly psychotherapy supervision as part of his psychiatric training. The patient, Jack, was completely the opposite of Philip in every way. He was an artist, flamboyantly attired, overtly gay and it seemed that he spent a good deal of each session describing his sex life in detail. As this continued it seemed that he was attempting to tantalise Philip with descriptions of one-night-stands and exciting but dangerous encounters with strangers. Philip had a rather fixed idea of his own heterosexuality and Jack's behaviour seemed to him to be wild and unbounded. As the therapy progressed Jack made more blatantly obvious moves towards his analyst; he teased in a way that began to feel intrusive and presented dream material incorporating sexual fantasies of being together with Philip.

Philip's discomfort was evident as he recounted this material. It seemed that this was in part because his own homosexuality was unfamiliar to him and therefore he saw Jack as completely 'other'. Whilst he was interested in the descriptions of this different life style, he could not identify with it. As we explored this, it became evident that Philip was meeting elements of himself with which he was unfamiliar. This is a delicate matter because a supervisor who attempts to set the agenda for his supervisee's analysis is intruding and yet it is sometimes necessary to indicate. It was a relief when Philip volunteered that he was working on this in his own analysis. Here again the analyst-as-person was inhibiting the use of the countertransference as a means of understanding the communications from the patient.

Once Philip's discomfort had been acknowledged in supervision, he relaxed. It was then possible to focus on the meaning of Jack's seductive behaviour. It gradually emerged that Jack's sexual behaviour was a distraction from the pain of relating. He was terrified of really relating to his analyst and so having to admit his vulnerability and dependency. His overt sexual behaviour was defensive. It was interpreted and, over a few weeks, began to be assimilated. Then it emerged that Jack was afraid of getting in touch with the pain of the rejection by his military father that had been compounded by his admission of his sexuality. The accounts of his exciting life had distracted his analyst in rather the same way as he distracted himself from the pain of this rejection. The sexual interest in Philip was not erotic in a relational sense; it was a means of keeping at bay the pain that would follow if he permitted Philip to witness his distress. When the sexual issues were laid aside, the flamboyant Jack was able to reveal a sad shadowy, figure overwhelmed by grief. A phase of mourning then followed in which he permitted Philip to accompany him.

In this case the erotic transference was at first a defence against being in touch with unhappiness. Initially both, analyst and patient had been arrested in their understanding, each by his fixed idea of his own sexual orientation. Philip was sure of his heterosexuality, and Jack was rebelliously claiming his identification as a gay man. Until this was mediated, and they could each move towards each other, the analysis was stuck. There was much drama in this supervision but it was a drama, at first, distant from the analytic relationship.

This was a male analyst/male patient pair and the supervisor, as a woman, was admitted to a male domain with the potential for feeling like a voyeur. In this case this would be in part the real relationship, in part the supervisory countertransference but also the parallel process.

Summary

In analytic case discussions and supervision it is still more common for the focus to be on the presence or absence of anger, envy or aggression than loving or sexual feelings. Perhaps that is because these engage the analyst-as-a-person more than any other aspect of analysis. In this chapter I hope to have shown how the role of the supervisor can facilitate presentation of this sensitive material. The supervisor, as witness, uses the supervisory countertransference as a guide to the nature of the analytic dyad. When the analyst is able to discuss openly this very sensitive material the psychological engagement is deepened.

References

Aristotle (1965) *On the Art of Poetry,* translated by T.S. Dorsch (London: Penguin Classics).

Freud, S. (1905) 'Three Essays on the Theory of Sexuality', *Standard Edition vol. 7*.

Freud, S. (1912) 'The Dynamics of Transference', *Standard Edition vol. 12*.

Freud, S. (1914) 'On Narcissism', *Standard Edition vol. 14*.

Freud, S. (1915) 'Observations on Transference Love', *Standard Edition vol. 12*.

Freud, S. (1917) 'Transference', *Standard Edition vol. 16*.

Gordon, R. (1989) 'The psychic roots of drama' in A. Gilroy and T. Dalley (eds) *Pictures at an Exhibition: Selected Essays on Art and Art Therapy*, (London: Tavistock/Routledge).

Greenson, R. (1967) *The Technique and Practice of Psychoanalysis* (London: Hogarth).

Guttman, H. (1984) 'Sexual Issues in the Transference and Countertransference between Female Therapist and Male Patient', *Journal of the American Academy of Psychoanalysis*, **12**(4), 187–97.

Jenkyns, M. (1996) *The Play's the Thing* (London and New York: Routledge).

Jones, E. (1980) *Sigmund Freud: Life and Work* (three vols, 1953, 1955, 1957) (London: Hogarth Press).

Jung, C. G. (1928) 'On Psychic Energy', *Collected Works Volume 8*.

Jung, C. G. (1946) 'The Psychology of the Transference', *Collected Works Volume 16*.

Jung, C. G. (1956) 'Symbols of Transformation', *Collected Works Volume 5*.

Langs, R. (1994) *Doing Supervision and Being Supervised* (London: Karnac Books).

McDougall, J. (1986) *The Theatres of the Mind: Illusion and Truth on the Psychoanalytic Stage* (London: Free Associations Books).

McGuire, W. (1974) *The Freud/Jung Letters* (London: Hogarth Press).

Peters, R. (1991) 'The Therapist's Expectations of the Transference', *Journal of Analytical Psychology*, **36**(1), January.

Pope, K. S., Sonne, J. L. and Holroyd, J. (1993) *Sexual Feelings in Psychotherapy* (London and Washington: American Psychological Association/Princeton Academic Press).

Rutter, P. (1989) *Sex in the Forbidden Zone* (London: Mandala).

Samuels, A. (1985) 'Symbolic Dimensions of Eros in Transference–Countertransference: Some Clinical Uses of Jung's Alchemical Metaphor', *Int. Rev. Psychoanalysis*, **12**, 199.

Schaverien, J. (1989) 'The Picture within the Frame' in A. Gilroy and T. Dalley (eds) Pictures at an Exhibition: Selected Essays on Art and Art Therapy, A. Gilroy and T. Dalley (editors). (London: Tavistock/Routledge).

Schaverien, J. (1991) *The Revealing Image: Analytical Art Psychotherapy in Theory and Practice* (London and Philadelphia: Jessica Kingsley Publishers).

Schaverien, J. (1995) *Desire and the Female Therapist: Engendered Gazes in Psychotherapy and Art Therapy* (London and New York: Routledge).

Schaverien, J. (1997) 'Men who Leave too Soon: Reflections on the Erotic Transference and Countertransference', *British Journal of Psychotherapy*, **14**(1).

Schaverien, J. (2002) *The Dying Patient in Psychotherapy: Desire, Dreams and Individuation* (Basingstoke, Palgrave Macmillan).

Wiener, J. (2001) 'Confidentiality and Paradox: The Location of Ethical Space', *Journal of Analytical Psychology*, **46**(3).

PART IV

Evolving a Theory of Supervision

11

Into the Labyrinth: A Developing Approach to Supervision

Christopher Perry

It is like passing through the valley of the shadow ... often the doctor [supervisor] is in much the same position as the alchemist, who no longer knew whether he was melting the *mysterious* [my italics] amalgam in the crucible or whether he was the salamander glowing in the fire. Psychological induction inevitably causes the two parties to get involved in the transformation of the third and to be themselves transformed in the process. (Jung, 1945, para. 399)

The complexity of supervision

Supervision is challenging, useful and an enjoyable complement to the more asymmetric analytic relationship. It can have a transformative effect on supervisor, supervisee and patient (which may be an individual, couple, family, group or institution). The complexity of the intersubjectives involved is, however, quite awesome and the process by which transformation takes place is as difficult to describe as the phenomenon of projective identification. These intersubjectivities include the personae and their impact on each other; body language; nuances of tone, pitch and volume of the voices; the sensation of the consulting room; mood and the intensity of feeling; somatic sensations and disturbances; the interplay of imagery; the triggering of complexes in both parties; the search for a common language; the

187

projections that fill the space between; the evolving transference–countertransference dynamic; shifts in closeness and distance; the search for meaning.

Finding a focus in supervision can be a daunting task. As Hobson (1985) states: 'we cannot report to others what we do not know has happened'. In teaching his Conversational Model of psychotherapy over many years in Manchester, he was fascinated by the discrepancies between trainees' verbatim reports and video footage of the same psychotherapy sessions. Further discrepancies emerged between patients and trainees concerning the emotional significance of certain events in sessions. These differences in perception arose largely from the trainees' countertransference. In seeking to reduce the complexity of the supervisory relationship, some authors, beginning with Doehrman (1976), suggest that problems arising in the therapeutic relationship are communicated unconsciously by the supervisee in supervision. This is called 'parallel process'. It is a useful formulation akin to Mattinson's 'reflection process', in which it becomes clear to the supervisor that the supervisee has identified with or been confused by the patient, or has identified with a projection from the patient (Mattinson, 1975). The same process can work in reverse, when the supervisor is experienced as persecutory and in an unholy alliance with persecutory aspects of the supervisee's superego. This may well lead to the supervisee 'acting-out' by becoming judgemental or sadistic through the defence of turning passive into active in order to cope with feelings of helplessness. It is not difficult to place parallel process in the context of sychronicity which Jung defined as

> not a question of cause and effect but of a falling together in time, a kind of simultaneity. Because of the quality of the simultaneity, I have picked the term 'synchronicity' to designate a hypothetical factor equal in rank to causality as a principle of explanation. (Jung, 1960, para. 840)

And again

> the meaningful coincidence between a psychic event and an objective event. (Jung, 1960, para. 850)

Let me give some examples from everyday life.

A young adolescent girl dreams of falling in love with a boy. The next evening she goes to a disco with some friends and actually does fall in love with a boy, who reciprocates the attraction.

Here, the archetype of the syzygy (the pair of opposites consisting of the archetypal image of the femininity pertaining to the man and the masculinity pertaining to the woman) has pushed its way into her consciousness where it is met by the real life carrier of her animus (contrasexual) projection. Subjectively, she finds the coincidence deeply meaningful – meaningfulness being a hallmark of synchronicity.

A man plays the lottery and 'decides' on some numbers for his ticket. Later he is overwhelmed to discover that his internal randomness (choice of numbers) has been matched by an external randomness, which makes him a millionaire.

In this example, the archetype of order, manifested in number, is activated internally and externally. He later realises that his numbers – multiples of seven – relate to the house number in his street, where he was very happy as a child.

It sometimes happens that, whilst listening to the supervisee, the supervisor will notice an image entering consciousness. This might *precede* the supervisee reporting the same image occurring to the patient some days before the supervision session. So the usual dimensions of space and time seem to have been transcended.

While the supervisee is sorting through her notes and seemingly finding it difficult to get started, the supervisor finds himself slightly disturbed by a picture of the inside of a Victorian prison. He is then told that the patient spent some time in a religious community. The supervisor verbalises the image of 'prison', by which the supervisee is bemused because that is precisely the image that the patient used.

Clearly 'prison' will have different meanings for patient, supervisee and supervisor. It may be of archetypal proportions and imbued with personal experience, fantasy and feeling. Holding to the image, experienced sychronistically, might lead supervisor and supervisee to an exploration of what exactly is imprisoned. How is that related to the patient's persistent symptom of constipation, the blocking and withholding of shadowy, shitty feelings? Is the supervisee reluctant to let go and confront the patient with something painful? Is the supervisor feeling imprisoned by the supervisee, whose occasionally muddled presentation imprisons him in a fog of mindlessness?

This example highlights again an inner psychic event (image of 'prison') foreshadowing an external event between analyst and patient, reported retrospectively, acausally connected, and demanding deeper and deeper meaning between all three parties.

Parallel process is one organ of information among many and does not do full justice to the complexity of the supervisory relationship and process. Not uncommonly, supervision is squeezed into an oedipal configuration, the characters in the triangle consisting of patient, supervisee and supervisor. But this is another oversimplification. Using my modification (Perry, 1997) of Jung's conception of the transference (Jung, 1945, para. 422), we can approach the complexity of what we are trying to understand (see Figure 11.1). (For a detailed exploration I refer the reader to Perry (1997). I would like to point out that behind the quaternio there is another – that of the analyst and patient).

To guide us through and out of this imbroglio I am suggesting a bilateral approach which relies on the *mundus imaginalis* as a centring principle of supervision and the notion of the *matrix* as a theoretical construct to use in the unravelling of the multiplicity of relationships, meanings and intersubjectivities that form the essence of supervision.

Supervision defined

I need to define what I mean by supervision. Zinkin (1995) described it as the 'impossible profession', because the 'supervisor is, all the time, both present and not present – which is impossible'. The term 'subvision' may be more evocative since both supervisor and supervisee are concerned with what happens beneath surface consciousness. 'Prismatic vision' seems to me to be an even better name for the

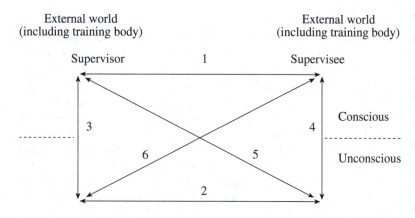

Figure 11.1 The supervisory, analytic or 'marriage' quaternio

process. My idea is borrowed from Jung (1960, para. 367) who wrote about the range of sound frequencies perceptible to the human ear and wavelengths of light visible to the human eye. He conceived of a lower and upper threshold for psychic events and thought that 'consciousness, the perceptual system par excellence, may therefore be compared with the perceptible scale of sound and light, having, like them, and upper an lower limit' (Jung, 1960, para. 367).

In supervision, I imagine the relationship and the process as an acoustic and luminous prism. The material for supervision may sometimes be brought as undifferentiated white noise or light which is then projected through the supervisory relationship, where 'noise' is broken down into its component sounds and 'light' into the colours of the rainbow. Jung (1960, para. 414) invoked the image of the spectrum as a simile of the archetype, suggesting that the infra-red pole holds instinct and the ultra-violet image-making and meaning. These two poles find each other in the unconscious where they form a *conjunctio*, which creates energy, which then appears in the conscious part of our psyche as needs, desires, thoughts, pictures, and so on.

For the purposes of supervision, we could schematise the material as shown in Table 11.1.

Table 11.1 A spectral scheme of the material and processes of supervision.

Colour	Analytic therapeutic interaction	Supervision
Red	Mindless impulses to act-out (no meaning)	Rigid case management
Orange	Sado-masochistic urges	Identifying with institutional superego
Yellow	Dawning of differentiation and consciousness	Creating a reflective space
Green	Growth through the transformation of envy	Facilitating the supervisee's personal style
Blue	Arriving at symbolic capacity	Dwelling in un-knowingness
Indigo	Growing into expansion of affectively laden meaning	Shared search for meaning
Violet	Constellating dissociated meaninglessness	Adhesion through helplessness to mindless dogma

I am proposing here a tentative guide for processing the *prima materia* (any communication, verbal or non-verbal between patient and analyst) through and across the matrix to the pole of the *mundus imaginalis* (see also Figure 11.2, p. 203)

The aims of supervision

Supervision is a mutual inquiry by supervisor and supervisee into the analytic relationship, and the inner world of the patient. Drawing on the alchemical metaphor, it is derived from the alchemist's use of the laboratorium (a place of work) and the oratorium (a place of prayer, reflection and contemplation). An engraving by Heinrich Khunrath in 1604 depicts the alchemist's *temenos* (Fabricius, 1976). Interestingly the engraving is circular. It depicts a huge hall. The portal, ceiling and chambers are covered in Latin inscriptions, one of which is particularly pertinent to supervisors and supervisees: '*Dormiens, vigila*' – while sleeping, be alert! On the left of the huge hall kneels the alchemist, arms outstretched in the oratorium space, a tent-like structure from whose roof hangs a plaque on which is written (translated) 'Do not speak of God without light' – that is, without insight (Fabricius, 1976). Jung's notion of psychotherapy – gaining insight, acting and then enduring the consequences – also has obviously relevance for supervision. The *temenos* is a quasi-metaphorical term used to describe the hermetically sealed, or well boundaried, container formed by the analyst and patient where oppositional forces meet and react together during analysis. For further discussion see Samuels *et al.* (1986).

These two containing spaces, of the laboratorium and the oratorium, are inextricably joined, but in my mind denote respectively the consulting rooms of supervisee and supervisor. The first is primarily a space for the personal individuation of the patient, the second for the professional development and individuation of the supervisee (see Chapter 10, pp. 169–70). It is in supervision that supervisee will begin to forge that deeply unique amalgam of life experience, personal analysis, theoretical knowledge and professional practice, all held within the personality of the supervisee with both its limitations and its capacity to grow, change and develop.

One aim of supervision is very close to Jung's aim in conducting psychotherapy:

> My aim is to bring about a psychic state in which my patient [supervisee] begins to experiment with his own nature – a state of fluidity, change and growth where nothing is eternally fixed or petrified. (Jung, 1945, para. 99)

Play

Supervision also offers an invaluable opportunity for both supervisor and supervisee to immerse themselves, like Jung in his daily play during his confrontation with the unconscious. The three processes of 'letting happen', 'considering' and 'confronting oneself with' all emerge in the dialectic between the conscious and unconscious and within the therapeutic and supervisory relationship (Humbert, 1988).

It is in this atmosphere of play, which I think takes place in 'the imaginal world, a *mundus imaginalis* that has its own processes and can also transform' (Schwartz-Salant, 1989), that supervision is most effective. The term *mundus imaginalis* refers to 'a precise order or level of reality, located somewhere between primary sense impressions and more developed cognition or (spirituality)' (Samuels, 1989). By 'spirituality' Samuels is not referring to religiosity, but rather to the apprehension of, and finding meaning in, the space 'located somewhere between'.

Jung played every day in the second half of his life, especially during his 'confrontation with the unconscious' (Jung, 1963). He played with stones he found on the lake shore, building towers, houses and whole villages. Also for a time Jung painted mandalas – symmetrical portraits of inner psychic states – during his researches into the Self. Far from freely associating away from these images and constructions, Jung chose to plumb their depths by a process of *circumambulatio*, walking round and round the image, feeling, mood – just as one would walk round a sculpture or cathedral. Like the nucleus of a complex magnetising experience towards it, so Jung's process of circumambulatio created an intellectual/cultural whirlpool into which images and myths were inexorably sucked. This resulted for Jung in the process of amplification, later extended by Edinger (1985) with his concept of 'cluster thinking'. The two processes of free association and cluster thinking form a pair of opposites, creating a tension, which lends supervision an energic intensity which can be highly creative. It results in Zinkin's notion of 'flexibility' in technique, imaged as a spiral process, forming a conjunctio between the line and the circle (Zinkin, 1969).

The artist Cecil Collins taught at the Central School of Art and

Design in London for several years. He encouraged his students in a practice that he undertook himself in a very disciplined way. While the dominant hand of the student was required to draw what was to be seen, the non-dominant hand was required to do another drawing hidden away under a board. His aim was to promote a discussion, so to speak, between what was consciously perceived and what was unconsciously apperceived in the space between the two – the *mundus imaginalis.*

Collins' approach highlights the difference of function between the left and right hemispheres of the brain and offers a helpful analogy that can be used in supervision.

Many supervisors require supervisees in training to produce verbatim notes of sessions. The usefulness of these notes is limited. It relies on the conscious processing of themes, motifs and interactions which are intrinsically non-linear, and it can exclude the exploration of the myriad events of a session such as the apperception of a mood, the non-verbal language created by the participants, and the 'unmentionable' associations and responses of the supervisee. These latter generally coagulate around anxieties about physical contact, erotic longings (see Chapter 10), increased availability through extra sessions, writing letters, telephone contact, the activation of a sado-masochistic complex, the use of tokens, the acceptance of gifts, succumbing to pressure to reduce fees, 'non-analytic' interventions or inexplicable failures in empathy. Talking about these in supervision is often shame-ridden but can lead to growth and the development of individual style.

Collins' practice of dual drawing perhaps may have its parallel in Jung's notion of directed thinking, which he called 'intellect' and the capacity for passive or undirected thinking which he called 'intellectual intuition' (Jung, 1971, para. 832). I have come to find that some supervisees can arrive at a point of healthy balance between the two, which creates a greater freedom in themselves as analysts and a tighter use of supervision through the presentation of aspects of the analytic relationship which are preoccupying them, fascinating them or bewildering them. Such freedom is fuelled by the dynamic opposition of a centripetal force to adhere to the material and a centrifugal energy to make imaginative leaps away from it. The creative use of this dynamic is determined by the typology of the supervisor and supervisee. Difference of attitude between supervisor and supervisee tends to irritate both parties to the limits of endurance; on the other hand, the opposition of primary functions – thinking vs. feeling, sensing vs.

intuiting – can foster the flowering of the inferior function in both parties. (See also a discussion of differences in typology of supervisor and supervisee in Chapter 2.) If the affinity between supervisor and supervisee is too close it can result in defensive collusion, stagnation or pseudo-mutuality. At the other extreme can lie a hopeless disconnectedness in which the supervisee feels unheld, misunderstood and undervalued. The 'other' (as supervisor) should ideally both attract and repel, so that difference and pluralism form the Ariadne's thread we can use to negotiate the labyrinth of supervision.

Containment

Part of the efficacy of supervision must of necessity depend on the provision by the supervisor of '[T]he *vas bene clausum* (well-sealed vessel) is a precautionary measure very frequently mentioned in alchemy, and is the equivalent of the magic circle. In both cases the idea is to protect what is within from the intrusion and admixture of what is without, as well as to prevent it from escaping' (Jung, 1953, rev. 1968, para. 219).

Such provision offers modelling to the supervisee and facilitates trust and mature interdependence. But the container poses difficult questions. The patient unfolds to the supervisee; the supervisee reports to the supervisor, who might consult with a colleague. In training institutions reports go to committees and, where the patient is suspected of or confesses to child abuse, for example, external agencies statutorily have to be involved (see Chapter 4). So where is the magic circle? Furthermore, little is known of the effects on the therapeutic relationship of supervision, clinical seminars or the writing of reports on patients for training purposes. I am not sure that there really can be a magic circle. Rather, I find it easier to think in terms of a series of permeable concentric circles rippling out from the patient, and containing all participants.

If the analyst is confronted with deeply disturbing shadow phenomena in the patient – such as violence, murder, the perpetration of child abuse and paedophilia or other paraphilias – the *vas bene clausum* is best incarnated in group supervision. In such cases, the analyst can feel very split, on the one hand filled with loathing and contempt for the patient and on the other drawn into over-identification with the victim. Defensive intellectualisation and somatic resonances (sexual arousal, severe headaches, localised and generalised body pain, visual and auditory disturbances and so on) can hold sway.

Group supervision within an institutional context provides a much stronger container, spreads the therapeutic load and injects a variety of perspectives on the work and the courage necessary to continue in the work through periods of hopelessness. (See Chapters 6 and 7 for discussion of supervision in institutions and groups.)

The supervisory relationship constellates a variety of archetypal processes and imagery that need humanising if the mutual learning of both participants is to reach an optimal level. Jung was very interested in images and imagery. In *Memories Dreams Reflections* (Jung, 1963, p. 199) he tells us how 'the years when I was pursuing my inner images were the most important in my life – in them everything essential was decided'. Through letting images surface to consciousness and by seeking to understand them Jung came to realise that they affected and directed behaviour. '[T]he term 'image' is intended to express not only the form of the activity taking place, but the typical situation in which the activity is released' (Jung, 1959, para. 152).

Archetypal images tend to exert a very powerful influence on the ego, which may become possessed by them or identified with them, leading to psychosis. Integration of the image comes about through searching for its meaning, meeting its dynamism and exploring the affective charge attached to it.

My schema is by no means exhaustive, it just beckons towards possibilities that can be confirmed or refuted through experience.

The labyrinth

Labyrinths contain a paradox. To the designer, the construction follows well-established principles based on the mathematical relationship between line and curve. Most of us, when entering a labyrinth, feel confused, disorientated, bewildered and irritated. From the vertex of super-vision, the design, entry and exit points are all too clear. On the ground we are faced with alluring pathways that so often end in dead-ends. So in one sense the journey towards the centre, traditionally the earth, is quite straightforward. In another sense the clearly comprehensible design throws us into confusion. Catapulted from our one-sided approach to linear journeying, we are thrown back on our need for a psychopomp – a soul guide.

The symbolism of the labyrinth took root in Europe in the fifteenth and sixteenth centuries, when it became inscribed in the houses of the aristocracy and in cathedrals. For the lay person there existed the dictum 'Just follow the path'. In the centre of the labyrinth stood the lover's maiden. Her lover would then have to run through the entire design without putting a foot wrong. Legend has it that, on reaching his beloved, he would then have to carry her all the way out again if he wished to keep her! (Martineau, 1996). Even closer to trainees' experience are stories emanating from France about the priests in cathedrals who, led by the Dean, would dance their way to the centre, three steps at a time, having first linked up as a chain. The Dean, at the head of the processional dance, would throw a large ball to his colleagues, beleaguered elsewhere in the labyrinth, who threw it back to him. The ball symbolised the sun, namely consciousness. The sun outside the cathedral signified a numinous power, which mediated by the iridescent and yet subdued colours of the stained glass, provided a much needed screen between I and not-I, ego and Self, conscious and unconscious; a screen, not a barrier.

The journey into and out of the labyrinth (of the analytic rela-tionship) tickles the archetypes of the hero and the anima (or their contrasexual counterpoint) and these can be transposed into the supervisory relationship. I agree with Redfearn, who maintains that these archetypes 'belong to the phase of separation from the maternal matrix, and are developed out of experiences of *separation, frustration and weaning*' [my italics] (Redfearn, 1979). Here, then, arises the possi-bility of a potentially creative unknowingness between supervisor and supervisee, disillusionment on the part of the supervisee and a nudge by the supervisor off the branch of security. There are, of course, ways of cheating our way out of the labyrinth but the cost, usually one of compliance, robs us of the hardship and reward of the journey.

The diabolus

Once inside the labyrinth, the dean and his priests can, of course, play games of a diabolical nature. I am not suggesting for a moment that supervision should consist of what is conventionally understood as 'game playing' – that is to say, identifying with the Trickster, a deeply unconscious activity. I am seeing the diabolus as a potentially creative archetypal predisposition in the supervisor to meet naivety and inno-cence in the supervisee – and even vice versa!

As young analysts (in terms of years of practice), most of us approach our work with all sorts of assumptions and preconceptions, consisting of shoulds and oughts and do nots and can nots and must nots. It is a veritably crippling constraint on the therapist's use of Self in the service of the patient's developing ego-Self axis, and a transposition from the clinical setting, where a patient's morality is undifferentiated and untested.

The diabolical is that which hurls things across assumptions, muddles our thinking, challenges boundaries and barriers, and invites us, as supervisees, to reposition ourselves from a sense of increasing authority and authenticity. The diabolical is also luciferian, the bearer of light, even though it feels to be of a hellish intensity.

During a war I was working with a military man, totally identified with the confrontational attitude of his leader and longing to be called to fight. I had been physically attacked by him twice although I was seeing him in an institutional setting on the advice of my supervisor. Again, twice, at the moment of greatest danger to myself (he was armed with a knife), I had managed to reach the feelings of humiliation engendered by my attempting (clumsily, in hindsight) to interpret his experience of my loss of contact with him (re-enacting a most significant abandonment in infancy). One day, during the height of the fighting, he derided me, sneered endlessly and KNEW of my contempt for his wish to go to war. The whole analysis had been conducted on a war footing, in terms of the frame, understanding, empathy (and my failures in that area) and his war-like use of analytic 'knowledge'. I was beside myself, and retreated into the mountainous caves of silence, hoping that his immense capacity for self-sabotage would bring an end to what felt like a thirty-year war. Longing for relief, shelter and respite, and hoping to dump the problem on my supervisor, I confessed my discontent in supervision. To my intense irritation, the first thing my supervisor did was to get up and say that he had forgotten to give me his bill. Then he settled down into a quiet reverie, and, after what seemed an endless silence, during which I became increasingly bellicose, quietly said 'Christopher, I have just been wondering to myself how are you getting on with your own war-mongering tendencies?'

That diabolical/luciferian quiet question, delivered in a very unthreatening way, remains as one of many crossroads in my training – an intersection between professional and personal development. I feel it emerged from my supervisor's imaginative reverie about what I could become both as an analyst and as a person (the two are inextricable). The posing of the question implied a faith in my willingness to grapple with it, personally and professionally.

Some time later, I read a passage in Jung 'the widening of consciousness is at first upheaval and darkness, then a broadening out of man to the whole man' (Jung, 1963, para. 209). In the analytic world, the broadening out of man to the whole man means joining the community, a community conjoined by the common purposes of offering analysis, deepening our understanding of humanity and providing a forum in which we can discuss our work.

Gatekeeper, authority and power

At the gateway to this community lie the gatekeepers, archetypically imaged by Cerberus and Janus. The former is represented mythologically as a three-headed monstrous dog, throat bristling with snakes, from whose mouth drips poisonous saliva. He/it is the guardian of Hades on the Stygian lake. Janus, facing backwards and forwards, symbolises past and future, and all pairs of opposites, including mutual sacrifice (de Vries, 1974).

Training is bedevilled by split transferences. Supervision can become injudiciously confused with the personal analysis of the trainee. Any intervention made by a supervisor is filtered through the supervisee's capacity for self-analysis. However in training situations, that intervention is transference-laden. As supervisees, we long to know and understand the inner workings of the mind of our supervisors. But in our minds, those very people act as gatekeepers to growing self-acceptance of ourselves as therapists and to entry into the ever-deeper burrows of our professional places of home.

In training institutions, supervisors are vested with authority, and with that authority goes the opportunity to exercise power: the power of inclusion–rejection, of knowledge and of magic. Authority can be dispersed along a continuum of authoritarianism towards a laissez-faire attitude. In these settings, authoritarianism tends to become predominant when the institution has failed to move from 'dependence on the founder to independent functioning' (O'Neill, 2000). Challenges to, or deviations from, the founder's vision, ideology and theoretical stance are seen as major threats, and the challenger is often scapegoated and expelled.

A very different approach to authority is offered by Haley (1963), who was interested in a certain type of permissiveness which he called meta-complementarity. It is the creation of a mutual, shared illusory space. The supervisee 'allows' the supervisor freedom of thought whilst retaining his own authority as therapist – the only person in the room with the patient. The supervisor is permissive to the degree that the development of the supervisee's personal style does not impinge negatively on the patient. The capacity to be permissive in this meta-complementary sense is governed in the supervisor by how much anxiety he can tolerate.

Anxiety within the Master–Apprentice pair can seep out at its negative pole in the form of the malign exercise of power by the Master and the undermining of authority by the Apprentice. There are many manifestations of this. Sometimes supervisors ascribe difficulties in the supervisory relationship to the supervisee by pathologising the latter. These difficulties may include problems of learning, envy, idealisation, over-identification and so on. The supervisory space, like any other relational space, contains projections from both sides. Where difficulties arise, these projections need to be examined, and an atmosphere cultivated in which difficulties in the supervisory relationship can be discussed and resolved in a way that sorts out and acknowledges the contribution of both parties.

In training institutions, the shadowy abuse of power can be reinforced by the institution itself. Whilst on the one hand the institution appears to be facilitative and supportive of its trainees, it can quite suddenly be tripped up by the emergence of doubts about a trainee. Doubts may have been building up over years, but the bearers have not had the courage of their convictions about saying 'No'. Then all hell is let loose. The quest for the Grail is flipped upside down and inside out and turns into a persecutory witch-hunt. The parties involved feel hurt, betrayed, tricked, angry and sometimes mystified. Often the candidate is the casualty. Doubts need to be voiced early and clearly. This is more easily done if we have in our minds the model of permeable concentric circles of containment, offering everyone involved secure holding and the chance to explore the difficulties.

In training bodies under threat of survival or riven by internal dissent, the shadow side of power can appear in the form of (un)conscious attempts to indoctrinate candidates into ways of thinking and working that squeeze the naturalness out of their practice. The imposition of rules and the insistence on adhering to a particular theoretical or technical approach, negate the whole notion of supervision as a dialectical process. They tyrannise the candidate, instil a fear of 'mistakes' and bypass the whole issue of how to handle authority and permissiveness in the consulting room (see Chapter 5, p. 96, and Chapter 8, p.147).

Initiation

Whatever the context, supervision is encompassed by the archetype of initiation, containing as it does the three stages of any *rite de passage* (Leach, 1976). The initiate is first separated from her former role by moving from one place to another, changing clothes (persona) and ritual washing. This is the phase of separation, and is accompanied by feelings of loss, fears of losing everything that was valuable in the former life and excited anticipation (and sometimes dread) of what is to come. This is followed by dwelling in a liminal area, often for an unspecified time. The initiate is kept apart from the main body of society and feels disoriented and uncertain. Holding onto old ways of thinking and practising no longer work. Finally, and often after struggles and ordeals of one kind and another, the initiate is reconnected to the larger group, reflecting a new level of integration on the inside. The rituals of circumcision, knocking out teeth, head shaving and all sorts of other bodily mutilations are metaphors not only of purification but also of death. The child must die before the adult is born. In the Mithraic rites, the young male initiate was separated from his mother and then thrown into a deep hole in the earth and left there. A bull was then ritually slaughtered, and its blood was used to baptise the initiate. The bull seems to have signified instinctuality which had to be overcome by will and determination.

Many of these qualities are needed in analytic training, where the initiates under tutelage are separated from the membership. They form a working group. Those training in individual therapy are given, and espouse, an implicit message that primacy of value is given to the dyads, of which there are:

(i) personal analysis
(ii) and (iii) two training patients (usually one of each sex) supervised by
(iv) and (v) two training supervisors (one of each sex).

We then have five pairs denoting amongst other things 'perfection' and the androgyne – 'the phallic, male, self-conscious 1 of the visible universe, followed by the vulva-shaped female, super-conscious 0 of the infinite' (de Vries, 1974). This nexus, with its permeable boundary, on the other side of which are other training groups (forming a trainee community), is held in mind by the parent organisation in all its positive and sometimes disillusioning aspects. It forms the backcloth across which each trainee traverses in the process of identifying with, and disidentifying from, the organisation, endlessly negotiating the tensions between inner and outer.

The matrix

The matrix is the concept that links inside and outside and offers a framework for thinking about the multiplicity of relationships and meanings in supervision. Jung speaks of the matrix as 'the hollow form, the vessel that carries and nourishes, and it thus stands psychologically for the foundations of consciousness' (Jung, 1945, para. 344), and again, when he says that the *mysterium conjunctionis* 'takes place in the retort or, more indefinitely, in the "natural vessel" or matrix.' (Jung, 1963, para. 657).

What I wish to attempt is a *conjunctio* of Jung's and Foulkes' notion of the matrix, actually the 'suprapersonal matrix', by which he meant interacting mental processes, both conscious and unconscious, which transcend the individual (Foulkes, 1990). Foulkes thought that the matrix consisted of two parts: the *foundation matrix*, which I would link with Jung's collective unconscious, and from which arises the *dynamic matrix* through interpersonal interaction and containing many levels of communication.

In Figure 11.2 construct a model of the matrix, a spiral model of interaction, crossed diametrically by polar opposites. The intersection of the diametric axes with any or all 'moments' on the spiral journey contains the possibility of finding intra-, inter- and trans-personal meaning in the service of the patient's ego and the analyst's potential to deepen the work, and eventually to assume the mantle of supervisor.

The model also offers the contrary motions, imagined as centrifugal and centripetal in relation to the Self of the therapist, so that the journey to and out of the centre of the labyrinth contains both movements. Both are contemporaneous and complementary, and are unthinkable the one without the other.

The spiral flow of the matrix is made verbally explicit and could be filled out by the reader. Movement and exchange signifies progress, growth and deepening relatedness, but there might be blockage at any point along the spiral or across the diametric axes, with the possibility of regression and the need for (a) further personal analysis of the analyst or (b) professional consultation by the supervisor or (c) both.

Each of the axes is polarised and many of them allude back to some of the ideas and material in the chapter. The *prima materia* of a supervision session is subjected to prismatic vision. Going clockwise around the compass, as it were, the therapeutic conversation is broken down into the transference–countertransference dynamic, in which

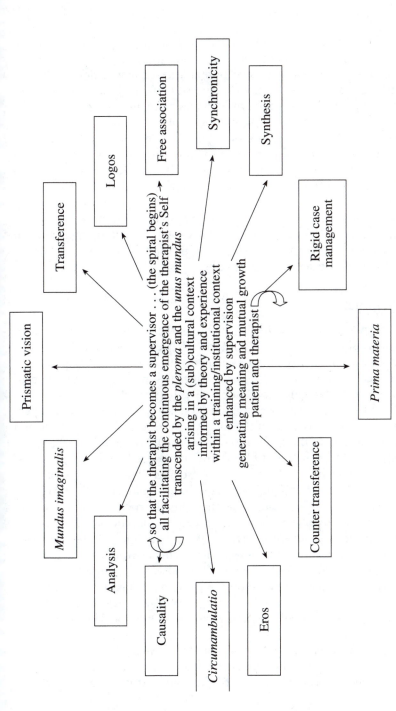

Transference

Logos

Free association

Synchronicity

Prismatic vision

Synthesis

Mundus imaginalis

Rigid case management

Analysis

Prima materia

Causality

Counter transference

Circumambulatio

Eros

so that the therapist becomes a supervisor . . . (the spiral begins)
all facilitating the continuous emergence of the therapist's Self
transcended by the *pleroma* and the *unus mundus*
arising in a (sub)cultural context
informed by theory and experience
within a training/institutional context
enhanced by supervision
generating meaning and mutual growth
patient and therapist

Figure 11.2 A spiral model of interaction between polar opposites in the matrix

differentiation through meaning (logos) and degrees of connectedness (eros) are thought about. Once prismatically broken down, the material is subjected to free association and circumambulation, leading to an exploration of synchronistic processes polarised by causal elements needing both analysis and synthesis extending into insight and action.

This mechanical boxing of the compass is totally arid and only spelt out for the purposes of explication. It is far better to see the matrix as a three-dimensional structure, upon every strand of which energy may alight in various forms, such as a non-verbal gesture, an utterance, dream, fantasy or interpretation. Then, like a spider's web, the whole matrix quivers, sending potential resonances of meaning and growth along each and every strand simultaneously. Each moment then forms a nodal point on the matrix, brought alive in what Pierre Teilhard de Chardin (1955) called the 'no-osphere', where meaning floats around, just waiting.

Summary

I began this chapter by highlighting the awesome complexity of supervision, a craft, which until the relatively recent arrival of formal courses, has been acquired by many of us through a long process of apprenticeship. Some supervisors envisage supervision as a triangular, oedipal configuration consisting of patient, analyst and supervisor. This seems to me an oversimplification, particularly when one superimposes the quaternio of the supervisory relationship in front of and over the top of the quaternio of the analytic relationship, thus creating a cubic structure. Others have introduced the idea of *parallel process,* which I link with Jung's seminal work on *synchronicity.* Drawing further on Jung's work, I introduce the nomenclature of *prismatic vision,* heralding an image through which communication from either or both quaternios can be passed. This is schematised along the continua: meaning–meaninglessness, rigidity–metacomplementarity. The concept of the *mundus imaginalis* forms a cornerstone of both my theory and practice, space between *sensation* and *spirituality.*

I suggest that the supervisory relationship brings into prominence three archetypal predispositions: those of *playing, containing,* and *being initiated,* which need mediating by the supervisor. The relationship also constellates six archetypal images: hero, *anima(us), labyrinth, diabolus, gatekeeper (authority and power),* and the *matrix.* These constellations are not exhaustive; they are embryonic.

I have used Jung's notion of the *matrix* to develop a theoretical construct. It consists of a spiral relationship between the two quaternios, which are incrementally contextualised. Across the spiral run axes of spectra, based on pairs of opposites. Any communication can alight, so to speak, on any strand of the *matrix* and will affect every other strand, generating the possibility of infinite meaning and connectedness, or their opposite. The *matrix* also implies, and has faith in, a developmental (including regressive) and teleological thrust in all the parties concerned.

I have touched on problems specific to training institutions and to work with the most disturbing and disturbed of the sufferers we encounter and try to meet.

On a rough count, spanning the 37 years since I was a volunteer at a University Settlement in London, I have been supervised by something like 30 people from a variety of disciplines and theoretical backgrounds.

I do not doubt that supervision works – in that it can enhance and deepen the work between the miner and the minefield (be that individual, couple, group or institution). At the same time, I am convinced that doubt ('dubium' – to be of two minds) is of the essence of supervision. Whilst a didactic approach is sometimes not only useful but also necessary, the fundamental attitude of a supervisor needs to be based on Jung's notion of *individuation*, insofar as the supervisee, like an adolescent, needs to be held up in two senses: supported, and limited. Thus he explores and develops an unique style within and apart from the 'parental', institutional context.

Robust debate, a sense of humour, appropriate humility, imaginative leaps, and the sharing of relevant theory and experience seem to me to be some of the qualities that foster good-enough supervision.

Running through the chapter is an invitation to play with your convictions, questions and doubts – surely part of the supervisory/professional individuation process, in which 'the two parties . . . get involved in the transformation of the third . . . to be themselves transformed in the process' (Jung, 1945, para. 399).

References

Chardin, P. Teilhard de (1955) *The Phenomenon of Man* (London: Collins).
de Vries, A. (1974) *Dictionary of Symbols and Imagery* (Amsterdam: Elsevier).
Doehrman, M. (1976) 'Parallel Processes in Supervision and Psychotherapy', *Bulletin of the Menninger Clinic,* **40**, 3–104.
Edinger, E. (1985) *Anatomy of the Psyche: Alchemical Symbolism in Psychotherapy* (La Salle: Open Court).

Faricius, J. (1976) *Alchemy: The Medieval Alchemists and their Royal Art* (London: The Aquarian Press).

Foulkes, S. H. (first pub. 1973) 'The Group as Matrix of the Individual's Mental Life', in E. Foulkes (ed.) (1990), *S.H. Foulkes Selected Papers: Psychoanalysis and Group Analysis* (London: Karnac).

Haley, J. (1963) *Strategies of Psychotherapy*, (New York: Grune & Stratton).

Hobson, R. (1985) *Forms of Feeling: The Heart of Psychotherapy* (London: Tavistock).

Humbert, E. (1988) *C. G. Jung: The Fundamentals of Theory and Practice* (Wilmette: Chiron).

Jung, C. G. (1945) 'The Practice of Psychotherapy', *Collected Works Volume 16*.

Jung, C. G. (1953, rev. 1968) 'Psychology and Alchemy', *Collected Works Volume 12*.

Jung, C. G. (1959) 'The Archetypes and the Collective Unconscious', *Collected Works Volume 9i*.

Jung, C. G. (1960)' The Structure and Dynamics of the Psyche', *Collected Works Volume 8*.

Jung, C. G. (1963) *Memories Dreams Reflections* (London: Collins and Routledge & Kegan Paul).

Jung, C. G. (1963, rev. 1970) 'Mysterium Conjiunctionis', *Collected Works Volume 14*.

Jung, C. G. (1971) 'Psychological Types', *Collected Works Volume 6*.

Leach, E. (1976) *Culture and Communication: The Logic by which Symbols are Connected* (Cambridge: Cambridge University Press).

Martineau, J. (1996) *Mazes and Labyrinths in Great Britain* (Presteigne: Wooden Books Ltd).

Mattinson, J. (1975) *The Reflection Process in Supervision* (London: Tavistock).

O'Neill, S. (2000) 'The Unseen Frame in Professional Cultures', *Psychoanalytic Psychotherapy,* **14**(3), 201–22.

Perry, C. (1997) 'Transference and Countertransference', in P. Young-Eisendrath and T. Dawson (eds), *The Cambridge Companion to Jung* (Cambridge: Cambridge University Press).

Redfearn J. (1979) 'The Captive, the Treasure, the Hero and the "Anal Stage of Development" ', *Journal of Analytical Psychology*, **24**(3), 185–206.

Samuels, A., Shorter, B. and Plaut, A, (1986) *A Critical Dictionary of Jungian Analysis* (London: Routledge & Kegan Paul).

Samuels, A. (1989) *The Plural Psyche* (London: Routledge).

Schwartz-Salant, N. (1989) *The Borderline Personality: Vision and Healing* (Illinois: Chiron).

Zinkin, L. (1969) 'Flexibility in Analytic Technique', *Journal of Analytical Psychology,* **14**(2), 119–35.

Zinkin, L. (1995) 'Supervision: The Impossible Profession', in P. Kugler (ed.), *Jungian Perspectives on Clinical Supervision* (Einsiedeln: Daimon).

12

Learning about Supervision

Ann Shearer

Introduction

What does it mean, really, to 'learn about supervision'? Is 'supervision' intrinsic to the practice of psychotherapy, a particular form of self-reflection awakened and fostered by the work? Or is it a specific skill, which may be theoretically learned and purposefully applied? Is there common ground between different theoretical schools, or is there something particular to each in their understanding of the supervisory task? What does the *process* of learning about supervision entail – a profound experience of initiation, a conscious career enhancement, the unfolding of a new relationship to organisational structures? Such questions begin to gather their own momentum and take me back into what I find important about Jungian psychology itself. This seems somehow essential to my own 'learning about supervision'. In this chapter I want to reflect on that in different ways: on the nature of supervision, and how its energy may engage us; on the place of theory, particularly Jungian theory; and finally on how learning may come about.

The nature of supervision

'Supervision is a process during which supervisor and supervisee are learning together – about the patient, about one another, and about themselves' (Jacobs *et al.*, 1995, p. 6). This perception of the mutuality of the process is also my own starting point. Yet the very word 'super-vision' hints at complexities and ambiguities behind that simple statement. A *super-vision* is lofty, superior, one which by its overview has a broader and longer perspective than that of the eye which is narrowly trained: so the supervisor can bring the dispassionate perspective of experience to the work of the usually neophyte supervisee, whose energy must be focused on the training case which leads through the narrow gateway to qualification. But we also know that the broad view must miss the details; how much of the significance of the tiny and exquisite carvings on ancient Cretan gems and seals would have been lost forever had they not fallen under the archeologist Arthur Evans' extremely short-sighted gaze? A supervisor is also an *overseer,* which may conjure images of protective guidance as well as brutal insistence on production-line quotas. But an *oversight* means too that something has been overlooked, something missed.

Supervision implies containment, a keeping of form and to task. Yet something may be leaking here too. The confidentiality of the analytical relationship is axiomatic to the practice of psychotherapy. For many Jungians, this involves more than the proper observance of ethical standards: they will draw on the alchemical imagery of the *vas bene clausum* to convey that the sealed vessel is no less essential to the process of individuation than it was to the seeking of the alchemical gold which was also the Self. Yet supervision, by its nature, must break the seal on the analytic vessel. How are we to understand the effects of this on all three parties involved? Depth psychologists need no telling about the painful energies of alliances and exclusions that ricochet around figures of three; every smoker knows that it is bad luck to take third light. Yet trinities are sacred too across time, place and culture, and three is nothing if not a moving number. The Axiom of Maria Prophetessa, taken by generations of alchemists as a key to the work, may also say something quintessential about the natural laws of psyche as expressed through the processes of analytical psychology: 'The one becomes two, two becomes three and out of the third comes the one as the fourth'.

'Supervision is a process during which supervisor and supervisee are learning together'. Yet that process is both brought to life and sustained by the essential third who must be psychically present even while physically absent if supervision is to happen at all. A sure indication that it *is* significantly happening is given when the patient brings to his next session something either so related to the supervisory discussion just past or so unexpectedly new, that all three parties can at once recognise that a profound psychic communication has taken place. In this often awe-inspiring evidence of the reality of objective psyche, it is no longer plain, to me at least, who is teaching and who learning; it seems to be psyche itself which is the educator. The mutuality of the supervisory process seems then to draw on a depth of unconscious process in which all three parties are equally engaged.

And at the same time, all three are vulnerable to the power-struggles that are mutuality's dark opposite. This seems inevitable once unconscious processes are engaged, an expression of the power-shadow which, as Guggenbuhl-Craig (1989) so valuably reminds us, is an inevitable part of the analytic relationship. Supervision brings its own particular flavour to this dynamic. As has often enough been remarked, supervisors have considerable potential power. The very nature of the supervisory relationship offers them a special opportunity to promulgate their individual versions of analytical psychology and so to shape its future while their supervisees shape their own practices. In the shadow-play that seems an intrinsic part of a training programme (Kimbles, 1999; Greene, 1999), supervisors may be particularly important gatekeepers to the institution. Yet finally, they are powerless too, their justification and their nourishment resting on sequences of events and exchanges that have already happened in their absence. They are both 'there' in the analytic encounter, and not there at all. 'Control' analysts, as they are still often known in German, are not in control.

So to 'learn about supervision' is to enter into an education in paradox. And here, it seems to me, Jung's psychology is uniquely suited, in that it takes the paradoxical nature of psyche as its starting point, and the union rather than the annihilation of psyche's manifold opposites as its goal. Not the least of these paradoxes is Jung's often-emphasised observation that 'in any psychological discussion we are not saying anything about the psyche, but . . . the psyche is always speaking about itself' (Jung, 1956a, para. 483). It is this which makes speaking and writing about psyche so problematical, and the recourse to symbolic language and imagery to describe the finally indescribable so central a part of Jung's psychological method. For him, it is the very image of paradox, the alchemical figure of the spirit Mercurius, which animates psyche just as he did the alchemists' labours. '(H)e is God, daemon, person, thing and the innermost secret in man; psychic as well as somatic. He is himself the source of all opposites, since he is duplex' (Jung, 1954a, para. 481).

Since for Jung '[t]his elusive entity symbolises the unconscious in every particular' (1954a), the practice of supervision can hardly fall outside its influence. So through the often baffling imagery of alchemical Mercurius, we may sense something more of the spirit and energy that animates it as much as any other psychic process. That imagery is further enriched by Jung's equation of Mercurius with Hermes, whose role as messenger to the Greek gods, guide of souls to the underworld, and deity of liminal places makes him a particular patron of depth psychologists. But both are the trickiest of guides. Hermes is keeper of boundaries and hermetic sealings; he is also wanderer, thief and cheat and his cloak of invisibility ensures that just when we think we have him in our sights, he disappears, as slippery as quicksilver itself. The alchemists said of Mercurius that he 'runs around the earth and enjoys equally the company of the good and the wicked'; they called him the 'egg of nature' who is also the 'poison-dripping dragon', highest and lowest, dark and light, the one who is known yet does not exist at all (Jung, 1953 rev. 1968, paras. 278–81; 284; 267). If this is the energy that underlies 'the innermost secret in man', it is no wonder perhaps that it leads us not only into all that is positive and healing in the supervisory process, but all that is shadowy as well. Mercurius will be equally at home in the poison-dripping envies of the elders for the coming generation and their most benign endeavours for its initiation into the analytic art. Supervision begins to sound a great deal less aloof than the word might at first suggest, its view less dispassionate altogether. We remember too that Hermes likes to wander in the market-place, right in the traffic of everyday life. The insights of supervision, it seems, can never be 'above' or separate from this hurly-burly of psychic exchange.

The search for theory

If it is indeed this mercurial figure that informs the vicissitudes and paradoxes of our supervisory, no less than our analytical, practice, then it is no wonder, perhaps, that we should also be in search of theory. As the alchemical law would have it, the volatile must become fixed, and alchemical Mercurius is also his Saturnine opposite, *senex* to his own *puer*. Theory is nothing if not a 'fixative' in this alchemical sense, dealing as it does with states of predictability, in which specific effects may be reliably expected from specific causes; it provides an important objective counterweight to subjective understandings. The image of Saturn devouring his children is often evoked in discussions of the shadow aspects of analytic training. But there are also positive *senex–puer* pairings, as theory provides structure and containment for individual flights of fancy. Theory offers at least the prospect of a universally applicable approach to psyche's questions; so the search for it feeds today's professional demands for accountability, transparency and fair play for supervisees, who should thereby be rendered less vulnerable to the individual quiddities of their elders. Not least, the pursuit of reliable theory bolsters a sense of ourselves as members of that 'professional' community whose welcome has been so long denied to us (see Introduction, pp. 8–13, Chapter 13, pp. 235–7).

This search for alchemical 'fixatives' in certainties of theory and practice has become a powerful collective endeavour; the present emphasis on supervision courses and qualifications, and for career-long supervision of practitioners and supervisors alike, can be seen as one expression of a larger appetite for certainty and reliability. There may be much that is positive in this collective movement. However, an awareness of the built-in limitations of such aspirations seems important too. *Theoria* originally had to do with *beholding, contemplation,* from the stem *thea, to look on.* A *theory* then could be a body of *theors,* sent by the state authorities not to check up on whether rules had been observed, but to *perform a religious rite or duty.* Once, a *therapist* was one who *waited upon, attended,* a great man, and a *psychotherapist* was an *attendant upon soul.* To call someone a *patient* was not to identify with our culture's mainstream model of 'healing', but to recognise him or her as capable of *suffering* or *experiencing* emotions and *passion, enduring* these through time. (In observing this book's convention, I use the term 'patient' with this in mind.) These etymological fragments may serve as reminders of how far we may have come in our modern usages from the respect for objective psyche encoded in the old understandings. Theories will always arise to fix our volatilities. But as Astor has remarked, 'theories tend to reduce experience and observation to conscious knowledge' (Astor, 1995, p. 216). The dangers of denying the essential *unknowingness* in analytical work, both in training programmes and in practice, have also been well explored (Miller, 2000). For analytical psychologists, what is conscious can be only part of the psychic story, just as unconsciousness, changeability and uncertainty must be another. The challenge, it seems to me, is to find an approach to theory that respects this.

A comparison of psychotherapy with other 'healing' professions may take us only so far in that search. The mythical centaur Chiron, the 'wounded healer' whom psychotherapists so often evoke as patron, lived not honoured at court, but in a solitary cave. His service to his wider community, which included the training of many of its heroes, can thus be seen as demanding a certain separation from its struggles and even its values. The alchemists knew this too: their hermetical art was known as an *opus contra naturam,* a work against nature. In its privileging of the individual over the collective, it seems to me, Jungian psychology in its own turn cannot but be counter-cultural. In its attention to and respect for the unconscious, it is engaged with values beyond those of ego – values that reveal themselves through the volatility, uncertainty and unboundedness of symbolic material. So, once more, any 'Jungian theory' must try to contain a tension of opposites: between the aspirations for a solid knowledge on which to base professional practice and the goals and processes of that very practice.

A 'Jungian' theory of supervision?

Jung himself wrote about the limitations of theory often enough. 'The human psyche is a thing of enormous ambiguity', he said.

> I must confess that I have so often been deceived in this matter that in any concrete case I am at pains to avoid all theoretical presuppositions about the structure of the neurosis and about what the patient can and ought to do. As far as possible, I let pure experience decide the therapeutic aims. (Jung, 1931, para. 81)

And more emphatically:

> Theories are to be avoided, except as mere auxiliaries. As soon as a dogma is made of them, it is evident that an inner doubt is being stifled . . . One could as little catch the psyche in a theory as one could catch the world. (Jung, 1945, para. 198)

This said, however, of course Jung had 'theories' about the nature of the human psyche, and these may help us discover a specifically 'Jungian' approach to supervision. Jung's theory of archetypes can encompass without difficulty both the striving for theoretical reliability and the inevitable uncertainty of the processes to which the theory is to be applied. In his definition of the archetypes as 'forms or riverbeds along which the current of psychic life has always flowed' (Jung, 1956b, para. 337), there is an image of exactly that bringing together of fixity ('form') and volatility ('current') which seems intrinsic to the work of psyche. So we can posit that by attempting to discern the archetypal pattern or patterns that underlie and inform the practice of supervision we may get nearer to understanding what a 'Jungian theory of supervision' might be. In this endeavour, we are immediately drawn into the symbolic because, as both theory and experience tell us, there is no way in which we may approach the archetypal realm directly without suffering the madness and ego-loss visited on those ancients who approached the Gods too near. So we turn instead to enduring understandings of human nature, mythic stories and recurrent imagery, in order to experience the reality of archetypal energy and its effects. As Jung said, 'we psychotherapists ought really to be philosophers or philosophic doctors – or rather we already are so' (Jung, 1942, para. 181).

Jung himself offers the imagery of midwifery – the archetypal act of enabling new life to enter the world. As early as 1912, he was calling analysis 'a refined technique of Socratic maieutics' (Jung, 1955, para. 519) and certainly the premise on which Socrates engaged with the souls of others finds a lasting echo in the traditions of Jung's own psychology. 'The many admirable truths they bring to birth have been discovered by themselves from within', Plato has Socrates say in *Theatetus*. 'But the delivery is heaven's work and mine' (quoted in Edinger, 1999, p. 55). In this relationship, the one coming-to-birth is far from passive or unformed but, on the contrary, full of hidden knowledge that can be realised through dialectical interaction. Here again, there is a striking consistency with Jung's quite central understanding of the human being as a powerhouse of archetypal potential with which consciousness can engage through the symbolic to activate and realise the energies of the Self.

A maieutic understanding of the analytic relationship thus carries quite some implications for the ways in which the analyst views both task and patient. The imagery should not, perhaps, carry us too far. As Beebe has cautioned, very few people come into analysis in the expectation of a 'whole new identity' being born rather than stress relieved or understanding gained; usually 'new birth' does not happen. But as he also points out, the one time when the birth of a new identity *is* expected is in supervision – 'because [the supervisee] is supposed to be turned into a psychotherapist or made into a more competent one' (Beebe, 1999, p. 484). So we can perhaps validly draw from the archetypal interactions of the midwife and the one coming-to-birth some pointers towards a 'Jungian theory of supervision'. These could include, for instance, a recognition that supervision is a dialogue between supervisor and supervisee, in which the skill of the first is to bring to consciousness that which the second already unconsciously 'knows'; a respect for the 'natural' timing of the supervisee, rather than an 'induced' understanding that has to do with external timetables or the midwife's workload; a recognition of internal/psychological or external/organisational obstacles to the natural birth rhythm which it is the supervisor's skill to detect, remove or mitigate, without harming the process itself; even the responsibility of deciding when the 'new identity' will be too damaged – or damaging to the life of the mother – to survive.

From midwife to mentor: Corbett offers a developmental unfolding in the imagery underlying supervision, from a premise that for many 'Jungians' (myself included) must remain a bedrock of both theory and practice: 'that we discern the workings of the Self and its archetypal constituents' (Corbett, 1995, p. 60). For him, it is the 'mentor archetype' which is at work in the supervisory process, and he evokes it through the image of the goddess Athene, who appears in *The Odyssey* under the guise of the nobleman Mentor when she guides and advises young Telemachus in his search for his father Odysseus. 'The search for the qualities of father among the young is facilitated by an older figure, father-like but not exactly father, who is able to embody wisdom, specifically Athena-like qualities' (Corbett, 1995, p. 62).

In his elaborations of the qualities of 'mentor', Corbett constructs a benign model for the relationship between supervisor and supervisee. Yet it is the nature of the archetypes' bipolar energy to take us beyond what we can consciously know or deliberately 'use'; as Jung emphasises, archetypal images are not allegories of known states or things (Jung, 1954b, para. 6n):

> The discriminating intellect naturally keeps on trying to establish [the archetypes'] singleness of meaning and thus misses the essential point: for what we can above all establish as the one thing consistent with their nature is their manifold meaning, their almost limitless wealth of reference, which makes any unilateral formulation impossible. (Jung, 1954b, para. 80)

So if we follow Corbett's chosen imagery, we may be led into some unexpected places. Observe the tactics of Athene, this most crafty of goddesses, when she first meets Telemachus (confusingly, as the nobleman Mentes, rather than as Mentor). The first thing she does is to make the lad feel good about himself and his heritage. 'But come, please', she says,' tell me about yourself now, point by point. You're truly Odysseus' son? You've sprung up so! Uncanny resemblance . . . the head, and the fine eyes – I see him now.' Then, having gained his trust, the goddess wastes no time at all in giving Telemachus a detailed plan of action. Finally, she reiterates her encouragement, her emphasis that he is now old enough to fend for himself: 'And you, my friend – how tall and handsome I see you now – be brave . . . so men will come and sing your praises down the years' (Homer, 1996, 1.238–42, 1.346–8):

> Off and away Athena the bright-eyed goddess flew
> Like a bird in soaring flight
> But left his spirit filled with nerve and courage,
> Charged with his father's memory more than ever now.
> He felt his senses quicken, overwhelmed with wonder –
> This was a god, he knew it well and made at once
> For the suitors, like a god himself.
>
> (Homer, 1996, 1.366–73)

In this exchange we might see an instilling of confidence, enabling focus on claiming a rightful place and a connection with the Self, all of which could well be part of the supervisory role. But Athene as Mentor has other lessons to teach as well. It was in this guise, for instance, that she helped Odysseus to set up the wooden horse which was so decisive in the fall of Troy and has left Western culture with an abiding image of gain through deceit and the false gift. It is in this guise, too, that the wrathful goddess goads Odysseus on to the blood-soaked slaughter of the suitors in reclamation of his kingdom. Athene the Many-Skilled, the Healer, is also the Contriver, the Deceitful, Driver of Armies, Marshaller of the Host, Goddess of Vengeance Deserved. Of the three virgin goddesses of the Greek pantheon, she alone is engaged in affairs of state; while Artemis roams the high mountains and Hestia privately tends the hearth, Athene, as her best-known images testify, is protector of cities, of the established order. Yet she is also a market-place deity, sometimes worshipped together with Hermes, and her legendary craft and guile in pursuing her own goals is one he would recognise (Shearer, 1998 p. 23–30).

Already then, the supervisor who turns to Athene's altar has also been led into ways of deceit, falsehood and ruthlessness in pursuit of goals and protection of favourites, towards a loyalty to the institution which is not entirely straightforward. And of course any or all of these qualities may manifest in supervisors too. But in any such exploration of symbolic idea and imagery, it seems inevitable that ego's carefully-constructed maps will finally give out, leaving us on the edge of the world known to consciousness. Another bedrock of Jung's 'theory' seems to be just this: we cannot, by our nature, know that nature, because we cannot stand outside psyche. If in any psychological discussion 'psyche is always speaking about itself' (Jung, 1956a, para. 483) then this, as Whan has pointed out (1999, p. 313), must mean that any theorising has to be 'just another expression of psyche'. Thus, there can be no such thing as 'objective' theory. 'Every psychology . . . has the character of a subjective confession . . . Even when I deal with empirical data, I am necessarily speaking about myself' (Jung, 1933a, para. 774) (see Chapter 7, p. 120).

This perception has important implications for a 'Jungian' approach to theory – whether of supervision, or of anything else. It suggests that in some sense there must always be a multiplicity of 'theories', each its own 'subjective confession', thus each with its own validities and invalidities, each both true and partial. It is this which makes any search for Jungian theory so slippery. Yet I suspect the hand of Mercurius here, drawing the argument away from theoretical 'fixity', casting his cloak over certainty and clarity, ensuring that the fixed is once more volatilised. For of course Jung offers a quite distinctive theory. But he also insists that it is the individual therapist's own philosophy which will not only guide his life but shape his therapeutic approach (Jung, 1942, para. 180) (see Chapter 1). So, for instance, my reading of Jung's theory of archetypes leads me to posit that each human being is born not as *tabula rasa*, but as already unconsciously 'knowing' all there is to know. This will inevitably colour my understanding of the nature of analysis and of supervision too; I will tend towards the maieutic fantasy, seeing my role as helping to lead out (*e-ducare*), bring to consciousness, what is already unconsciously formed.

Others, of course, see things differently. And if each theory, being in part at least the product of its own 'subjective confession', is both in and of psyche, we are led towards something radically egalitarian which will inform discussions of learning, or teaching, about supervision. Indeed, in this perspective, the one cannot be discussed without the other, for the teacher is also student and the student is also teacher. This is not to deny the importance of Jung's theoretical understandings, nor is it to underestimate the value of theoretical knowledge, or especially of experience. But it does perhaps give these a particular place in the mutual work of psyche which is the supervision session: they are not all that matters there.

The essential multiplicity of 'Jungian theory' offers a challenge to institutions as well as individuals, as a recent exchange in the *New York Journal of Jungian Theory and Practice* helped to highlight. In his contribution to a symposium on 'Issues in Supervision', Ventimiglia (2000, pp. 23–30) evoked the image of the circumcised heart as symbol of the grounding of both analysis and supervision in the religious function of the psyche, and of what he perceived as the 'sacred responsibility' of training. He amplified this image to speak of the issues of power, of longing to be 'chosen', of initiation, and of moving beyond ego concerns, that he sees as part of becoming an analyst. In his reminder that it is an anathema to eat the sacrifice intended for the Lord, he raised questions not only about issues of transference between supervisor and supervisee, but more generally about where the duty of the supervisor lies between the needs of the institution and those of individuals. For me, then, this was a thought-provoking, even moving, attempt to engage openly with painful realities in the shadow of supervision, and to offer an image and energy of containment and purification. Ventimiglia's *Journal* respondents, however, found in it, among other things, a 'romanticised disregard for organisational structure and accountability', an advocacy of 'authoritarian and non-responsive training programs', the creation of an atmosphere of 'power differential' and a fealty to the Self that is 'very hard to conceptualise' (Ekstrom, 2000, pp. 31–2; Cwik, 2000, p. 33). So the multiplicity of 'Jungian theory' can reveal an often-painful polarity between the essential unknownness of the psychic realm and the demands of the organisation for a coherent and generally-accepted theoretical underpinning to its training practices. The tension between the psychological and the organisational seems intrinsic to any 'Jungian' training, and brings another dimension to the search for a 'Jungian theory of supervision' as well.

This tension can also be understood as lying between the individual and the collective, and in the end any such theory will also be informed, and its validity continually tested, by the experience of individual supervisory relationships. What Jung says about the nature of the analytic relationship seems as applicable to the supervisory one:

> By no device can the treatment be anything but the product of mutual influence, in which the whole being of the doctor as well as that of the patient plays its part. In the treatment there is an encounter between two irrational factors, that is to say, between two persons who are not fixed and determinable qualities but who bring with them, besides their more or less clearly

defined fields of consciousness, an indefinitely extended sphere of non-consciousness. Hence the personalities of doctor and patient are often more important for the outcome of the treatment than what the doctors says and thinks. (Jung, 1933b, para. 163)

Supervision brings an extra dimension to this encounter. As the alchemists would have it, 'the two becomes three': it seems inescapable that the 'imponderable factors which bring about a mutual transformation' (Jung, 1933b, para. 164) must also be at work in and between all three parties to the supervisory relationship. For me, that offers an approach to both a specifically 'Jungian' theory and a 'Jungian' practice of supervision.

Learning about supervision

People who set out more or less formally to learn what it is to be a supervisor will already have a considerable experience of this art. First and foremost, they will have learned at least some of its conventions, expectations and limitations from having been supervised; importantly, they will know from the receiving end what supervision *feels* like. They may also have had quite some experience of 'doing supervision', starting with case discussions under the tutelage of a senior analyst during their training, and subsequently in discussions with peers. All this may have happened – as it did for me – before undertaking any 'formal' work as a supervisor at all. So people will most likely bring to any new learning table their own prejudgements of what constitutes supervision, and some pretty heartfelt ideas of what is 'helpful' and what is not, what is enjoyable and what is horrible, and which experience seems, in the end, to have taught them most. We will all, in short, come with the makings of a personal 'theory' of supervision, for if 'theory is experience of a kind' (Fordham, 1995, para. 154), then experience also makes for theory.

For this reason, I suspect, the form of any programme may be as important as its content: the learning may come as much from opportunities to exchange 'theories' built on experience as from informational and didactic input. Lectures on a variety of theoretical approaches will offer intellectual frameworks and containers for experience. But the very nature of analytical psychology – the inextricability of theory and practice, object and subject – demands something else as well; unless we can find a fit between what Jung called our own 'personal equation' and the theoretical material, it will remain of only intellectual interest and so limited applicability. The Society of Analytical Psychology addressed this in its *Thinking About Supervision* events in the late 1990s, by offering a balance in each session of lectures and small group discussions of issues that had arisen for participants in their practices, whether as supervisor or supervisee, against which they could also discuss the theoretical input.

This interweaving of theory and experience, so central to the construction of 'Jungian theory', may offer a particular contribution to one of the current debates about supervision, and so teaching and learning about it: what is the breadth of theoretical approach that supervisors should properly be expected to have? In my own main supervision, I learned about developmental, developmental/classical and psychiatric/eclectic approaches. But I learned about them from three different people, for each of whom this truly seemed a 'subjective confession' rather than a dutiful covering of the theoretical ground. For many other practitioners, a synthesis of many different approaches is equally true to themselves. What seems important is that each should express their particular intellectual, experiential and psychological reality. As Jung said: 'Every therapist not only has his own method – he himself is that method' (Jung, 1945, para. 198).

So a 'Jungian approach' to learning about supervision will equally be one that enables each participant to bring their own 'method' to the continuing work of constructing theory and also testing its validity against experience. Kalsched writes warmly of the case seminar as his favourite place of education in 'the art and science of psychotherapy': this for him really is where to learn about the workings of the unconscious through the varied perceptions of group members, about transference by observing and identifying with that of colleagues, and about doing supervision through the opportunity to comment on colleagues' work in the company of others doing the same thing. Importantly too, group-participants have an experience of 'a psychological culture instead of a political one' – provided that the leader encourages an atmosphere of exploration, hunch, intuition and play, in a recognition that an honouring of the unconscious means there can be no 'right' or 'wrong' interpretations. If it works, as Kalsched says, 'the group has a better chance of understanding the patient's unconscious communication than any individual in it, including the supervisor'. Of course there are darker sides to the group, as Kalsched also explores, identifying among them a 'shadow' side of supervision itself: the danger of the supervisor's inflation, the temptation to infallibility

(Kalsched, 1995, pp. 110–11). But shadows can bring their own education, and I share Kalsched's enthusiasm. Some of my own most enlivening, enthusing, playful, effective and also profound experiences of supervision have been in case seminars and discussions.

The feeling-emotional quality of such experiences suggests that the door has been opened to let in the charge of psychic, that is archetypal, energies. So an understanding of how that may happen seems important to both teaching and learning about supervision – not least because, as Kalsched says, the group thus enlivened has a better chance of understanding than any individual in it. Some of the answer may, of course, concern the dynamics of case seminar groups. But some of it may also relate to an approach to psyche, which need not be unique to groups at all. Kalsched evokes an atmosphere in which there is freedom to engage freely with psychic material, free from judgements about right and wrong or considerations of politics – in alchemical terms, perhaps, to bring volatility into places which have become fixed. This seems to be the sort of environment which favours an opening to the unconscious, and to the archetypal energies which may be at work.

The link to these energies, for Jung, is 'the bridge of emotion' (Jung, 1961, para. 589). So does the supervisor have a particular responsibility to enable the building of that bridge, even to lead by example? Elsewhere, Kalsched (1999) writes vividly about his own contribution to a loss of the capacity to engage with psyche, to work symbolically; this started to return when he recognised that although his technical and theoretical approach has been both elegant and sound, he had become internally and interpersonally disconnected, and spoke of this. This happened in a case seminar group. But are there lessons about the need for an awareness of the 'bridge of emotion' thrown between the consciousness and the archetypal in any place where people are 'learning about supervision'? In his evocation of the supervisor as midwife to the psychological identity of the supervisee, Beebe (1999) emphasises just how emotionally charged the supervisory relationship must be. The supervisee, he suggests, disavows this: he was amazed at the discrepancy between his own unowned transferences towards his supervisors and the intensity of his now-conscious transference feelings towards his supervisees. When he recalled the people he had supervised over nearly thirty years, he says, he immediately touched feelings in himself that were by turn erotic, angry and hate-filled, or highly anxious; he realised the extent to which aggression, dependency and competition give this field its 'weight'. 'It seems to me that we really need to begin to let the cat out of the bag – acknowledge that there is something else going on in analytic supervision, and perhaps all supervision, than simply a very controlled professional relationship' (Beebe, 1999, p. 483).

An exploration of that 'something else going on' seems a quite crucial aspect of learning about supervision. The people who will know most about the proverbial cat and best understand its colour, contours and character are of course the experienced supervisors. Their sharing of their personal experiences of 'doing supervision' seems invaluable to the subtle understanding of theory in practice. It can help beginning supervisors, for instance, to learn to discriminate more finely between interactions with their supervisees that have to do with 'parallel process' and those which are going on between the two people who are actually in the room. But more generally, this sharing of the experience of 'doing supervision' seems essential to the constellation and bringing to consciousness of the archetypal patterns that underlie the supervisory relationship and the psychic energy that fuels it.

Summary

Once more we return to the 'personal confession'. In this chapter I have tried to explore something of the nature of supervision, and of Jungian psychological theory and theorising, and to begin to suggest how these might begin to lead towards a distinctive 'Jungian theory of supervision'. At each stage, I have found myself returning to Jung's insistence that there can be no theory that stands 'outside psyche', thus outside the individuals involved. This leads to an understanding of theory as a continuing interaction between psychic energy, experience and consciousness, and of 'learning about supervision' as becoming more aware of how these are at work in the personal and archetypal relationship between supervisor, supervisee and patient. At the same time, there must be a shared and radical 'unknowing', which goes beyond the hierarchy of conscious roles. In the end, 'learning about supervision', as much as any other endeavour of analytical psychology, is a work of psyche itself.

References

Astor, J. (1995) 'Supervision, Training and the Institution as an Internal Pressure', in P. Kugler (ed.), *Jungian Perspectives on Clinical Supervision* (Einseideln: Daimon).

Beebe, J. (1999) 'Some Special Features of the Transference in Consultation and Supervision', in M. A. Mattoon (ed.), *Florence 98: Proceedings of the Fourteenth International Congress for Analytical Psychology* (Einseideln: Daimon).

Corbett, L. (1995) 'Supervision and the Mentor Archetype', in P. Kugler (ed.), *Jungian Perspectives on Clinical Supervision* (Einsiedeln: Daimon).

Cwik, A. (2000) 'Response to William Ventimiglia', *Journal of Jungian Theory and Practice*, **2**, 33 (New York: C. G. Jung Institute).

Edinger, E. (1999) *The Psyche in Antiquity: Book One: Early Greek Philosophy*, (Toronto: Inner City Books).

Ekstrom, S. (2000) 'Response to William Ventimiglia', *Journal of Jungian Theory and Practice*, **2**, 31–2.

Fordham, M. (1995) 'Suggestions towards a Theory of Supervision', in P. Kugler (ed.) *Jungian Perspectives* on *Clinical Supervision* (Einsiedeln: Daimon).

Greene, T. (1999) 'The Group Shadow in Jungian Training', in M. A. Mattoon (ed.), *Florence 98: Proceedings of the Fourteenth International Congress for Analytical Psychology* (Einsiedeln: Daimon).

Guggenbuhl-Craig, A. (1989) *Power in the Helping Professions* (Dallas, TX: Spring Publications).

Homer (1996) *The Odyssey*, trans. by R. Fagles (New York: Viking Penguin).

Jacobs, D., David, P. and Meyer, D. (1995) *The Supervisory Encounter* (New Haven: Yale University Press).

Jung, C. G. (1931) 'The Aims of Psychotherapy'. *Collected Works Volume 16.*

Jung, C. G. (1933a) 'Freud and Jung: Contrasts', *Collected Works Volume 4.*

Jung, C. G. (1933b) 'Problems of Modern Psychotherapy', *Collected Works Volume 16.*

Jung, C. G. (1942) 'Psychotherapy and a Philosophy of Life', *Collected Works Volume 16.*

Jung, C. G. (1945) 'Medicine and Psychotherapy', *Collected Works Volume 16.*

Jung, C. G. (1953) 'The Spirit Mercurius', *Collected Works Volume 13.*

Jung, C. G. (1954a) 'The Philosophical Tree', *Collected Works Volume 13.*

Jung, C. G. (1954b) 'Archetypes of the Collective Unconscious', *Collected Works Volume 9i.*

Jung, C. G. (1955) 'The Theory of Psychoanalysis', *Collected Works Volume 4.*

Jung, C. G. (1956a) 'On the Psychology of the Trickster-Figure', *Collected Works Volume 9i.*

Jung, C. G. (1956b) 'Symbols of Transformation,' *Collected Works Volume 5.*

Jung, C. G. (1961) 'Symbols and the Interpretation of Dreams', *Collected Works Volume 18.*

Kalsched, D. (1995) 'Ecstasies and Agonies of Case Seminar Supervision', in P. Kugler (ed.) *Jungian Perspectives on Clinical Supervision* (Einsiedeln: Daimon).

Kalsched, D. (1999) 'Getting the Analytic Baby Back in the Bathwater', in M.

A. Mattoon (ed.), *Florence 98: Proceedings of the Fourteenth International Congress for Analytical Psychology* (Einseideln: Daimon).

Kimbles, S. (1999) 'Panacea and Poison', in M. A. Mattoon (ed.), *Florence 98: Proceedings of the Fourteenth International Congress for Analytical Psychology* (Einseideln: Daimon).

Miller, J. (2000) 'Training: Fears of Destruction and Creativity. Reflections on the Process of Becoming an Analyst', *Harvest: Journal for Jungian Studies*, **46**(2) (London: C. G. Jung Analytical Psychology Club).

Shearer, A. (1998), *Athene: Image and Energy* (London: Penguin Arkana).

Ventimiglia, W. (2000) 'Supervision and the Circumcised Heart', *Journal of Jungian Theory and Practice*, **2** 23–30.

Whan, M. (1999) 'Registering Psychotherapy as an Institutional Neurosis: or Compounding the Estrangement between Soul and World', *European Journal of Psychotherapy, Counselling and Health*, **2**, December, 309–23. (London: Taylor & Francis).

13

From Practice to Theory: Evolving a Theory of Supervision

Richard Mizen, Jan Wiener and Jenny Duckham

The indivisibility of supervision and analysis

Supervision is such an established part of analytic work that the question, 'What is it for?' would be considered rather ridiculous if it were ever asked. The need for supervision is intuitively understood. Supervision is a manifestation of an internal process that is inseparable from the work of analysis and cannot be considered as an essentially different activity, but only as part of it. One cannot think about analysis without supervision because, to borrow Winnicott's idea, one can no more think about analysis without supervision than one can think about a baby without a mother. In both cases, the former could not exist without the latter. The link between analysis and supervision seems to be absolute, whether supervision is considered as a meeting between two people or as an internal dialogue (Knight, Chapter 2).

It is less easy to argue the contention that supervision is an essentially separate activity from analysis. Indeed it has not always been considered to be separate (see Introduction, pp. 4–8). Wharton (Chapter 5) and Martin (Chapter 8) have both described the way in which supervision as a separate activity emerged from the need felt by the early analytic pioneers to discuss their experiences with each other. In part this was because of the unique demands made upon analysts to combine the professional and personal. In the early days of psychoanalysis, it was common practice to combine personal analysis with supervision. The contradictions that this may have engendered in the neophyte analyst's analysis may explain why Freud distinguished 'didactic analysis' – the analysis to be undertaken by novice analysts – from analysis as a treatment for 'patients'. Implicit in this distinction is the assumption that there is a need for an educational component that is separate from personal analysis, even if these activities are combined. In the period up until the 1920s the convention had arisen, exemplified by the practice of the Hungarian Psychoanalytic Society, that a trainee's analyst was also his or her supervisor. In Vienna and Berlin however, a different convention developed whereby different analysts took on the respective roles of analyst and supervisor. Formal consideration of the matter at the Four Countries Conferences in 1935 and 1937 (Kovacs, 1936; Bibring, 1937), reinforced the Viennese/Berlin position, but the Hungarian arrangement persists today, particularly amongst those following in Ferenczi's footsteps and in small societies where the limited number of available training analysts makes expediency a more important priority than principle.

The tradition in analytical psychology has been more diverse, but until the 1960s, the practice of combining analysis and supervision was common for reasons of *both* principle and expediency. Some 'classical' Jungian trainees were required to have two or more analysts as a way of deterring the development of infantile transferences. Jung considered these transferences undesirable in much the same way that Freud had originally considered the development of the patient's transference to the analyst a hindrance to analytic work. In both these situations, analysis emphasised the patient's 'objective' material – dreams and other imaginative activity as the main source of knowledge and insight – without its rather more subjective, personal role, that has higher value today. The Society of Analytical Psychology considered the matter during the 1960s (Fordham, 1995) and, influenced by psychoanalytic colleagues, gave much more weight to the complexities of transference and countertransference. In consequence, the practice of separating analysis and supervision, already widespread, was systematically adopted. Since that time other societies within the Jungian tradition have followed suit.

The choice made by analytical societies to separate analysis and supervision institutionalised matters in a way which has tended to foreclose on some of the thorny issues that their relationship raises. These issues concern the establishment of the main focus for supervisors and how this differs from analysts' area of responsibility. There are some things that supervisors are 'allowed to say' without stepping outside their remit and other things that are in danger of trespassing into analysis. This is equally relevant for analysts, although presumably the analyst will be less constrained than the supervisor. A common position taken by supervisors is to reflect on the patient's emotional impact upon the supervisee, but not on the supervisee's infantile transference to the supervising analyst. An analyst may choose not to comment upon material concerning a trainee's patient, except perhaps as a projection of the trainee analyst.

Thinking about countertransference

What may be lost in supervision is a place to consider the kind of material Freud seems to have had in mind when he developed his original concept of countertransference. Freud thought of counter-transference as

> a result of the patient's influence on [the physician's] *unconscious* feelings. [authors' italics] (Freud, 1910, p. 144)

At the time Freud thought of countertransference in terms of the analyst's unanalysed neurotic transference to the patient and therefore a potential impediment to the analytic work that required analysis. It was literally 'a counter-transference'. Consistent with his view that both analyst and patient possess an objective psyche as well as a personal unconscious, Jung did not consider the unconscious elements in either patient or analyst to be necessarily neurotic. Jung (1946, p. 176) believed that in any thorough analysis, both patient and analyst are equally engaged in the processs. This has been subsequently modified by Fordham's remark that it is an asymmetrical arrangement (Fordham, 1993). Jung was clear, however, that the analyst needed a *confidante* to avoid the risk of patient and analyst becoming unconsciously over-identified with each other. He stated that analysts

> should have a father confessor or a mother confessor . . . If the analyst does not keep in touch with his unconscious objectively, there is no guarantee whatever that the patient will not fall into the unconscious of the analyst . . . Then the condition of participation happens, or more strictly speaking a condition of personal contamination through mutual unconsciousness. (Jung, 1968, pp. 157–8)

There is little reason to think that present-day analysts are any more free of developing such transferences, even allowing for developments in analytic understanding and the observation that contemporary analyses are longer and more thorough than those conducted in 1910. From this perspective, the availability of the supervisee's unconscious material might be considered essential for the work of the supervisor. Over the last half century, however, most notably under the influence of the British neo-Kleinians, the concept of countertransference has been broadened to include the totality of the analyst's responses to the patient, in a way, that has tended to obscure the implications of countertransference according to Freud's and Jung's original definitions. This is a position that the separation of supervision and analysis has tended to institutionalise, and raises the question of what a supervisee is bringing to the analysis. In this way it may be problematical as to whether the 'self' that the supervisee is bringing to supervision is a well-attuned, sensitive instrument with which the supervisee is listening to the patient, or whether the patient is generating so much 'feedback' in the supervisee that the patient is excluded or cannot be heard. Of course this is (hopefully) a caricature and the neurosis of the supervisee does not necessarily (but certainly may) disable, rather than facilitate understanding of the patient. The difficulty that this situation can raise for supervisors, especially as to how supervisees' communications are thought about and taken up by supervisors, is an ongoing concern. This is one of the most common themes discussed in this volume.

The operation of the split transference

There is no consensus about how to manage a split transference in supervision. A variety of approaches have been proposed including direct exploration and elucidation of supervisee's personal difficulties, albeit with the analytic focus on the work with the patient (Martin, Chapter 8) or indirectly through the work with the patient (Astor, Chapter 3). Others believe it should be carefully excluded (Gee, Chapter 9). It can become complicated if analysts are approached for supervision and the request subsequently turns out to be an indirect wish for personal analysis. Sometimes, the supervision explicitly changes into analysis despite the considerable problems that are frequently disregarded. The process of supervision can covertly allow auxiliary analysis (Perry, Chapter 11). More commonly, analysts with 'trainees' as patients will be familiar with defensive attempts to turn analytic sessions into supervision sessions.

Supervisors' definitions of countertransference, whether in its broad or its narrow form, are likely to be of crucial importance in determining their treatment of their supervisees' material. Fordham's (1996a) view, for example, is that countertransference and projective identification are identical concepts and he argues against the expanded concept of countertransference on the grounds that it has a

> tendency to cover all the affective responses by the analyst which are not necessarily transferred and so not necessarily an illusion (Fordham, 1996a, p. 28)

This narrower definition of countertransference explicitly separates the material produced by the patient in the analyst from that which is personal to the analyst, but evoked in the analytic relationship. This separation may be less important in clinical practice and supervisees' responses to their patients may be addressed as if it is their patients' material that is evocative, even if it has a dimension that is personal to the supervisee. This retains the possibility of supervisors addressing them separately if appropriate.

In supervision, the broader concept of countertransference has tended to cast the supervisee's emotional states in a different light from that envisaged by Fordham, so that all affects induced can end up being referred back to the patient without distinction. Other analysts have found distinctions between these definitions false, maintaining that the processes of analysis and supervision are actually the same. It is only the treatment of the material that is different. It has a different focus. From this perspective, the transference and countertransference are not used to elucidate the internal world of the supervisee but rather to elucidate the quality of the supervisee's experience of the patient that, by extension, then illuminates the patient's own experience.

Fordham (1995) describes how he went to the psychoanalyst Donald Meltzer for what Meltzer called 'supervision' of Fordham's internal world. Fordham used the couch and observed that he was unable to make a distinction between the supervision he received and his analysis. Elsewhere, Redfearn (2000) thinks there are advantages to combining analysis and supervision, with the caveat that this is only suitable for older and more experienced analysts. Presumably, this combination would only become possible in certain circumstances, when the 'self' is capable of tolerating primitive or archetypal experiences without disintegration (see Chapter 9, p. 155).

In practice, combining supervision and analysis seems to have been thought about more in terms of intrusive elements in analysis on the one hand, and as a potential for doctrinaire or 'incestuous' collusions between analyst and supervisee/patient on the other. This was a particular problem when it led to the establishment of groupings around particular analysts and their ideas. Although separating analysis and supervision is unlikely entirely to prevent this it does go some way to opening matters up.

Equally important may be the management of regression that is likely in both analysis and supervision. In analysis, the oedipal configuration is likely to explicitly facilitate regression to infantile levels of functioning (see Chapter 8, p. 136). In supervision, however, regression may happen implicitly, depending in part on the way the supervisee's material is treated. Urban (Chapter 4, pp. 69–73) limits herself to 'translating' rather than 'interpreting', although it is difficult to prevent unconscious regression if the discussion between supervisee and supervisor produces an object (the patient) which easily lends itself to the projection of infantile material. Regression in analysis and in supervision can facilitate development or potentially take a malignant form. In supervision, the malign is more likely to be obscured by projection into the patient, and there is only the likelihood (but not the certainty) of the supervisee's greater individuation to limit this.

In summary, it is our view that supervision is not identical to analysis but rather the expression of a particular aspect of analytic work that may be considered separately from analysis itself. Both analysis and supervision can be considered interpersonally or intrapsychically, although in the case of supervision this is complicated by the inevitable triangulation and oedipal constellations that take place. At an interpersonal level, supervision may be a dialogue between two people, supervisor and supervisee, paralleled by intrapsychic dialogues between both parties. Over time, this external dialogue may become less important, may become intermittent or cease. Assuming satisfactory progress in the supervisee's development, an internal dialogue will flourish to the point where an adequate 'internal supervisor' becomes established (Casement, 1985). A qualified analyst is likely to need supervision on an occasional basis and this may more usefully be distinguished as *consultation* (Knight, Chapter 2) and talked about in terms of a process of *modelling*. This is not a simple matter, however, involving as it does projective and identificatory processes that may also be used in defensive ways rather than in the service of personal and professional development. Narcissistic processes and defences, such as adhesive identification, for example, may distort personal and professional development (Britton, 1998).

The psychological difficulty of separating analysis and supervision may be one reason for the widespread view that a qualification to analyse also equips practitioners to supervise. Implicit is the notion that the skills required of the supervisor are identical to those of the analyst and these skills may be acquired as if by osmosis. This is a theme developed implicitly and explicitly by several authors in the book. Only recently has the assumption that good analysts are also likely to possess relevant supervisory and didactic skills to make them into good supervisors begun to be questioned (Martin, Chapter 8 and; Astor, Chapter 3).

A mental space in which to reflect

Developments in both psychoanalysis and analytical psychology led practitioners to conceptualise the need for a mental space for reflection in a systematic, psychological fashion. However, even before it was ever called 'supervision', the need for this sort of reflection in the presence of another arose out of the nature of the relationship between the sufferer and his therapist – 'one who serves' (Shearer, Chapter 12). Jung's (1952, para. 219) metaphor of the *vas bene clausum*, the well-sealed vessel, introduces the idea of an analytic frame or container which creates a space inside it in which something vital – a relationship between two selves, patient and analyst – can evolve. It has, however, been the analytic relationship that has been the main object of attention (Gordon, 1993; Ogden, 1994), leaving the supervisory process as a mere adjunct. For the most part it is treated as axiomatic that a reflective space is essential to both. The only topic for consideration or dispute is the question of whether this should be a matter limited to internal reflection, should take place in a group, with a mentor, with peers or in some combination of these. Regardless of the form that supervision takes, its task remains the same: to create a space in which a human interaction can be considered in the context of affects often intensely felt by patient and analyst alike, whether syntonic or dystonic, symmetrical or asymmetrical, of an intensely personal kind and simultaneously requiring a response that is strictly disciplined and professional. The intensity of the personal affects underlines the need for the strict professionalism.

The correspondence between Jung and Freud about Jung's relationship with Sabina Spielrein (Kerr, 1994; see Chapters 8 and 7) bears testament to the delicate balance between the personal and the professional, and illustrates how easy it is to fail. Perry (Chapter 11) quotes from the correspondence between Freud and Ferenczi, which touches on similar issues. Other historical examples may be found with ease (Gabbard and Lester, 1995), but most analysts will be aware that from time to time colleagues are revealed to be breaking critical professional boundaries, entering into inappropriate social contact or even sexual relationships with their patients (see Chapter 10). The complicated projections, introjections, identifications and projective identifications that form the backdrop to such boundary-breaking are highlighted in Freud's careful attention to the division between the personal and professional in his letters to Jung (McGuire, 1974). Jung's pained, sometimes deceitful, and what may now be considered self-deceiving responses, to Freud testify to the strength of the emotional forces at work.

The need for *a* space to think about feeling is essential but also fraught with inherent difficulty, not least because of the tendency to idealise either thinking on the one hand or feeling on the other. The early correspondence between analysts can be seen as the beginning of formal training to become an analyst, moving away from its vocational aspects. Academic work and supervision on the one hand became more separate from personal analysis. By the 1920s, formal programmes of training had been set up and supervision, as an institution, was here to stay (Wharton, Chapter 5).

Thinking about feeling

In order to consider carefully the specific role of supervision, it is necessary first to pose the question, 'What tasks do analysis and the analyst perform?'. In the light of our argument so far concerning the strong connections between analysis and supervision, the answer to such a question is likely to have considerable influence on the ways in which supervision is thought about and practised, both by supervisor and supervisee. Patients frequently raise the question with their analysts, and analysts with other analysts, of whether or not analysis is a 'real' relationship. Is there some inherently special quality to the analyst–patient relationship? (Covington, 2002; Schaverien, Chapter 10). One approach might be to view analysis as a purely technical enterprise with phenomena such as transference and countertransference as the consequence of the analytic work and the establishment of the analytic frame. Certainly Freud claimed transference as uniquely engendered by the psychoanalytic method. An alternative position would be to see this view as basically defensive and transference rather as the stuff of everyday life. Analysis merely constellates and frames transference dynamics in a way that facilitates their systematic examination. From this vertex, the analytic frame merely amplifies matters in the way that, to borrow Baynes' image, a dye placed on a slide might amplify the internal structure of a histological specimen (Baynes, 1947). From this point of view analysis is an ordinary matter, instinctually or archetypally driven and an aspect of an epistemophilic drive (Britton, 1998). It is reflecting upon it that is extra-ordinary.

From this second vertex, for example, patients present analysts with real erotic possibilities, albeit in their infantile manifestations (Schaverien, Chapter 10). Consistent with Jung's view (Jung, 1963) that *both* patient and analyst are in the analysis, if the analyst does not understand this, then the patient is failed. It is essential that the erotic is not enacted, because to do so would be an attack on the parental couple and therefore any 'sex' is not sex at all but violence masked by defensive eroticisation and therefore anti-erotic. Searles, (1979) described his intense erotic sensations for a mute, schizophrenic woman, for whom he felt in sessions that he would give up everything. He came to think about her as his 'oedipal love object', objectifying his subjective experience and making it available for analysis. R. D. Laing (1965), in contrast, refers to Freud's use of transference as a 'shield'. Freud, like Perseus, is seen as protecting himself against Medusa's gaze by looking at the image indirectly through the shield. Perseus' fear was that to gaze directly would mean turning to stone. Laing argued in favour of direct gaze, but becoming an analyst means maintaining an analytic attitude and avoiding friendship, advice, sex, or any participation in a *folie à deux*. Laing's omnipotent position risks overlooking analysts' need for protection as a means of creating a thinking space. Whether as an internal or an external activity, supervision is essential to enable analytic work to continue, discriminating between its more modest aims and the siren songs of omnipotent narcissism.

Supervision and theories of analysis

Our point here is that different views about the nature of the analytic endeavour, including the tension between the personal and the professional, are likely to reverberate between supervisor and supervisee and affect the kind of 'thinking space' that exists between them. Their actual meetings will hopefully come to model an internal space in the supervisee that the patient, too, acquires and this space will affect their developing relationship and the analytic work that evolves within it.

The supervisory space, whether internal or external, needs to be well-boundaried in order to protect it from intrusions that could disable the enterprise permanently or beyond a point where the thinking capacity can be restored. Systems theory (Durkin, 1983) considers that boundaries can be opened to receive the stimulus of the new, the surprising, or previously neglected but may also be closed if there is an inner crisis and the system needs to return to task or re-find its thinking capacity. Once sufficiently restored, the boundaries may become permeable again and growth and adaptation to the environment can take place. Ideally there is room for some degree of provocation or intrusion into the system: a learning process of confession, elucidation, education and transformation (Jung, 1929, paras 123–70), so that internal change is possible and individuation facilitated (Crowther, Chapter 6). The supervisory space is a container with appropriate boundaries, which can be opened or closed as necessary. If, for example, analysts are unwell or under pressure, they may 'consciously' tighten the boundaries so that they can keep going. It is difficult to envisage a situation in practice without some intrusions connected with the setting in which the analysis takes place: training, the limits of what can be contained by the analytic frame, time, money and, not least, the abilities of the analyst and the capacities of the patient.

There will inevitably also be theoretical and temperamental differences between supervisors and their supervisees. Whether or not these can be accommodated creatively as well as the degree of regression – benign or malignant – in the relationship may make the difference between a supervisory setting that becomes a container or a *claustrum*. Difficulties may arise consciously or unconsciously. McGlashan (Chapter 1) has considered some of the stereotyped ways in which supervisors may unconsciously relate to their supervisees. It may not be possible to separate theory from underlying unconscious processes as ultimately, theory is an expression of unconscious phantasy (see Introduction). It is possible, however, to think about the way in which theory affects the approach to supervision of both supervisee and supervisor. One example might be the ways in which supervisors variously think about 'infantile' material. For an analyst following

Freud the ego is a body ego, and emotional and intellectual life has its roots in bodily, sensory experience. This model is one that charts the development of psychic life from somatic roots in normal development towards a more sophisticated and differentiated mental state. The 'alimentary' aspect of this model is not then an analogous one, but charts a conception of mental life, initially concrete and relatively devoid of mind, but latterly taking on more complex mental forms (Bion, 1977). This may be contrasted with a model that considers such material as merely analogous, symbolic or suggestive where the notion of infantile material is a potent myth to be understood hermeneutically (Samuels, 1993; Hauke, 2000).

These differences are fundamental, and, although often unstated, may be of profound importance in the relationship between supervisor and supervisee. Despite claims to the contrary and the operation of strongly-felt allegiances and convictions, perhaps all that can be asserted is belief (Britton, 1998). Some authors have suggested a solution based on giving equal status to a multiplicity of plausible interpretations (Samuels, 1989), but such an approach may also tend towards the abstract and lack depth or conviction. It may be advocated that such fundamental assumptions should be explicitly addressed, but this may take away time spent on the patient and in any case, most analysts naturally tend to use theoretical conceptions which are incomplete, tentative or in a state of flux (see Introduction). Discussions may be hijacked for defensive purposes in the face of painful or difficult emotional exchanges that are hard to address between supervisee and patient, supervisor and supervisee. For these reasons, differences in approach may be treated pragmatically or cynically (depending upon your position), as though they are not there or are unimportant. The question is, 'Does it matter?'. The answer is probably 'yes' at times, and 'no' at times. Sometimes difference is fruitful in the relationship between supervisor and supervisee but, in extreme cases, it can result in a disastrous dialogue of the deaf. It is more likely to matter if there is another unacknowledged antagonism in the relationship between them. It works best when both parties can hold to their convictions, retaining an open mind and the possibility that they could be wrong. Deceit is unlikely to facilitate any supervisory relationship.

Differences in aim or approach may be illustrated in the following example.

A supervisee reports meeting with a prospective patient for the first time. The patient is very late, arriving in a breathless and flustered state with a torrent of explanations and apologies. The therapist says to the patient that there is no need to hurry and he can take his time to say what he has got to say. The supervisor asks the supervisee about her comment. She explains that she wishes to 'contain' the patient's anxiety and provide a place in which the man can articulate the difficulties with which he feels burdened.

The therapist's response is based on an identification with a conscious characteristic of her patient. It is consistent with an approach to difficulties based on sympathy. If the therapist's approach to her patient is based on an assumption that includes relieving him of his distress, a supervisor may feel that the therapist's response is entirely appropriate. It may also be the case that the supervisor agrees with the therapist's contention that there are certain matters which the patient has 'got to say'(under some sort of external obligation), and the therapist is facilitating this.

A more analytic supervisor might value the patient's unconscious communication – his need to hurry, but his inability to do so for reasons which, for the moment, are unclear. It could be due to his ambivalence towards the analyst, his fears of what might be painfully revealed or his hatred for any changes that analysis could bring. Such an approach might hold that the therapist has received an unspoken invocation to reassure him and she has acted on it. She has colluded with her patient, not to suffer the prospects inherent in analysis. A question could also be raised that is less about what the patient wants to say, but more about what he needs to say, but may well not want to say at all. The analytic supervisor might help the supervisee hear what the patient *needs to say,* not what he wants to say with which he is defensively invested. It is not that either of these approaches is 'wrong' but rather that they can be seen as expressing different therapeutic aims.

Theory-making in analysis

We have now considered some of the conscious and unconscious factors at work in the supervisory relationship and we are in a position to consider whether or not there are any central theories of supervision which attract general agreement, over and above the need for a 'thinking space'. The concept of parallel process (Ekstein and Wallerstein, 1958) is much used by supervisors as a model for thinking about the relevance of the interaction between supervisor and supervisee. It suggests that the processes of transference and counter-transference are not only observable in the analyst and patient relationship, but also that the dynamics are capable of direct replication or repetition between the supervisor and the supervisee. Little work has been done to elucidate the mechanism at work although it is assumed that the operations of unconscious projection, identification and projective identification, especially at the archetypal level or the level of unconscious phantasy, are central. Perry (Chapter 11) develops a possible link between parallel process and Jung's original concept of synchronicity. This is the primary material for analytic work, but the means by which it is repeated in the supervisory relationship is less clear. Parallels are so striking, however, that they have tended to become widely accepted as established fact.

An often-neglected distinction that causes confusion is the *difference between meta-theory making and micro-theory-making*. This confusion applies as much to analysis as to supervision and arises out of undifferentiated concepts of 'theory'. *Meta-theory* refers to the process of developing overarching theories of psychological functions, or at least aspects of them, whereas *micro-theory* is the theory-making that evolves with patients in the consulting room. Meta-theory is likely to be important in supervision as it may be used to understand patients' material or, on occasion, to obscure it (Shearer, Chapter 12). Theoretical prejudices and preconceptions led Jung to his idea of a new theory for each patient (Jung, 1963), Fordham to 'not knowing beforehand' (Fordham, 1996a) and Bion to advocating the setting aside of knowledge, memory and desire (Bion, 1977).

An approach operating on the basis of interpreting patient's material in the light of *meta-theory*, contrasts with an approach in which supervisor and supervisee come together to develop *micro-theories* about the patient. This will emerge out of the sessions the supervisee has with the patient. Some prefer to 'build up a picture' of the patient over time, like Jung; others make a new theory for each session like Fordham.

In the latter case, the patient does the analysis facilitated by his analyst. He explores areas where knowledge is lacking, in which that significance may be found and which hold within them the potential for new development and individuation. In the former, it is the analyst who does the analysis and it is accumulated knowledge about the patient that is significant. These are differences in approach likely to be of considerable importance for any supervisory process, representing as they do different vertices. They hold potential for creative tension while at the same time there lurks the shadow possibility of dogma and destructiveness powerful enough to close the 'system' rather than keeping it open and flexible (see Fuller, Chapter 7, p. 119; and Shearer, Chapter 12, p. 210).

Conclusion

At the beginning of this chapter we suggested that analysis and supervision are inseparable. They share similar structures, language and values. Both are applied to an analytic relationship. Their differences are in approach and the ways in which patient material, as presented by the supervisee, tends to be handled. We have argued that the conceptual separation of supervision from analysis has distinct disadvantages and tends to create a false dichotomy, making significant aspects of what the analyst brings to an analysis unavailable. In part, this may have been fostered by a traditionally broad definition of countertransference that aggregates the analyst's affective responses to the patient without adequately differentiating between that which belongs to the analyst and that which is truly transferred onto the analyst by the patient. All analysts hopefully develop an 'internal supervisor', a capacity which may be brought to bear both in their analytic work with patients and in the developing capacity to become good supervisors themselves. It is this internal supervising capacity that ultimately is externalised when qualified analysts and therapists turn their hand to supervising and can be refined with further learning (see Wharton, Chapter 5, p. 87).

The disadvantages of separating supervision and analysis need to be set alongside the need to respect the maturity of the supervisee in the context of the regressive aspects of supervision, especially supervision during training. This includes supervisors evaluating their supervisees' capacity for deintegration/reintegration, as opposed to defensive splitting (McGlashan, Chapter 1). The problems inherent in a broad definition of countertransference may also be mitigated by making a distinction between the illusory quality of the transference and that which is not transferred, but can be held in mind by supervisors to facilitate the development of a capacity for making such distinctions in their supervisees. The contributions by Astor (Chapter 3), Martin (Chapter 8) and Gee (Chapter 9) have suggested different ways to do this, making use of the analyst's affects even when they are not 'truly transferred' or when they are neurotic in character. Even if the totality of the supervisee's self in relation to the patient's self is not explicitly addressed, this does not mean that the responses evoked by the patient in the supervisee cannot be appropriately explored in supervision.

A tendency towards an incestuous, narrow approach to supervision is also mitigated by the fact that in practice most analysts, even by the time that they come to train, have already had several supervisors (Perry, Chapter 11, p. 205). Indeed, most training institutions now recognise the need for trainees to have at least two supervisors. An experience of different approaches makes it easier for developing analysts to become aware of the distinctions between knowledge and belief (Britton, 1998). They learn to develop a capacity for patience, and to tolerate anxiety, doubt, difference and uncertainty, which is the bedrock of the analytic attitude, and the art of timely interpretation.

It is arguable whether in practice there is likely to be any greater degree of variation between supervisors than might be expected between analysts. A range of issues receive attention in supervision sessions and there is also diversity of method, both analytic and supervisory. Some supervisors will attend to the interaction between supervisee and patient, others will focus primarily on the material presented by the patient. Still other supervisors will attend to the interaction between the supervisor and supervisee with different emphases on the sessions presented. In this book, some of the different perspectives and approaches will have been apparent even from within a broad-based 'Jungian' tradition. This diversity could be seen as a barrier to thinking about 'patterns' in supervisory practice (Zinkin 1991), but, contained, this is the engine of creative development. Containment is more likely to be achieved by supervisors who are consciously aware of their assumptions or at least of their capacity to operate on the basis of basic assumptions.

This book had its genesis in an attempt to think about what is meant by the word 'supervision' and the nature of the supervisory task. Our subtitle 'A practice in search of a theory' has been an attempt to articulate the ambiguous relationship of theory with supervision as it has arisen spontaneously in direct consequence of the need for a place to reflect about analytic work. We have not produced a well-articulated 'theory of supervision'. Indeed we have argued that to separate the theory of supervision from the theory of analysis is not possible (although paradoxically this *is* a theory of supervision). We have, however, attempted to consider the place of theory in supervision and how it is used in order to differentiate the role of 'analyst' from the role of 'supervisor'. What is fundamental is that the generation of theories about the patient is the essential task of supervision, along with the capacity to test and evaluate critically these theories, both within the supervisory session and in the mind of the supervisee in the course of his or her analytic work with the patient.

References

Baynes, H. G. (1947) *The Mythology of the Soul* (London: Balliere Tindall & Cox).

Bibring, E. (1937) 'Methods and Techniques of Control-analysis', *International Journal of Psycho-Analysis*, **18**, 369–70.

Bion, W. R. (1977) *Two Papers: The Grid and the Caesura* (London: Karnac Books).

Britton, R. (1998) *Belief and Imagination* (London: Routledge).

Casement, P. (1983) *On Learning from the Patient* (London: Tavistock).

Covington, C. (2002) 'The Myth of Pure Analysis', *Journal of Analytical Psychology*, **47**(1).

Durkin, H. E. (1983) 'Some Contributions of General Systems Theory to Psychoanalytic Group Psychotherapy', in M. Pines (ed.), *The Evolution of Group Analysis* (London: Routledge & Kegan Paul).

Ekstein, R. and Wallerstein, R. S. (1958) *The Teaching and Learning of Psychotherapy* (New York: Basic Books).

Fordham, M. (1993) *The Making of an Analyst* (London: Free Association Books).

Fordham, M. (1995) *The Fenceless Field* (London: Routledge).

Fordham, M. (1996a) 'Theory in Practice,' *Journal of Child Psychotherapy*, **22**(1), 28.

Fordham, M. (1996b) 'Suggestions towards a Theory of Supervision', in *Analyst–Patient Interaction* (London: Routledge).

Freud, S. (1910) 'The Future Prospects of Psycho-Analytic Therapy', *Standard Edition volume, XI*, 144–5.

Gabbard, G. O. and Lester, E. P. (1995) *Boundaries and Boundary Violations in Psychoanalysis* (New York: Basic Books).

Gordon, R. (1993) 'The Location of Archetypal Experience', *Bridges: Metaphor for Psychic Processes* (London: Karnac Books).

Hauke, C. (2000) *Jung and the Postmodern* (London: Routledge).

Jung, C. G. (1929) 'Problems of Modern Psychotherapy', *Collected Works Volume 16*.

Jung, C. G. (1946) 'The Psychology of the Transference', *Collected Works 16*.

Jung, C. G. (1952) 'The Symbolism of the Mandala', *Collected Works Volume 12*.

Jung, C. G. (1963) *Memories, Dreams, Reflections* (London: Collins and Routledge).

Jung, C. G. (1968) 'Analytical Psychology; Its Theory and Practice', *The Tavistock Lectures* (New York: Pantheon Books), 157–8.

Kerr, J. (1994) *A Most Dangerous Method* (London: Sinclair-Stevenson).

Kovacs, W. (1936) 'Training and Control-analysis', *International Journal of Psycho-Analysis* **17**, 346–54.

Laing, R. D. (1965) *The Divided Self* (Harmondsworth: Penguin).

McGuire, W. (1974) *The Freud/ Jung Letters* (Cambridge, MA: Harvard University Press).

Ogden, T. H. (1994) *Subjects of Analysis* (London: Karnac Books).

Redfearn J. (2000), 'Possible Psychosomatic Hazards to the Therapist: Patients as Self Objects', *Journal of Analytical Psychology*, **45**(2).

Samuels, A. (1989) *The Plural Psyche* (London: Routledge).

Samuels, A. (1993) *The Political Psyche* (London: Routledge).

Searles, H. F. (1979) 'The "Dedicated Physician" ', in *Countertransference and Related Subjects*, (Madison, CN: International Universities Press).

Zinkin, L. (1991) 'The Klein Connection in the London School: The Search for Origins' *Journal of Analytical Psychology*, **36**(1).